Interest Rate Risk in the Banking Book

A Best Practice Guide to Management and Hedging

BEATA LUBINSKA

WILEY

Library of Congress Cataloging-in-Publication Data

Names: Lubinska, Beata, 1973- author.
Title: Interest rate risk in the banking book : a best practice guide to
   management and hedging / Beata Lubinska.
Description: Chichester, West Sussex, United Kingdom : John Wiley & Sons,
   Ltd., 2021. | Includes bibliographical references and index.
Identifiers: LCCN 2021028310 (print) | LCCN 2021028311 (ebook) | ISBN
   9781119755012 (hardback) | ISBN 9781119755029 (adobe pdf) | ISBN
   9781119755036 (epub)
Subjects: LCSH: Interest rate risk. | Asset-liability management. | Banks
   and banking.
Classification: LCC HG1621 .L83 2021 (print) | LCC HG1621 (ebook) | DDC
   332.1068/1—dc23
LC record available at https://lccn.loc.gov/2021028310
LC ebook record available at https://lccn.loc.gov/2021028311

Cover Design: Wiley
Cover Image: © in-future/iStock/Getty Images Plus/Getty Images

Set in 10/12pt Sabon LT Std by Straive, Chennai, India
Printed and bound by CPI Group (UK) Ltd, Croydon, CR0 4YY

C9781119755012_200921

"To my Father. Thank you for inspiring me, for guiding me and for your fantastic lectures about the Universe".

Contents

Preface

There are so many well-written books and articles focused specifically on Interest Rate Risk in the Banking Book (IRRBB) and, more broadly, on Asset Liability Management (ALM). Therefore, the concepts related to IRRBB are already well understood by market practitioners. Recently I have found Paul Newson's (2017) book, which is fully dedicated to the topic of IRRBB, very useful and well written. I have read many books on ALM that I have found extremely useful in my career as a treasurer in a small bank.

In general, I love reading all books on ALM and treasury as I truly believe there is always something new to learn, and I am interested in seeing how the same concept is approached by other market practitioners. As an author I appreciate the amount of time and effort spent on preparing any book and I am grateful that some authors have shared their knowledge and experience. Every book reflects years and years of hard work and learning, and usually the objective of any book is to share the best of the author's knowledge and experience. This is exactly the case for this book.

Having said that, my intention here is to complement existing writing on IRRBB and ALM over the past years. My **main objective** is to share my experience and knowledge gathered over years of working in the banking industry with the focus on the importance of this risk category. It is based almost exclusively on practical **case studies** and **examples** which I have examined in my work as a treasurer, head of IRRBB and other positions. The theory lying behind the IRRBB concept is deliberately reduced to the minimum required so that the main attention is dedicated to various case studies such as **identification of IRRBB sources** in a number of banks, **enhancement of IRRBB framework**, **IRRBB stress testing** and even an example of an **ALM report** with the focus on IRRBB, which I hope will be of value to the reader.

The second objective of the book is to share with the reader practical examples of an **integrated approach to the management of ALM risks in the treasury,** i.e. the integrated approach for building the hedging and funding strategy in one holistic exercise. This is an increasingly important task for treasurers in financial institutions, and brings quantifiable benefit in terms of reduction of the funding costs of these institutions.

As already mentioned, the theoretical part of the book is reduced to a minimum based on the rationale that there are many great books already available which explore the IRRBB metrics and other concepts in details. This book mainly consists of **walk-through practical case studies** presented for hypothetical banks and challenges in daily management of IRRBB – for example, how to fund and hedge the Banking Group's subsidiary and integrated approach for set up of the funding plan. However, the book also contains a brief summary of main concepts related to IRRBB.

Another important point which needs to be highlighted, in order to be crystal clear about the approach undertaken in articulating the book structure, is that case studies and examples are mainly based on the standardised approach proposed by the Basel Committee on Banking Supervision (BCBS) in 2016, which is already incorporated widely by national legislations across the globe. This book already envisages the compliance with the Basel approach. Therefore, the case studies and examples are built on that basis. Consequently, if the reader is looking to enhance the IRRBB framework outside the Basel recommendations this book won't provide the solution.

The audience for the book is envisaged as treasury professionals, i.e., treasurers of medium and small sized banks who have adopted the BCBS standardised approach as an IRRBB framework. In addition, this is a perfect guide for challenger banks which are growing fast, are capital constrained and need to optimise their funding and hedging strategy. I truly believe this book will help treasury professionals in building the overall enhanced IRRBB framework based on the Basel Standards; meanwhile Risk and Audit professionals will gain the knowledge necessary to challenge the strategies undertaken by a treasurer.

Driven by the simplicity and elegance of the Basel approach this book is also well suited to practitioners who are just starting the IRRBB journey and want to equip themselves with practical tools to manage this risk.

About the Website

Thank you for purchasing this book.

You may access the following additional complementary resources provided for your use by visiting: www.wiley.com\go\lubinska\interestraterisk.

(Password: Lubinska123)

■ IRRBB Model

Introduction

Interest Rate Risk in the Banking Book (IRRBB) has become a hot topic over recent years and there is a clear trend towards standardisation of the IRRBB approaches for measurement, modelling and monitoring in the banking industry. From a regulatory perspective, the journey started in April 2016 when the Basel Committee on Banking Supervision (BCBS) published the final Standards (BCBS Standards) on IRRBB that replaced the 2004 Principles. The new standards set out the Committee's expectations on the management of IRRBB in terms of identification, measurement, monitoring, control and supervision, and reflect changes in supervisory practices due to the exceptionally low interest rates, whilst providing methods and models to be used by banks in a wider and enhanced risk management framework. BCBS Standards had an important impact on the global adoption of standardised metrics and emphasised a clear difference between market risk (inherent in the trading book) and IRRBB (inherent in the banking book). However, IRRBB is not only a regulatory term. It has an impact on the profitability of financial institutions and its mismanagement leads to losses. There are many cases where banks have suffered from margin compression in the aftermath of the financial crisis when interest rates started going down. These banks failed to hedge the banking book against rates going down and, consequently, Current Accounts and Saving Accounts (CASA) and equity liabilities were reinvested at lower rates. Additionally, a non-transparent and deficient internal transfer pricing framework from business to the central unit caused open positions and margin at risk. The robust balance sheet management presupposes that customer business and financial risks are clearly separated with sound methodology. Therefore, the understanding of the interrelation between IRRBB and Funds Transfer Pricing (FTP) is an imperative in order to ensure effectiveness in the risk management process and allocation of clear responsibilities between stakeholders within the financial institution.

Without any doubt, the main driver for IRRBB evolution is a persistent low-rate environment. In some locations rates even moved into negative territory. The concept of negative rates is against a fundamental paradigm in finance that money has a time value that results from different investment opportunities. A fixed income security bought today for a specified term will return the payoff or future value that is dependent on both the compounding method and interest rate employed. Interest rates paid or charged for money depend, to a great extent, on the length of the term of investments. Therefore, the interest rate represents the price paid to use money for a period of time, which is commonly referred to as the time value of money.

In recent years, central banks in Europe have employed negative rates as an unprecedented measure to combat recession and foster recovery. The idea of being charged for lending is counter-intuitive and puts into question the concept of time value of money described above. Such a move is viewed as controversial by economists as there is a clear impact on the banking system. One of the primary concerns over negative rates is fuelling of cash hoarding behaviours as depositors are penalised instead of being compensated. Consequently, they are incentivised to hold cash. There is also a clear impact on the banks' profitability. Negative rates increase costs for banks with excess liquidity, resulting in a search for ways to offset these costs through raising account fees and charges and, in extreme cases, cutting back lending to the real economy. Indeed, the interest rates concept is extremely important because changes in interest rates affect a bank's earnings and its risk situation in different ways. This is exactly the reason why the regulator advocates the need for appropriate and precise methods for the measurement of the interest rate risk which enable the revelation of all its significant sources and the evaluation of its impact on the operative profile of the bank.

The regulatory aspect which reflects the changes in the market landscape is an important driver for IRRBB evolution and enhanced framework. However, the author believes there is another reason for the change in approach for the management of financial risks, in particular IRRBB and liquidity risk. It is beneficial for banks to adopt holistic and proactive management of financial risks. In her book *Asset Liability Management Optimisation* (Lubinska, 2020), the author examined the interrelation between interest rate risk and liquidity risk and quantified the benefits in terms of the reduced cost of funding achieved by the optimisation exercise and the holistic management of both risk categories.

The first attempts to integrate the interest rate risk and another type of risk (credit risk) has been proposed by Drehmann et al. (2010), and Alessandri and Drehmann (2010). The work performed by Drehmann et al. constructs the general framework for measuring the riskiness of banks, which are subject to correlated interest rate and credit shocks. The results show a strong interaction between credit risk and interest rate risk, sufficient to influence net profitability and capital adequacy: in particular, the magnitude of each risk component and the speed with which profits return back to equilibrium after the hypothesised shocks depend, among other things, on the re-pricing characteristics of the positions in the banking book and the cost of funding (Baldan et al., 2012).

The literature has thoroughly debated both the liquidity risk and interest rate risk and, until the regulatory updates on stress testing, IRRBB and liquidity, there seems to be little contribution from scholars on the integrated management of these types of risk. The link between financial risks can be seen in one of the main functions of credit institution, i.e., maturity transformation. Banks finance their investments by issuing liabilities with a shorter maturity than that of their investments; the resulting imbalance between the terms for the assets and liabilities means that they take on the interest rate risk and liquidity risk (Resti and Sironi, 2007). Baldan et al. (2012) launched the hypothesis that there is a direct relationship so that reducing the exposure to the liquidity risk induces a reduction in the interest rate risk as well. Their study analysed a small Italian bank during the years 2009 and 2010 which had to modify its liquidity profile in order to comply with the Basel III requirements. As a result, it generated the simultaneous reduction in its exposure to the interest rate risk. The authors conclude that there is a need to arrive at integrated risk management in which the control of each of these risks is placed in relation to the bank's different functions and influences its strategic decisions (Baldan et al., 2012).

After the regulatory updates, the *silo basis* approach is being slowly replaced by more integrated management of ALM risks. This is because profitability remains a key concern for the banking sector. The low profitability and widespread dispersion for some countries, along with high operating costs, continues to dampen the profitability prospects, especially for the European banking sector. Thus, there is a need to come up with new approaches which could address shrinking profitability, a heavily regulated landscape and exposure to financial risks. This necessity has been highlighted by Choudhry (2017) in "Strategic ALM and Integrated Balance Sheet Management: The Future of Bank Risk Management". In this article Choudhry suggests that the discipline of ALM, as practised by banks worldwide for over 40 years, needs to be updated to meet the challenges presented by globalisation and Basel III regulatory requirements. In order to maintain viability and a sustainable balance sheet, banks need to move from the traditional "reactive" ALM approach to a more proactive, integrated balance sheet management framework. This will enable them to solve the multi-dimensional optimisation problem they are faced with at present. In his book *The Moorad Choudhry Anthology: Past, Present and Future Principles of Banking and Finance* (2018), Choudhry describes a "vision of the future" with respect to a sustainable bank business model. This vision of the future contains the concepts of strategic, integrated and optimised ALM. The need for integration is now getting recognition from treasurers, risk managers and regulators. It is also starting to be considered among the ALM systems providers. They are attempting to build ALM solutions which focus on the integration between IRRBB, liquidity and FTP, supporting the view that, today, more holistic balance sheet risk management is required. Interest rate risk in banking cannot be viewed in isolation from liquidity risk, funds transfer pricing or capital management. Balance sheets have become more volatile – a result of changing term structures, optionality, better informed customers and the use of derivatives.

The objective of this book is to serve as a practical support in the daily management of IRRBB through the examples, case studies and solutions which have been developed during the author's career. It is a summary of many practical ideas related to hedging of the exposure to IRRBB subcategories, i.e., yield risk, option risk, gap risk and basis risk. The book represents the author's attempt to provide an insight into the practical aspects of IRRBB management along with the description of the main metrics and their calculation methods. It presents the concept of immunisation and natural hedging strategy showing the benefits from the optimisation exercise and a holistic view for funding and hedging strategy adopted by the treasury. The book contains case studies which walk the reader through different aspects of building the hedging and funding strategy through the holistic and integrated approach as opposed to the silo basis approach, which is still so often adopted in this process. Therefore, one of the objectives of this book is to focus on the optimisation of hedging strategies and proactive management of IRRBB both on the short part of the interest rate curve (*directional gap* strategy) and on the medium-to-long part of the curve (*riding the yield curve* strategy). Additionally, the author walks the reader through the IRRBB stress testing, policy and instruments used in the daily management of the treasury.

Chapter 1 of this book introduces the subcategories of IRRBB and provides the practical examples of identification of the risk sources in the banking book. This part highlights the main regulatory developments, sheds light on the results of the IRRBB stress test performed by the European Central Bank (ECB) in 2017 and provides examples of historical interest rate shocks which could be applied for the measurement of changes in Economic Value of Equity (EVE) or in the IRRBB stress testing framework. In this section the author answers the question why it is so important to adopt the enhanced IRRBB framework and examines the concept of *margin compression* faced by banks worldwide.

Chapter 2 contains a number of practical case studies for identification of the IRRBB sources, practical approaches for hedging some products with behavioural nature such as reversions or lifetime mortgages and how to enhance the IRRBB framework in a bank. This chapter walks the reader through the dual nature of IRRBB, the *trade off* between Net Interest Income (NII) volatility and change in EVE and the calculations methods for the main metrics. Additionally, it extends the concept of *rate transformation* and *riding the yield curve* strategy. There are case studies related to the calculation of NII sensitivity through *flows* and *stock* approach and analysis of the impact driven by the existence of automatic options in the banking book. Chapter 2 summarises the main IRRBB metrics such as Earnings at Risk (EaR), Value at Risk (VaR) and static IRRBB methods.

Hedging instruments and hedging strategies are the main subject of Chapter 3 which, additionally, provides the reader with the practical example of the Asset Liability Management (ALM) report with key information to be communicated to the Asset Liability Management Committee (ALCO) members. It contains an extensive analysis of the IRRBB position of an illustrative bank. In this section the natural hedging and synthetic hedging strategy are analysed in detail supported by practical examples.

The concept of *behaviouralisation* is covered in Chapter 4 with the main focus on modelling of Non-Maturing Deposits (NMDs). This chapter emphasises the reason for modelling items without deterministic maturity and the impact on an IRRBB position driven by *behaviouralisation* both on the asset and liability side. It walks the reader through a simple approach for modelling of balances volatility, rate sensitivity and average life of the product. The chapter introduces also the term of structural and financial prepayments.

The concept of the application of optimisation methods in ALM, interrelation between liquidity risk and IRRBB is the crucial point of Chapter 5. It shows how to set up an integrated approach between funding and hedging strategy as the holistic view for the balance sheet. There is a case study related to the optimisation of hedging strategy and, in the same exercise, reduction of cost of funds.

The second part of Chapter 5 is fully dedicated to the strategic tool which the treasury has at its disposal to support the optimisation exercise, i.e. the Funds Transfer Pricing (FTP) process. It shows several examples of a methodological approach to the correct transfer of both types of risks, i.e., liquidity and IRRBB from business to the central unit.

Chapter 6 is divided into two parts. The first part walks the reader through the proposal of methodological approach for IRRBB stress testing and ICAAP. It shows practical examples of the implementation of the stress test and ICAAP with illustrative numbers. The second part of this chapter addresses IRRBB governance and the Risk Appetite Statement (RAS).

Appendix 1 illustrates the practical example of the IRRBB policy compliant with BCBS Standards, walks the reader through the main section of the policy with the emphasis on the calculation of the value of the automatic option in a negative rates environment and an illustrative example of the treatment of NMDs for IRRBB purposes.

Appendix 2 illustrates a practical example of the IRRBB model manual compliant with BCBS Standards. This section has been included to support the reader with the implementation of methodological changes required by the Standards. Appendix 2 is meant to support smaller banks where they intend to apply the standardised approach as the IRRBB measurement framework.

CHAPTER 1

What is IRRBB and why is it important?

The common definition of Interest Rate Risk in the Banking Book (IRRBB) describes the threat to the capital position and earnings of a bank driven by changes in the interest rates in the market. Though the definition is simple, the underlying threat to the bank's resilience is potentially serious if IRRBB is mismanaged. There are multiple ways that the interest rate curve can change its shape, i.e., it could take the form of a steepener, a flattener, a humped or an inverted curve. Changes to interest rates threaten a bank's earnings by impacting its Net Interest Income (NII) which is the main source of earnings for a bank. It is estimated that, in the composition of the total income of a bank, NII contributes, on average, about 60% (Figure 1.1).

Changes to interest rates also threaten the underlying value of bank's assets, liabilities and off-balance sheet instruments, given the adverse impact which may arise on the present value of items, in particular their future cash flows. This is known as the impact on economic value of the banking book, which is understood as the sum of the net present value of assets, the net present value of liabilities and the net present value of off-balance sheet items.

We can already see that there is a dual view under which interest rate risk in the banking book should be analysed and these two views are complementary. The short-term view relates to the impact on earnings of a bank and this is known, in the IRRBB parlance, as the *short end* curve impact. The time horizon for this kind of analysis is short, spanning from 12 months to a maximum of 36 months. Under short-term analysis we are looking at the negative impact on a bank's earnings (NII) driven by the fluctuation in the interest rate curve. One can argue that not only negative impact should be considered but the earnings variability as well. Excessive earnings sensitivity is considered bad practice in IRRBB management. We will tackle this point at a later stage.

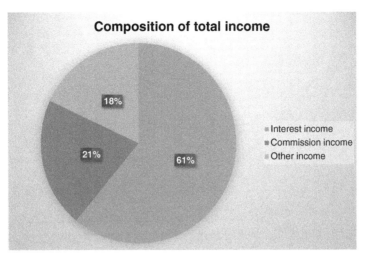

FIGURE 1.1   Composition of the total income in a bank.
Source: own elaboration

The medium-to-long-term view relates to the impact on economic value of a bank and looks at a much longer horizon, i.e., it includes all risk sensitive positions in the banking book. The outcome of the economic value analysis provides the fundamental number both for the financial institution and for the regulator as it describes the extent of structural mismatching between assets and liabilities. It indicates embedded, although not crystallised, losses or gains in the economic value of a bank.

Managing IRRBB properly is vital due to it being a major source of income. IRRBB has an impact on a bank's capital base as it is a potential threat to capital, and interest movements create sensitivity to the NII. Therefore, a proper framework creates an opportunity for income generation both under near-term and longer-term horizons. This is what is meant by a steering approach or trade-off between the NII and EVE metrics. This point is analysed in detail in Chapter 6.

As already shown in Figure 1.1, in the composition of the total income of a bank NII contributes on average about 60%, 85% of which is considered to be gained through margin differential and the remaining 15% resulting from maturity transformation. Additionally, IRRBB creates a capital demand under Pillar 2. Mismanagement can be very expensive and can have implications across different areas of a bank. In the first place, both incorrect assumptions and risk underestimation can affect the P&L of the treasury, which is responsible for ALM profitability. Secondly, it affects P&L results of the business units through FTP rates and FTP margins and the correct IRRBB assumptions impact the product profitability assessment through the interest income split. Figure 1.2 shows an example of NII compression in a banking group. This group lost billions because it failed to hedge itself against rates going down and, consequently, reinvested CASA and equity liabilities at lower rates. Interest rate risk was not fully transferred from the businesses to ALM, causing open positions and margin at risk.

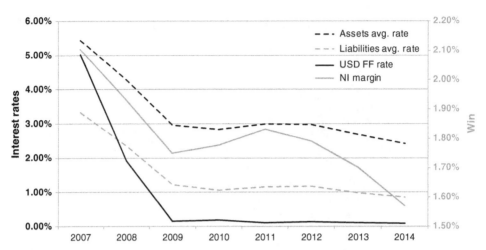

FIGURE 1.2 Example of margin compression caused by lowering interest rates and an inefficient FTP process.
Source: own elaboration

SUBCATEGORIES OF INTEREST RATE RISK

There are four main subcategories (subtypes) of IRRBB to be identified, managed and reported by a financial institution. The bank's banking book usually is exposed to all subtypes to a lesser or greater degree dependent on its business model. For example, banks with a conventional business model, i.e., where the medium-to-long-term assets are funded by short-term repricing liabilities, mainly run the risk of exposure to repricing and yield risk. This is known as *riding the yield curve* strategy or *rate transformation*. This is because, in the case where rates go up, the bank incurs embedded losses in terms of EVE and negative P&L impact on NII (this case is described in detail in the following section).

Commercial banks with vast depositors' base are exposed to behavioural risk given that deposits without deterministic maturity need to be modelled for the purpose of Asset Liability Management (ALM). This behavioural option both on the customer side (a depositor can withdraw money at any time) and on the bank's side (the bank can change the interest rate on the product at any time) is known as optionality risk and represents an important risk category to be managed. Hedging of IRRBB is based on the behavioural basis, which means that getting the behavioural assumptions wrong may easily lead to the over- or under-hedging of an interest rate risk position.

In some countries, for example the UK or the Middle East, assets at the floating rate are strongly correlated to the base rate. However, these banks finance their assets through the interbank market and/or behavioural liabilities (deposits). Given that there is no perfect correlation between market rates and the administered rate (where the interest rate of behavioural liabilities and assets can be changed by banks at will), and there is always a time lag between administered rate adjustment resulting from market rate changes, banks are vulnerable to exposure from basis risk. As described later, basis risk itself has a number of subcategories.

Repricing risk (gap risk)

Repricing risk, known also as gap risk, represents an important category of IRRBB. It arises because assets have a different repricing frequency to liabilities. For example, if assets reprice before liabilities, we say that a bank runs repricing mismatching, and it is *asset sensitive*. On the other hand, if liabilities reprice before assets a bank is *liability sensitive* and it is exposed to the increase in the interest rates level. However, before going into detail we need to introduce the concept of gap.

Gap represents the difference between the outstanding amount of Risk Sensitive Assets (RSA) and Risk Sensitive Liabilities (RSL). The residual gap is negative when there is more RSL than RSA in a certain time bucket. For example, let's imagine this in simple terms: we have 100 GBP of floating rate asset repricing within the next 1 month funded by 100 GBP of fixed rate time deposits which matures and therefore resets its rate in the next 6 months (see Figure 1.3).

The gaps in Figure 1.3 show the short-term repricing asset funded by longer term repricing liability. As already mentioned, these gaps are called *gaps in repricing* and drive the bank's exposure to the repricing risk.

This exposure needs to be quantified (Chapter 2) and drives the impact on a bank's NII where rates move up or down during the period of analysis. If the rates go up the exposure shown in Figure 1.3 has a positive NII impact because assets are earning more in terms of interest. On the other hand, if rates go down there will be a negative NII impact for the same reason (assets earn less in terms of interest).

It is important to highlight, at this point, that repricing and yield risk are measured through gap analysis, i.e., the tool which shows the residual gaps allocated to

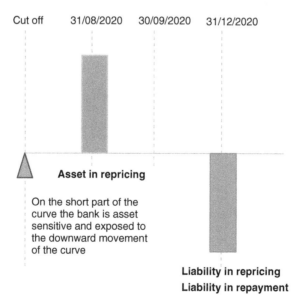

FIGURE 1.3   Illustrative example of repricing risk.
Source: own elaboration

the corresponding time bucket (time slot). BCBS Standards has introduced 19 time buckets. The banking book items are allocated according to their first repricing date or maturity date (this is analysed in detail in Chapter 2).

Yield risk

This kind of IRRBB subcategory refers to the potential adverse change in the Economic Value of Equity (EVE) of a bank and, therefore, it refers to the medium-to-long part of the curve. It forms the structural risk exposure of a financial institution and is driven by non-parallel shifts in the yield curve. This exposure is driven by IRRBB strategy and the steering approach (discussed in Chapter 6). For example, let us imagine that a bank runs a *riding the yield curve* strategy, i.e., it extends fixed rate mortgages to retail clients which are funded by retail current and saving accounts (CASA) with a shorter repricing period. There is a positive NIM impact related to this particular strategy because under the upward sloping shape of the curve the rates associated with longer tenors are higher than the rates on the short part of the curve. The *rate transformation* ensures earnings but, at the same time, it exposes the risk of rates moving up (see Figure 1.4).

The yield risk relates to the changing relationship between interest rates of various maturities (tenors) of the same curve. In the example shown in Figure 1.4, the risk arises between two tenors, i.e., the 2Y and the 10Y tenor. As we will see in Chapter 2, the yield curve risk is captured through the application of a number of interest rate risk shocks and under different scenarios (for example, a contractual versus behavioural scenario, or a balance sheet growth assumption).

The potential increase at the 2Y interest rates will affect the economic value of the banking book as the *present value* of the asset side will become lower after an increase in interest rates and there is no offsetting reduction in the *present value* of liabilities (there is an open risk position).

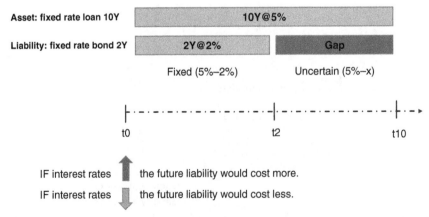

FIGURE 1.4   Riding the yield curve strategy and yield risk.
Source: own elaboration

Optionality risk

As underlined in the BCBS Standards there are two types of optionality risk in the banking book, i.e., behavioural optionality and automatic options. The behavioural option is the most common phenomenon in the banking book. It arises when a customer of a financial institution has the right but not obligation to influence the timing and/or the magnitude of the cash flows of an asset, liability or off-balance sheet instrument. Sight and savings deposits (CASA) whose maturities are uncertain for the institution entail a risk for the banking book in the form of a right of withdrawal at any time (current accounts) in relation to the assumed (by the bank) maturity. This is the behavioural optionality on the client (depositor side). From the other side, a bank has the optionality to change the price (or customer rate) for these products, giving the client only short notice, or no notice at all. This is the option on a bank's side.

Behavioural risk arises also from the assets side and is driven by the early redemption option (full prepayment or partial prepayment) of mortgages or some customer loans. The client has the right to repay the loan whenever he/she decides, without any penalty (or with a penalty in some cases).

Another important source of the interest rate risk which is driven by the behavioural assumptions is pipeline risk. It is driven by the time difference between agreement of the mortgage product rate and draw down of balance and the consequent risk that repricing in an interest rate move will compress the margin of the product.

Early redemption of assets, if not accounted for in the hedging strategies of a bank, may cause *over-hedging* because the amount of the payer swap is higher than the actual amount of fixed rate assets (which has been repaid). Consequently, the bank has to adjust hedging positions and, in the meantime, is left with the time bucket sensitivity and negative impact in terms of the PV01 metric. The prepayment pattern will change as a function of the interest rates movements. In the case of a low interest rate environment, i.e., higher differential between the committed interest rate paid by the client and external market rates, the prepayment events tend to increase as clients want to refinance their loans in order to pay lower rates. The early redemption of mortgages (prepayments) and *behaviouralisation* of deposits have an important impact on both the gap risk and yield risk discussed earlier.

The automatic options, as opposed to the behavioural optionality, always follows a rational pattern, i.e., if the agreed event happens the option is executed. Otherwise, it is not. This is the case with floors, caps or collars embedded in the banking book. Quite often, especially in European banks, the embedded floors are an important part of the asset base (either floors at 0% or at 1%) as they protect the Net Interest Income from losses in a negative rates environment. In a negative interest rate environment, the implicit floor at 0% on a bank's liabilities (current accounts) cannot be ignored, even though no institution has the intention of selling interest rate options outright.

EXAMPLE 1

Impact of automatic options embedded in the banking book of Bank X.
    Bank X has the banking book composed as follows:

ASSET SIDE

EUR 1.2bn of corporate loans with the contractual floor at 0%. These assets are repricing over a period of 1 month.

LIABILITY SIDE

EUR 900m of client deposits with the implicit zero floor at 0% slotted on the uniform basis between 1 month and 12 months.

    Bank X has a material amount of automatic interest rate options (IROs) which are implicitly embedded in the corporate loans on the asset side. Therefore, Bank X is a holder of those options (a long option position on the asset side). In addition, Bank X has the short option position at 0% strike on the liabilities side (deposits) as there is no willingness to cut depositors' rates below 0% in the case of rates entering negative territory. Bank X's senior management does not want to lose depositors who could potentially leave for another bank due to unfavourable repricing.

    In a negative interest rates environment, the floor on the asset side is executed (the option is *in the money*) limiting the potential squeeze of the NIM.

    Bank X measures the impact of interest rate movements on EVE under seven interest rate shocks, in particular:

- – Short up
- – Short down
- – Parallel up
- – Parallel down
- – Steepener
- – Flattener
- – 94 crisis scenario

    In the example, the interest rate curve is assumed as of 30 April 2019 and floor values have been calculated using the Bachelier model (see Chapter 3).
    The illustrative values of floors embedded in the corporate loans, under different interest rate shocks are shown in Table 1.1.

TABLE 1.1 The economic value of floors embedded in Bank X corporate loans under seven interest rate shocks.

Base	94 crash	Parallel up	Parallel down	Short up	Short down	Flattener	Steepener
29,465.95	—	—	204,102.78	—	170,503.41	—	92,643.43
1,327.13	—	—	8,634.67	—	8,728.39	—	5,471.54
3,414.68	—	—	23,652.56	—	19,758.88	—	10,736.03
2,123.47	—	—	14,708.72	—	12,287.38	—	6,676.37
735.25	—	—	5,092.87	—	4,254.48	—	2,311.68
9,929.38	—	—	68,778.19	—	57,455.94	—	31,218.82
4,653.29	—	—	32,232.13	—	26,926.08	—	14,630.35
178,998.07	14,226.24	—	468,567.96	16,544.04	389,659.37	63,796.69	260,860.87
83,221.10	—	—	577,544.01	—	485,780.27	—	265,529.53
4,807.03	319.12	—	12,261.89	—	11,362.15	643.93	8,034.37
13,817.34	1,874.26	—	35,149.48	—	33,374.66	1,680.23	23,866.38
19,902.79	1,343.78	—	50,766.39	—	47,060.44	2,654.99	33,283.46
91,403.48	6,067.98	—	233,154.02	—	216,046.00	12,243.94	152,769.75
27,319.31	—	—	213,810.92	—	155,520.23	—	72,694.01
14,519.18	—	—	116,984.86	—	82,359.69	43.43	37,124.68
39,452.99	—	—	323,984.43	—	216,059.97	128.72	90,379.30
78,548.47	—	—	680,733.96	—	425,893.91	16,592.81	180,359.90
92,036.66	—	—	797,604.54	—	500,302.61	20,076.86	213,313.20
118,003.16	—	—	1,000,935.39	—	649,344.84	13,595.19	278,132.76
242,388.78	—	—	2,290,385.64	—	1,305,475.61	124,425.35	559,780.06
29,846.13	—	—	281,980.25	—	156,593.76	14,900.41	63,816.46
27,721.68	—	—	257,023.45	—	145,511.26	12,363.16	59,302.11
105,546.81	—	—	1,062,119.56	—	553,832.10	69,783.21	225,717.39
38,252.60	—	—	283,500.18	—	217,401.13	—	108,298.98
59,567.98	—	—	571,668.01	—	312,873.64	32,057.23	127,573.97
130,237.61	—	—	1,312,945.25	—	692,785.96	87,445.45	290,419.43
137,516.21	—	—	1,427,951.59	—	728,909.59	101,774.68	302,803.92
1,132,201.09	23,549.88	—	3,240,632.64	423,803.70	2,010,941.31	873,444.13	1,111,980.69

Source: own elaboration

(Continued)

(Continued)

In order to understand the impact on the economic value of the bank, resulting from interest rate changes, Bank X calculates the change in the value of the optionality component as a difference between the option value under a shock scenario (KAO_{shock}) and base scenario (KAO_{base}). This is shown in equation 1.

$$\text{Change in the value of the automatic option} = KAO_{shock} - KAO_{base} \quad (1)$$

The positive economic value of floors, which are contractually embedded in corporate loans, offset the embedded loss on the liability side where rates move downwards. This offset depends on the maturity of the floor and its strike. Usually, assets have longer behavioural maturity than deposits, i.e., there is positive *maturity transformation* in the banking book. Also, the floor for assets is usually set up above 0%. Therefore, the potential positive value of the floor on the asset side fully offsets the loss on the liability side, resulting from the short option position on deposits when the rates go down.

The numbers in Table 1.2 are illustrative and invented by the author to represent the concept.

In Example 1, Bank X is exposed to the downward movement of the interest rate curve (see negative values in terms of ΔEVE under all downward scenarios). In fact, it can be clearly seen because there is an embedded loss under parallel down (EUR 31m), short down (EUR 25m) and steepener (EUR 11m) scenario (the detailed definition of the scenario is provided in BCBS Standards). This is because the floating rate assets are funded by behavioural liabilities (see Figure 1.5).

TABLE 1.2   The impact of automatic options on ΔEVE of Bank X.

	Economic value analysis – behavioural	
	ΔEVE	ΔEVE + Options
94 crash	30.456	24.028
Parallel up	30.513	24.085
Parallel down	(31.424)	107.429
Short up	24.756	24.535
Short down	(25.466)	(6.491)
Flattener	16.686	45.221
Steepener	(11.453)	(11.204)
Worse	(31.424)	(11.204)

Source: own elaboration

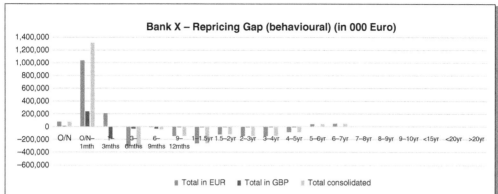

FIGURE 1.5 Repricing Gap of Bank X.
Source: own elaboration

However, the economic value of automatic options (floors on the asset side) which are *in the money*, under the assumption that interest rates are in negative territory, fully offset EVE loss under downward scenarios. As a result, the total change in EVE is as follows:

– Parallel down: +107m

– Short down: –6m

– Steepener: –11m

As already mentioned, Bank X is funded by CASA. Consequently, given the negative interest rates territory, it holds a short option position with strike at 0% on the liability side. This short option position, from an economic perspective, decreases the economic value of the bank's equity under downward scenarios.

The 0% floor on deposits (especially retail deposits) should not be underestimated in the negative rate environment. This is because, from the theoretical standpoint, the potential loss is a function of interest rates going down. From the practical standpoint banks often charge negative rates on deposit holders through commissions applied and charges on transactions.

Basis risk

Basis risk forms an important category of IRRBB. It is defined as the risk arising from imperfect correlation between risk factors of products with similar characteristics. By the risk factor we intend the underlying term structure of interest rates, for example the government bond curve versus money market curve. A good example of basis risk exposure is funding the 1Y government bond with 1Y deposit repricing on a quarterly basis and indexed to LIBOR 3M. Even though both products have the same maturity of 1Y, their underlying market factors are different, i.e., they are priced off on different curves, which are not perfectly correlated. This example represents a typical understanding of basis risk but there are also additional subcategories of this risk.

FIGURE 1.6 Example of basis risk exposure arising from different risk factors.
Source: own elaboration

The floating rate assets indexed to LIBOR 3M and funded by liabilities linked to LIBOR 6M cause basis risk exposure. This is because the movement of LIBOR 3M and LIBOR 6M are not perfectly correlated, i.e., the increase in LIBOR 3M is not followed by the same magnitude of increase in LIBOR 6M.

Another example consists of funding floating rate assets indexed to LIBOR with administered rate liabilities (a common case in Europe). Although it is true that a bank can reprice the behavioural liabilities when it wants, even if it does so there is always a time lag between the movement in market rates and the adjustment in the administered rate. Another example of basis risk is the loan priced on the prime rate but funded by liability indexed to LIBOR. The prime rate would be adjusted only by discrete amounts and its differential with money market rates could drift substantially.

Figure 1.6 shows the exposure to the movement of spread *Base rate – LIBOR 3M* and *Administered rate – LIBOR 3M*.

Frequently, the exposure to basis risk in the banking book is driven by interest rate swaps which are taken on to hedge the structural exposure of a bank.

EXAMPLE 2

Example of basis risk exposure of Bank Y.

Bank Y has £100m of fixed rate deposits which fund the portfolio of commercial mortgages indexed to the Bank of England (BoE) rate, i.e., tracker loans. These are called trackers because they follow the movement of the Bank of England base rate.

The bank enters into receiver swaps (it receives fixed rate and pays SONIA rate). The bank is exposed to the movement of the spread between a SONIA rate and a BoE rate it receives on the asset side (see Figure 1.7).

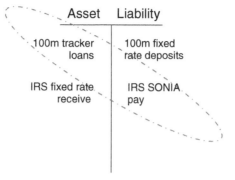

FIGURE 1.7   Basis risk exposure: BoE rate – SONIA.
Source: own elaboration

REGULATORY OVERVIEW FOR IRRBB – WHAT HAS CHANGED?

There is increasing regulatory attention towards IRRBB and it has become one of the hot topics for regulators in recent years, as we show below. The section below focuses on the IRRBB requirements in Europe.

The regulatory roadmap starts in May 2015 when the European Banking Authority (EBA) issued the "Guidelines on the management of the interest rate risk arising from non-trading activities". The *Guidelines* are addressed to financial institutions in Europe, and replaced the Committee of European Banking Supervisors (CEBS) Guidelines as of January 2016. Subsequently, in April 2016, the Basel Committee on Banking Supervision (BCBS) published the final *Standards* on IRRBB that replaced its 2004 *Principles*. The new standards set out the Committee's expectations on the management of IRRBB in terms of identification, measurement, monitoring, control and supervision. The updated IRRBB Principles reflect changes in market and supervisory practices due to the current low interest rate environment, and provides methods and models to be used by banks in a wider and enhanced risk management framework. On 31 October 2017, the EBA published a consultation paper on the update of its "Guidelines on the management of interest rate risk arising from non-trading book activities". The long-awaited update for the management of IRRBB builds on the original guidelines published in May 2015, but compared to the 2015 version it has increased in size significantly. It is also effectively the translation into European law of the IRRBB Standards published by BCBS in April 2016. The EBA is still working on a number of technical standards as part of the ongoing Capital Requirements Directive (CRD) and Capital Requirement Regulation (CRR) revision in which the regulator will prescribe disclosure requirements and a standardised approach for IRRBB. These technical standards will be published separately at a later stage.

The final IRRBB guidelines known as the "Final Report" were issued by the EBA on 19 July 2018 and posed significant challenges for banks. As a result, adequate IRRBB management needs to be considered in several dimensions, not only in terms of the integrated software solution, revision of metrics and introduction of the model validation framework. With the new guidelines and more restricted manoeuvring capabilities banks will have to revise their IRRBB strategy and measures for its implementation.

There are several changes introduced in the final EBA Guidelines. First is a major overhaul of the supervisory outlier test which measures how the EVE responds to interest rate shocks. The Supervisory Outlier Test (SOT) is an important tool for supervisors to spot excessive exposure of banks driven by the interest rates movements. The previously existing SOT measured changes arising from a +/–200 bps parallel yield curve shift. In the BCBS Standards and EBA Final Report, a different SOT definition was proposed introducing a 15% trigger compared to Tier 1 capital in combination with six interest rate scenarios that also include non-parallel shocks. The EBA has decided to implement both SOTs (20% and 15%).

In the updated EBA Guidelines the section on governance is significantly increased in size compared to the previous version published in 2015. It includes new guidelines on the risk management framework, risk appetite and model governance. While the guidelines on the risk management framework and risk appetite can be considered as a more detailed explanation of the original guidelines, the main addition is on model risk management. This requires banks to set up a model governance process, not only for behavioural models, but for all IRRBB management methods that traditionally have not always been within the scope of model governance. Various challenges have to be mastered when defining suitable governance – for example, the separation of and allocation of interest income to Business Units (BUs) and the treasury through FTP is highly controversial and emotional. Therefore, there should be the possibility, from the ALM system perspective, of providing clear-cut responsibilities through separation of books, for each component of interest income, and a transparent calculation methodology.

The technical implementation of a NII simulation is a major challenge for larger financial institutions. This is because the results of future NII are required for different purposes across the bank and an integrated and flexible approach is needed. We have seen that NII simulation is required for EBA stress tests, ECB IRRBB stress tests, and the Short-Term Exercise (STE). Now, we also have the EBA Guidelines disclosure. These different views required for NII simulation require solutions which ensure consistency between NII and EVE and serve the various purposes of NII simulation. Figures 1.8, 1.9 and 1.10 summarise the key changes and challenges introduced by the EBA Final Report.

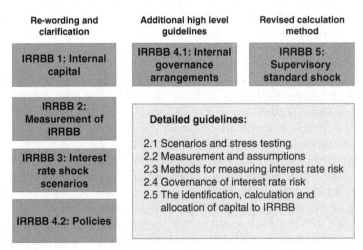

FIGURE 1.8   EBA Guidelines on IRRBB – key sections.
Source: own elaboration

Key changes

- **Credit spread risk in the banking book (CSRBB)** has been included in the scope of the Guidelines in the form of high level guidelines for institutions to identify their CSRBB exposures and ensure that CSRBB is adequately measured, monitored and controlled;
- **Guidance has been added for the internal IRRBB measurement** such as for institutions to consider negative interest rates in low interest rate environments;
- **Guidance has been added in the governance section** with regards to the assessment of new products and activities in terms of IRRBB and model validation.

Key changes

- **A number of changes have been made to the existing supervisory outlier test.** A set of new principles has been added to the calculation such as the removal of the zero bound floor and the inclusion of NPEs;
- **The revised outlier test** introduced by the BCBS Standards (threshold 15% of Tier 1 capital) has been included as an **early warning signal** on top of the current outlier test;
- **Lower bound of –100 basis points** (linear function between –100 and 0 bps) to be applied.
- The new threshold of 15% of Tier 1 will only apply to SREP category 3 and 4 institutions 6 months after the guidelines enter into force. It allows for a timely preparation for the calculations of the new outlier test and provides the smaller institutions with a longer *phase-in* period.

FIGURE 1.9   EBA Guidelines on IRRBB – key changes.
Source: own elaboration

Another area of concern is the guidance on capital calculation. In particular, the revised calculation of capital add-on for IRRBB requires the coverage for earnings risk and value risk so that both types of risks should be integrated in a consistent framework without duplication. Usually, if the bank's ΔNII shows a loss under certain interest rate scenarios then we can easily expect that its ΔEVE will be showing a positive number. Given that the EVE is nothing more than the discounted value of future cash flows over the whole life of the banking book, those two metrics are showing the same things but under different time frames (although for the estimation of ΔNII the cash flows are not discounted). Consequently, the interpretation of the EBA Guidelines related to the capital add-on assessment could be that the impact for earnings needs to be considered only if it is showing a loss and ΔEVE is positive. Otherwise, there is a risk that the negative impact will be double counted.

Strategy	Steering approach	Risk appetite	Limit system

GOVERNANCE	METHODS	IT INFRASTRUCTURE
• Organisational setup • Roles and responsibilities • Efficient processes • Incentive system • Reporting • Validation	• NII approach • EVE approach • Stress testing (inc. reverse stress testing) • Deriving interest rate scenarios • Modelling NMDs and options • Outlier test	• Integrated data basis as *single point of truth* • Flexible, modifiable data model • Adequate software support for EaR and EVE calculations

FIGURE 1.10   EBA Guidelines – implementation challenges under the microscope.
Source: own elaboration

Another addition to the guidelines which did not originate from the original guidelines nor from the BCBS Standards is the requirement to include market value changes in earnings metrics. This change will require banks to start modelling the true IFRS P&L and to consider the increase or reduction in total earnings and capital. This is a very important point since, traditionally, earnings metrics just focus on NII and ignore interest rate sensitivity in other areas of P&L. This is a clear attempt at convergence between accounting and risk management techniques, which have always been treated on a separate basis. The accounting treatment of instruments will determine how the earnings metric will be impacted.

The updated IRRBB EBA Guidelines impose the inclusion of the non-performing exposures (NPE) into the IRRBB "equation". NPE should be included as general interest sensitive instruments whose modelling reflects expected cash flows and their timing. NPEs should be included net of provisions. This point is of relevance given that the gradual increase of NPL stocks in Europe, in particular in Mediterranean countries, stresses the importance of a more integrated approach between credit risk and active management of interest rate risk in the banking book. As such, this requirement gives rise to the new trend in modern Treasury/ALM and risk management where default probabilities will be applied while hedging the volatility of NII. In this case the financial structure of the hedging derivative would match the credit risk adjusted cash flow profile of the asset portfolio. Therefore, considering the interaction between ALM and credit risk has become a methodological challenge both in light of the updated EBA guidelines and IFRS 9 Principles. Figure 1.11 shows the evolution of the IRRBB regulatory requirements in Europe from 2015 onwards.

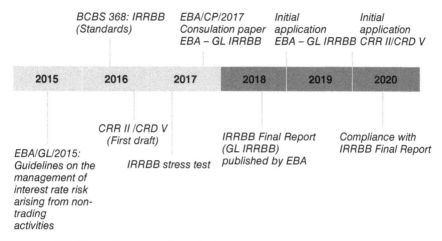

FIGURE 1.11   IRRBB regulatory roadmap in Europe.
Source: own elaboration

ECB 2017 IRRBB STRESS TEST

In 2017 the European Central Bank (ECB) conducted a sensitivity analysis of IRRBB based on year-end 2016 numbers across European banks. This exercise was designed to provide the ECB with sufficient information to understand the interest rate sensitivity of European banks' assets and liabilities in the banking book and the impact on net interest income. Additionally, the exercise covered the changes in the economic value of the banking book assets and liabilities resulting from applied shocks and the development of net interest income generated by assets and liabilities under a shock scenario. ECB Banking Supervision applied six hypothetical interest rate shocks, shown in Figure 1.12, to determine how the economic value of equity and net interest income projections would change in an evolving interest rate environment. The starting point of the analysis was the end of 2016.

The results indicated that NII of European banks would decrease under most of the applied scenarios. The most severe decrease (under parallel down shock) was associated with the assumption that retail deposits would not be renumbered below 0%. Therefore, banks can see it as a short option position on the liability side at 0% strike. The more rates go down the higher economic value of the option. NII would recover with an increase in interest rates, i.e., under the upward movement of the interest rate curve.

There was a rather limited impact on EVE instead shown in Figure 1.13. The worst outcome can be seen under the parallel up scenario equal to −2.7% of Common Equity Tier 1 (CET1).

Under an interest rate increase European banks would benefit from NII perspective, however the rate increase would have a negative impact on EVE. This is clearly seen in Figure 1.14, which shows the overall IRRBB position of banks in Europe. This is the case for 57% of banks which participated in the stress test exercise. The positive impact on NII is driven by floating rate assets on the short end of the interest

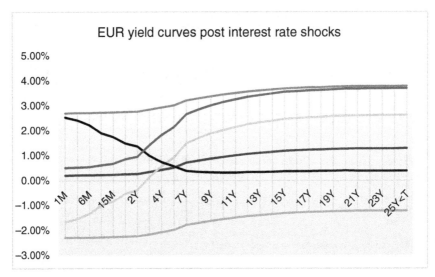

FIGURE 1.12 Interest rate shocks applied for the EUR currency in EBA stress test exercise.
Source: IRRBB – ECB (2017) Stress test

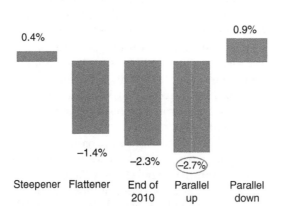

FIGURE 1.13 Average change in EVE by interest rate shocks.
Source: Sensitivity analysis on IRRBB – ECB (2017) Stress test – Final results

rate curve (up to 12 months). The negative impact on EVE is driven by the *net asset* position on the medium-to-long part of the interest rate curve, i.e., assets with long-term repricing are funded by short-term repricing liabilities. For 19% of banks the increase in interest rates leads to a positive impact on NII and EVE. In this case the positive impact on NII is driven by *asset sensitive* position on the short end (the repricing velocity of assets is higher than liabilities). These assets are funded by liabilities

	Delta EVE > 0	Delta EVE < 0
Delta NII > 0	19%	57%
Delta NII < 0	4%	20%

FIGURE 1.14 Distribution of changes in NII under 1-year horizon and EVE in parallel up IR shock.
Source: Sensitivity analysis on IRRBB – ECB (2017) Stress test – Final results

with long-term repricing, for example *behaviouralised* liabilities (the stable portion of deposits).

The important result coming from IRRBB stress test is the bank's dependence on behavioural modelling both on the asset and liability side of the balance sheet, i.e., stability of Non-Maturing Deposits (NMDs) and loans prepayments. Both the magnitude and the sign of the IRRBB exposure can change as a result of *behaviouralisation*. The IRRBB stress test shows that if NMDs are considered as an overnight liability the average EVE impact will be –28.1% CET1 under a parallel up shock of 200 bps instead of an average –2.7% CET in the case where the NMDs are *behaviouralised*.

Banks use behavioural models to better measure and manage IRRBB and hedging is performed on a behavioural basis. Modelling of deposits is particularly important, as deposits are the main funding source for banks. Incorrectly modelled stability of deposits might lead to extensive losses in an increasing rate environment. Based on the results of the IRRBB stress test provided by ECB, retail transactional core deposits exhibit the highest model stability (4.9 Y) and highest share of core deposits (77%). It has been pointed out that modelled by banks the duration of wholesale core deposits is surprisingly long (3.2 Y) and, in some cases, the same calibration for all customer types has been used. Figure 1.15 shows the weighted average repricing profile of core deposits based on the results of the ECB stress test.

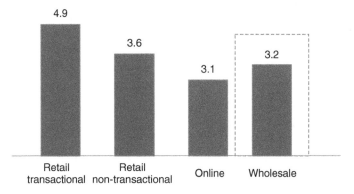

FIGURE 1.15 Repricing period in years of core deposits split by customer segment.
Source: Sensitivity analysis on IRRBB – ECB (2017) Stress test – Final results

The IRRBB stress test performed has shown the importance and the impact of the prepayment model in the IRRBB position of a bank. Prepayment models are the second most relevant model for IRRBB as borrowers pay back or renegotiate some of their loans ahead of schedule, especially when market rates decrease, and penalty fees are low. Prepayments shorten the duration of some loans, in particular if long dated and fixed rate (mortgages). Without loan prepayments models the average EVE impact in a +200 bps shock would be –11.1% CET1 instead of –2.7% CET1.

Interesting points have been highlighted in the results of the IRRBB stress test performed by the ECB related to derivatives in the banking book which are crucial for interest rate risk management. In particular, banks use derivatives not only for risk mitigation to manage the mismatches in the repricing profile of assets and liabilities but also to reach a target Interest Rate (IR) profile. The target IR profile is a combination of NII and EVE stability or to position themselves in a certain way [Sensitivity analysis on IRRBB – ECB (2017) Stress test – Final results].

It is emphasised throughout this book that using derivatives has additional risk for financial institutions which cannot be underestimated. Derivatives represent effective tools for the management of interest rate risk but generate exposure to other risk categories such as:

- counterparty credit risk – when the contract has positive value for the bank, the counterparty default leads to credit losses.
- liquidity risk – the negative mark to market of derivatives poses requirements to exchange cash collateral with the counterparty. In the case of bilateral trading the exchange of collateral happens after the predetermined threshold is exceeded in terms of negative mark to market. In the case of central clearing the derivative position is cleared on a daily basis.
- P&L volatility and hedge accounting – derivatives in the banking book have to obtain the hedge accounting designation, otherwise there is P&L volatility on a daily basis due to the mark to market fluctuations.

Additionally, hedging is subject to transaction costs and hedging charges and transaction unwind can impact P&L negatively. In case of swap transaction, the cost depends on the transaction tenor as it drives the risk position and capital allocation for the counterparty. The longer the tenor is the higher the hedging cost incurred by a bank. In the case of interest rate options (IRO) there is a premium paid by the option buyer.

INTEREST RATE SHOCKS

This section provides an overview of interest rate shocks which can be applied in the calculations of delta EVE (ΔEVE). These are both historical and hypothetical interest rate shocks. The regulators in Europe and the UK recommend the use of interest rate shocks determined in the BCBS Standards issued in April 2016 (BCBS 368). However,

TABLE 1.3 IRRBB shocks defined by BCBS.

	O/N	O/N–1mth	1–3 mths	3–6 mths	6–9 mths	9–12 mths	1–1.5 yr	1.5–2 yr	2–3 yr	3–4 yr	4–5 yr	5–6 yr	6–7 yr	7–8 yr	8–9 yr	9–10 yr
Parallel up																
EUR	2.00%	2.00%	2.00%	2.00%	2.00%	2.00%	2.00%	2.00%	2.00%	2.00%	2.00%	2.00%	2.00%	2.00%	2.00%	2.00%
USD	2.00%	2.00%	2.00%	2.00%	2.00%	2.00%	2.00%	2.00%	2.00%	2.00%	2.00%	2.00%	2.00%	2.00%	2.00%	2.00%
GBP	2.50%	2.50%	2.50%	2.50%	2.50%	2.50%	2.50%	2.50%	2.50%	2.50%	2.50%	2.50%	2.50%	2.50%	2.50%	2.50%
Parallel down																
EUR	-2.00%	-2.00%	-2.00%	-2.00%	-2.00%	-2.00%	-2.00%	-2.00%	-2.00%	-2.00%	-2.00%	-2.00%	-2.00%	-2.00%	-2.00%	-2.00%
USD	-2.00%	-2.00%	-2.00%	-2.00%	-2.00%	-2.00%	-2.00%	-2.00%	-2.00%	-2.00%	-2.00%	-2.00%	-2.00%	-2.00%	-2.00%	-2.00%
GBP	-2.50%	-2.50%	-2.50%	-2.50%	-2.50%	-2.50%	-2.50%	-2.50%	-2.50%	-2.50%	-2.50%	-2.50%	-2.50%	-2.50%	-2.50%	-2.50%
Short up																
EUR	2.50%	2.47%	2.40%	2.28%	2.14%	2.01%	1.83%	1.61%	1.34%	1.04%	0.81%	0.63%	0.49%	0.38%	0.30%	0.23%
USD	3.00%	2.97%	2.88%	2.73%	2.57%	2.41%	2.19%	1.94%	1.61%	1.25%	0.97%	0.76%	0.59%	0.46%	0.36%	0.28%
GBP	3.00%	2.97%	2.88%	2.73%	2.57%	2.41%	2.19%	1.94%	1.61%	1.25%	0.97%	0.76%	0.59%	0.46%	0.36%	0.28%
Short down																
EUR	-2.50%	-2.47%	-2.40%	-2.28%	-2.14%	-2.01%	-1.83%	-1.61%	-1.34%	-1.04%	-0.81%	-0.63%	-0.49%	-0.38%	-0.30%	-0.23%
USD	-3.00%	-2.97%	-2.88%	-2.73%	-2.57%	-2.41%	-2.19%	-1.94%	-1.61%	-1.25%	-0.97%	-0.76%	-0.59%	-0.46%	-0.36%	-0.28%
GBP	-3.00%	-2.97%	-2.88%	-2.73%	-2.57%	-2.41%	-2.19%	-1.94%	-1.61%	-1.25%	-0.97%	-0.76%	-0.59%	-0.46%	-0.36%	-0.28%
Flattener																
EUR	2.00%	1.97%	1.89%	1.77%	1.62%	1.49%	1.30%	1.08%	0.79%	0.48%	0.24%	0.06%	-0.09%	-0.20%	-0.29%	-0.36%
USD	2.40%	2.37%	2.27%	2.10%	1.92%	1.75%	1.51%	1.23%	0.87%	0.48%	0.17%	-0.07%	-0.25%	-0.39%	-0.51%	-0.59%
GBP	2.40%	2.37%	2.27%	2.10%	1.92%	1.75%	1.51%	1.23%	0.87%	0.48%	0.17%	-0.07%	-0.25%	-0.39%	-0.51%	-0.59%
Steepener																
EUR	-1.62%	-1.60%	-1.52%	-1.40%	-1.26%	-1.13%	-0.95%	-0.73%	-0.45%	-0.15%	0.08%	0.26%	0.40%	0.51%	0.60%	0.67%
USD	-1.95%	-1.92%	-1.82%	-1.65%	-1.47%	-1.30%	-1.06%	-0.78%	-0.42%	-0.03%	0.28%	0.52%	0.70%	0.84%	0.96%	1.04%
GBP	-1.95%	-1.92%	-1.82%	-1.65%	-1.47%	-1.30%	-1.06%	-0.78%	-0.42%	-0.03%	0.28%	0.52%	0.70%	0.84%	0.96%	1.04%

Source: Based on BCBS Standards, 2016

TABLE 1.4 The interest rate shock under the "Oil Supply Crisis" scenario for USD currency.

Oil Supply Crisis	0.25	0.5	0.75	1	2	3	4	5	6	7	8	9	10	15	20	30
USD Scenario	24	14	35	53	71	80	80	80	80	80	71	60	51	55	55	55

Source: own elaboration

banks can apply additional scenarios which capture the particularities of their banking book. For example, a bank with a significant amount of Treasury book can apply the 1994 bond market crisis scenario (*Great Bond Massacre*) to stress the portfolio value. The 94 crisis shock includes a sudden drop in bonds market prices which began in the United States and spread through the rest of the world. The yields in 30-year Treasury bonds rose by 200 bps in the first 9 months of the year.

Table 1.3 shows interest rates shocks defined by the BCBS Standards.

Additional scenarios could potentially include for a number of currencies as follows.

Oil Supply Crisis

In 1973, the global economy was rocked by an oil crisis caused by an OPEC oil embargo, which dramatically cut the available oil supply and significantly increased world oil prices. The "Oil Supply Crisis" scenario simulates the shocks of another oil supply crisis to test the impact on the market.

The scenario is defined in terms of the upward movements of the curve (in bps) by tenor (Table 1.4).

HY/LBO/Default Risk

High Yield/Leverage Buyout/Default Risk refers to the risk posed by less stable entities and the resulting effect which their default could have on the market rates.

The scenario is defined in terms of the downward movements of the curve (in bps) by tenor (Table 1.5).

TABLE 1.5 The interest rate shocks under the "HY/LBO/Default Risk" scenario.

HY/LBO/ Default Risk	0.25	0.5	0.75	1	2	3	4	5	6	7	8	9	10	15	20	30
USD Scenario	−13	−24	−26	−28	−32	−32	−32	−34	−34	−32	−28	−24	−21	−21	−21	−21

Source: own elaboration

TABLE 1.6   The interest rate shocks under the "Inflation Expectation" scenario.

Inflation Expecta- tion	0.25	0.5	0.75	1	2	3	4	5	6	7	8	9	10	15	20	30
USD Scenario	55	55	55	55	55	62	70	75	78	80	80	80	80	70	70	70

Source: own elaboration

Inflation expectations

Inflation expectations play a significant role in interest rates and their perceived "real" value. Environments with high inflation leads to lower returns on nominal interest rates, as inflation erodes interest rates. Greater expected inflation will lead to lower expected returns.

The scenario is defined in terms of the upward movements of the curve (in bps) by tenor (Table 1.6).

Great Bond Massacre – 94

Additional *event-driven* scenarios which are calibrated on historical financial shocks could be added to the interest rate shocks list. The scenarios below replicate relative changes in interest rates for selected historical events. A far from exhaustive list of examples, on which potential interest rate changes could be based, is as follows.

- October 1973: First OPEC Oil crisis;
- 1979: Iranian Revolution & Second OPEC Oil Shock;
- August 1982: Mexican Debt Crisis;
- September 1985: The Plaza Accord to Weaken the USD;
- October 1987: Black Monday in US Stocks;
- September 1992: Speculative Attack on the European ERM;
- February 1994: Dramatic Federal Reserve Tightening;
- July 1997: Asian Currency Crisis;
- August 1998: Russian Default – Emerging Market Debt Crisis;
- September 1998: Long Term Capital Management Failure;
- 2000–2001: Dot.com Bust;
- January 2002: Argentine Peso Devaluation;
- March 2008: Bear Stearns Rescue;
- September 2008: Lehman, AIG, FNMA & FHLMC Collapse;
- April 2010: Greece Sovereign Downgrade – Euro Crisis;
- February 2014: Ukraine/Crimea Crisis.

TABLE 1.7 94 crisis scenario.

94 crash	O/N	O/N–1mth	1-3 mths	3-6 mths	6-9 mths	9-12 mths	1-1.5yr	1.5-2yr	2-3yr	3-4yr	4-5yr	5-6yr	6-7yr	7-8yr	8-9yr	9-10yr
EUR		0.38%	0.48%	0.73%	1.180%	1.63%	1.76%	1.965%	2.17%	2.27%	2.37%	2.315%	2.26%	2.2067%	2.1533%	2.10%
USD		2.75%	3.13%	3.44%	3.660%	3.88%	3.90%	3.605%	3.31%	3.20%	3.02%	2.875%	2.73%	2.6767%	2.6233%	2.30%
GBP		0.56%	1.24%	1.90%	2.325%	2.75%	3.36%	3.275%	3.19%	3.18%	3.10%	3.035%	2.97%	2.9167%	2.8633%	2.77%

Source: own elaboration

CHAPTER 2

How to identify and measure Interest Rate Risk in the Banking Book

IDENTIFICATION OF IRRBB – CASE STUDIES OF THE EXPOSURE TO IRRBB

The first part of this chapter is dedicated to an analysis of the exposure to IRRBB and its different subcategories. It presents several case studies and the proposal of hedging solutions to mitigate a bank's exposure. The case studies presented are illustrative and numbers are elaborated by the author.

In the second part, the dual nature of IRRBB is explained along with the measurement methodologies and metrics to quantify the IRRBB exposure in financial institutions.

CASE STUDY 1: Analysis of the NII, EVE and margin compression of Bank A.

The asset side of the banking book of Bank A comprises corporate mortgages which use an administered rate, i.e., a rate which can be changed at will by the bank, usually as a result of the movements in the central bank base rate.

Corporate mortgages are funded by fixed rate deposits with 3 months, 12 months and 24 months residual maturity. Additionally, Bank A has a liquid asset buffer (LAB) composed of government bonds with a short-term maturity of 3 months.

The IRRBB position of Bank A is analysed from several perspectives:

1. Impact on net interest income (ΔNII).
2. Impact on economic value of equity (ΔEVE).
3. Level of the term structure of interest rates (positive or negative territory).
4. Behavioural optionality embedded in the banking book of Bank A.
5. Existence of automatic options embedded in banking book items, for example interest rate floors or caps.
6. Basis risk exposure.

Below is an analysis of the potential drivers for IRRBB exposure of Bank A.

There is an impact on the net interest income due to the movements in the interest rate curve – this is driven by the short-term repricing assets. The downward movement of the curve has a negative impact on the net interest income of Bank A as it is *asset sensitive* over the gapping period of 12 months.

This impact needs to be quantified. Where the treasurer of Bank A is convinced there is no imminent downward pressure in terms of the short end curve movement then this directional gap position is beneficial. Otherwise, in expectation of downward pressures on the short end of the curve, the treasurer has to "close" or diminish the extent of the total *GAP* within a 12-month time horizon.

The management of the directional gap, on the short end of the curve, is an important tool as it mitigates potential NII sensitivity which needs to be monitored on at least a monthly basis (NII sensitivity is presented and discussed in the ALCO report of a bank). The easiest way to manage the extent of the directional gap is through natural offsetting. The interbank placement or borrowings are common practice to deal with it. In our example, Bank A would need to diversify its funding base and borrow in the interbank market to offset the sensitivity driven by administered rate loans or to raise short-term repricing deposits (for example *Instant Access* deposits). Figure 2.2 shows the management of a directional gap through natural offsetting.

Interbank placement or borrowing are not the only tools to manage a directional gap. There are other instruments to manage it which are described in Chapter 3.

In terms of ΔEVE, Bank A is positioned as a *net liability* position. This is because on the medium-to-long part of the curve (beyond 12 months) it has more repricing liabilities than assets. Such a structure exposes Bank A to the downward movement of the curve as the *Present Value* of liabilities is higher in comparison to the base scenario (no interest rate shift). This situation is shown in Figure 2.3.

The regulatory guidelines related to IRRBB practices require banks to perform an analysis of the EVE impact under at least 6 interest rate shocks which are defined by BCBS and endorsed by the regulators worldwide. The worst outcome drives the exposure of a bank. In our example, Bank A faces embedded, although not crystallised, loss under all downward interest rate shocks. The worst outcome is achieved under parallel down scenario and equals to –£225K. It is important to highlight that Bank A represents the example for illustrative purposes only, so we are not analysing, at this point, if the exposure is limited or significant. The objective of this section is to present the IRRBB subcategories which are incorporated in the banking book structure of a bank and create the risk exposure.

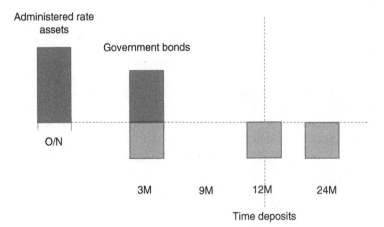

FIGURE 2.1   Asset sensitive position of Bank A within the gapping period of 12 months.
Source: own elaboration

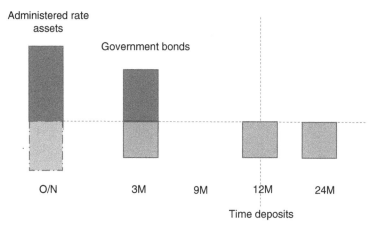

FIGURE 2.2   Reduction of NII sensitivity through natural offsetting.
Source: own elaboration

The impact on EVE can be easily reduced through Interest Rate Swaps (IRS) if the exposure is considered excessive. Where Bank A decides that its exposure, in terms of EVE, is too high it will enter into the *receiver* swap (pay floating and receive fixed). In this way the exposure is mitigated as per Figure 2.4.

The level of interest rates is another point to be considered while analysing the overall exposure of Bank A. The level of interest rates impacts the NII sensitivity directly. The aftermath of the financial crisis brought in the concept of negative rates, which was never considered in ALM models before, and NII shocks was locked at 0% level, meaning that interest rates could never go below zero. In that case, the magnitude of any downward shock was limited. For example, if the rate for a certain time bucket was equal to 1%, and the intention was to apply a –2% parallel shock, then the magnitude of the shock applied was –1% instead of –2% due to the 0% floor.

The introduction of negative rates and, subsequently, the BCBS Standards published in 2016 removed the zero bound from ALM models, stating explicitly that the full extent of the shock should be applied. Coming back to our example, we can easily realise that Bank A, under downward shocks, would face potential margin compression and this is driven by the following reasons:

1. variable rate assets
2. fixed rate deposits

	ΔEVE
94 crash	459
Parallel up	194
Parallel down	(225)
Short up	(46)
Short down	33
Flattener	(120)
Steepener	157
Worse	(225)

FIGURE 2.3   The ΔEVE under various interest rate scenarios (numbers in thousands of GBP).
Source: own elaboration

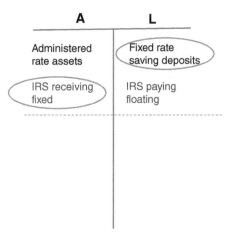

FIGURE 2.4   Management of the IRRBB exposure through receiver swap.
Source: own elaboration

Meanwhile, the asset side will reprice following the downward pressure from the market; the repricing capacity on the liability side is limited because the interest rate is fixed. In general, many banks do not reprice current accounts or saving accounts fearing the loss of customers. In some jurisdictions there is a regulatory requirement to keep the customer rate at a certain minimum level. For example, in Belgium there is a product known as the Regulatory Saving Account (RSA) and the minimum level of return rate to customer is 11 bps.

The level of interest rates not only involves the risk of margin compression as per Figure 2.5. It also determines whether the automatic options, either explicit or implicit, are *out of money* or *in the money*. Case study 2 will focus exactly on the impact of automatic options on ΔNII and ΔEVE.

Needless to say, behavioural liabilities introduce a behavioural optionality risk. Bank A is funded by customer deposits, but these are fixed rate deposits. Therefore, if clients withdraw funds before the expiration of the product (the phenomenon known as early redemption of time depo), they may lose the beneficial rate locked in and, in some cases, be subject to penalties. Consequently, in the case of Bank A,

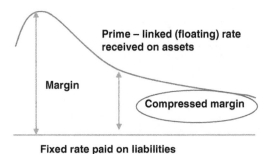

FIGURE 2.5   Margin compression resulting from a reduction in interest rates.
Source: own elaboration

FIGURE 2.6   Basis risk exposure of Bank A.
Source: own elaboration

behavioural optionality risk is contained. However, it shouldn't be neglected. Analysis of the past behaviour of depositors is still imperative. Behavioural optionality lies also on the asset side. There is the potential risk of early redemption of the mortgages. However, given the nature of assets (variable rate assets) the impact on IRRBB, from the asset side, is limited.

Assuming that Bank A enters the *receiver swaps* there is also basis risk exposure. Basis risk is driven by an imperfect correlation between the SONIA rate and the base rate. Bank A receives the base rate on the asset side and pays the SONIA rate on the liability side. The SONIA rate on the liability side comes from the floating rate on the Overnight Index Swap (OIS) which Bank A entered into to manage its IRRBB exposure. This exposure could be considered significant with the growth of the tracker mortages book and management of this exposure will depend on the future commercial strategy of the Bank.

Figure 2.6 shows the basis risk exposure driven by an imperfect correlation between the indexes on the asset side and the liability side.

CASE STUDY 2: Analysis of the impact of automatic options embedded in the banking book on NII and EVE

Bank B shows a positive mismatching related to gaps in repricing within the next 12 months. This positive total gap is driven mainly by the repricing frequency of the floating rate assets. However, it has to be highlighted that Bank B has limited NII sensitivity in a downward scenario driven by the existence of automatic options (floors) which lock the rate at the strike level (mainly at 0% level). Instead, the sensitivity in an upward scenario is significant and is driven by the faster velocity of repricing of assets rather than behavioural liabilities, which have an average repricing maturity of between 2 and 3 years.

On the medium-to-long part of the curve Bank B carries a *net liability position* due to the portion of behavioural liabilities with longer repricing. Those liabilities are distributed between the 1.5- and 5-year time buckets. In addition, Bank B has a smaller amount of fixed rate time deposits with maturities between 1 and 5 years. Figure 2.7 shows the repricing gap of Bank B.

Bank B is exposed to option risk as a result of the existence of automatic and behavioural options in its banking book structure. The common practice is to measure the impact of the automatic options under a number of interest rate shocks and the change in the options value is added to the final ΔEVE number (as per the methodological approach presented in the BCBS Standards 2016). As far as behavioural optionality is concerned, the easiest way to measure the impact is to compare IRRBB metrics under behavioural and contractual analysis, i.e., under the assumption that non-maturing deposits are modelled versus the assumption that they simply follow the contractual maturity.

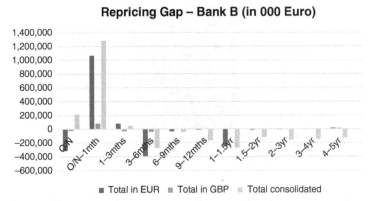

FIGURE 2.7 Repricing gap of Bank B.
Source: own elaboration

Bank B is also exposed to gap risk (often known as repricing risk) which arises because the rate of interest paid on liabilities increases after the rate of interest received on assets or reduces on assets before liabilities. The extent of gap risk depends on whether changes to the term structure of interest rates occur consistently across the whole yield curve (parallel risk) or differently by period (non-parallel risk). The common practice is to measure and to control gap risk through the repricing gap technique and the analysis of the net mismatch for every time band and split by material currency. As per regulatory guidelines, this is the simplest technique for measuring interest rate risk exposure to the short end interest rate risk. The gap risk is measured through the application of the parallel shift to the interest rate curve and the calculation of the change to the net interest income (ΔNII) although more advanced techniques require the simulation of a bank's NII under a number of interest rate shocks (Figure 2.8). The methodologies for the calculation of NII sensitivity are described in detail later in this chapter.

From the economic value perspective, the structure, as per Figure 2.7, gives rise to the exposure to the downward movement of the curve as a decrease in the medium-to-long-term rates has a negative impact on the value of equity. This situation is reflected in the EVE sensitivity metric, i.e., Bank B faces a negative impact on equity under a downward scenario (and positive under an upward scenario). The worst result is driven by the steepener scenario. Under the steepener scenario, interest rates increase gradually by scalar, which applies the higher negative magnitude of shock to the shorter rates rather than medium-term rates. Consequently, given that interest rate options are exercised only when the rates are below the strike level (in most cases set at 0%), on the medium-to-long part of the curve, they are not exercised (under assumption of positive slope of the curve), and the impact of floors is limited only to

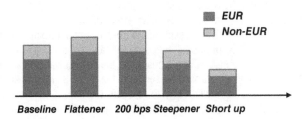

FIGURE 2.8 Simulation of NII under a number of interest rate shocks.
Source: own elaboration

	Short down		
	ΔEVE	ΔOptions	ΔEVE + Options
Consolidated	(25,349)	38,472	13,123
EUR	(23,062)	29,620	6,557
USD	–	–	–
GBP	(2,152)	7,940	5,788

FIGURE 2.9 The impact of automatic options on ΔEVE under short down shock.
Source: own elaboration

	Parallel down		
	ΔEVE	ΔOptions	ΔEVE + Options
Consolidated	(20,385)	152,127	131,742
EUR	(17,448)	117,434	99,986
USD	–	–	–
GBP	(2,797)	34,693	31,896

FIGURE 2.10 The impact of automatic options on ΔEVE under parallel down shock.
Source: own elaboration

the short-term time buckets. For this reason, the steepener scenario represents the worst outcome for Bank B driven by limited beneficial impact of automatic options.

The reduction in interest rates will cause an increase in value of the automatic options embedded in corporate loans both under a base scenario and under all downward scenarios (for negative market rates). The positive value of options can significantly outweigh the losses driven by the structural exposure of Bank B. In fact, this can be clearly seen in Figure 2.9 and Figure 2.10.

As seen in Figure 2.10 the impact of automatic options is much higher in a parallel down scenario. This is driven by the fact that under a short down scenario the option protection becomes less effective on the longer end of the curve as the curve shift applied is lower than in the parallel down scenario.

It can be clearly seen that the ΔEVE result is highly dependent on the intrinsic value of the automatic options embedded in the banking book structure and the volatility of the interest rates (EUR rates which are in the negative territory).

Analysing in detail the NII sensitivity, under the assumptions that Bank B performs analysis of the NII sensitivity in a parallel up and parallel down interest rate scenario and that the full amount of shock is applied, the impact of automatic options (floors) is clearly seen under a −2% interest rate shock. This is the case in the following Balance Sheet (BS) items:

1. Treasury Securities (TS).
2. Corporate Loans (CL).
3. Behavioural Liabilities (BL).

NII sensitivity parallel down – Assets	1-year horizon (in 000 Euro)	NII sensitivity parallel down – Liabilities	1-year horizon (in 000 Euro)
Cash and central bank balances	–3,996	Behavioural CASA	2,341
Treasury securities	0	Corporate time depo	338
Placed interbank	0	Borrowed interbank	0
Corporate loans	–2,350	Other liabilities	0
Revolving loans	0		
Other loans	0		
Derivatives	1,516		
	Total	**–2,151**	

FIGURE 2.11   NII sensitivity of Bank B under a parallel down scenario.
Source: own elaboration

In a –200 bps interest rate scenario, the impact on TS, CL and BL is limited and we can deduce that this is driven by automatic optionality which is *in the money* under a –2% shock. On the other hand, under a parallel up scenario the TS, CL and BL are subject to the full extent of a 200 bps scenario which results in higher sensitivity.

Therefore, in a downward shock, the negative impact on NII is limited (let's remember that Bank B is *asset sensitive* on the short part of the curve). This is clearly seen in Figure 2.11. On the contrary, Figure 2.12 shows the positive impact on NII under +2% which is exactly what we expect for the *asset sensitive* position on the short part of the curve which, in our example, is equal to a 1-year time horizon. The zero floor on the deposit side is related to the Bank B decision not to pass on negative rates to clients. Therefore, it can be seen as a short option position (floor) with strike at 0%.

It is worth highlighting that Bank B has significant variability in terms of NII result (22m under +200 bps versus –2m under –200 bps) which is not well perceived by investors and by the regulator. NII variability means that, in comparison to the expected annual NII, the change that is driven by interest rate curve movements (both up and down) is high.

Assuming that expected NII of Bank B equals to 24m its NII sensitivity under +200 bps would be 22m/24m = 91%.

NII sensitivity parallel up – Assets	1-year horizon (in 000 Euro)	NII sensitivity parallel up – Liabilities	1-year horizon (in 000 Euro)
Cash and central bank balances	3,996	Behavioural CASA	–7,204
Treasury securities	1,629	Corporate time depo	–339
Placed interbank	0	Borrowed interbank	0
Corporate loans	25,746	Other liabilities	0
Revolving loans	0		
Other loans	0		
Derivatives	–1,516		
	Total	**22,312**	

FIGURE 2.12   NII sensitivity of Bank B under a parallel up scenario.
Source: own elaboration

CASE STUDY 3: Review of the hedging strategy of a bank

The objective of this case study is to analyse the exposure of Bank C, its hedging strategy and the potential improvements which could be made to the hedging strategy in place.

Let's assume that Bank C has the following products in the banking book:

ASSETS

Product	Balance at 31 Dec 2020 (£m)	Brief description
Commercial Lending	218	Fixed and variable rate loans
Retirement Mortgages	31	A lifetime mortgage where the customer is required to pay the fixed interest on the loan each month. Capital is repaid following customer death or entry into long-term care.
Lifetime Mortgages	33	A fixed rate lifetime mortgage secured against the borrower's home. Interest rolls up into the loan which is repayable on death or entry into long-term care. Borrowers can repay their loan early but in the early years an early repayment charge is payable at between 0–5% of the capital borrowed.
Reversions	60	Customers receive a cash lump sum in return for a percentage of their home.
Treasury Assets	275	Variable rate bank securities, cash deposits and fixed rate assets.
Fixed Assets	10	
Other Assets	17	

LIABILITIES

Product	Balance at 31 Dec 2020 (£m)	Brief description
Wholesale Funding	18	Variable rate funding
Current Accounts	11	Administered rate
Fixed Term Deposits	499	Fixed rate deposits
Notice Accounts	158	Administered rate
Other Liabilities	12	Tax and other liabilities
Capital & Reserves	133	

HEDGING STRATEGY OF BANK C

Bank C hedges its fixed rate assets through entering into hedging derivatives (swaps) over the long-time period. Since lifetime mortgages are fixed rate for 20–25 years Bank C enters into pay fixed derivatives. Mortgages are held at amortised cost and the interest rolls up until the redemption of the loan. The notional of the interest rate swaps increases over time as the product interest rolls-up.

Bank C also hedges the reversion products through entering into pay fixed interest rate swaps.

Commercial lending at a fixed rate is mostly offset by fixed rate deposits. The same applies for fixed rate securities. The residual exposure is managed through interest rates swaps. Index linked gilts from the investment portfolio are hedged through index linked swaps.

Bank C does not hedge core deposits, fixed assets, capital and reserves (also known as structural hedging program discussed later in Chapter 3).

Given the particularities of the products offered by Bank C it is worth providing a more detailed description of risks implied by products offered in this example.

LIFETIME MORTGAGES

Lifetime mortgages have a fixed rate for the term of the product funded by shorter-term repricing liabilities. This means that Bank C is exposed to interest rate risk over the term of the product. As already mentioned, the interest rate risk is managed through the execution of pay fixed receive floating interest rate swaps. Interest rate swaps have a term equal to the expected life of the product. This expected life of the product is a function of borrowers' mortality, morbidity and lapse rates and is determined through regular review of these assumptions and the modelling of the impact of these assumptions on expected lifespans.

The following assumptions are used in the behavioural life modelling of these products and can be provided by the Office for National Statistics (ONS):

1. Percentage of mortality table
2. Female mortality table
3. Male mortality table
4. Future longevity improvements
5. Lapse rates

The notional of the interest rate swaps increases over time as the product interest rolls up. These swaps have no optionality, which means Bank C is exposed to the extent that the actual life of the product is different to the expected life of the product. To minimise this risk, the assumptions need to be back tested and reviewed on at least an annual basis.

REVERSIONS

Table 2.1 shows the illustrative example of the reversion product.

The relevant reversion rate is the discount rate to obtain Bank C's share of the expected property value (£200,000) to the £50,000 advanced on Day 1. The pay fixed interest rate swaps hedge this inherent unwind. This unwind of the initial discount to property value is effectively a notional interest amount.

The following assumptions need to be taken into account in the behavioural life modelling of these products:

TABLE 2.1   The illustrative example of reversion product.

Lump sum (cash) released to the customer on Day 1	£50,000
Share of property value acquired by Bank C	50%
Property value on Day 1	£250,000
Expected property value at expected repayment date	£400,000
Bank C share of expected property value at expected repayment date (50% of £400,000)	**£200,000**

Source: own elaboration

1. Valuation discount rate
2. Property sale delay from death/lapse
3. Sale expenses
4. Male mortality table
5. Inflation rate for costs

NON-INTEREST-BEARING ITEMS (NIBS)

It is assumed that, in comparison to the peer group where the hedging of non-interest-bearing items (NIBs) is the common practice, Bank C undertakes no hedging of its non-interest-bearing balances, which principally reflect capital and reserves and core deposit accounts.

ANALYSIS OF THE IRRBB EXPOSURE OF BANK C

Bank C's approach for ALM modelling of interest roll-up mortgages is based on the assumption that the interest roll-up on the Lifetime mortgage is funded through liabilities. Therefore, Bank C hedges the interest rate risk on the mortgage principal plus interest roll-up for the expected life of the product (i.e., through the execution of an initially accreting swap which then amortises in line with the expected life of the product).

Table 2.2 sets out a numerical example for illustrative purposes.

TABLE 2.2   Example of lifetime mortgages funded by variable rate liabilities.

Balance Sheet category	Day 1	After 1 month
Assets		
Mortgage (principal)	100,000	100,000
Fixed interest accrual	0	500
Liabilities		
Variable rate funding	−100,000	−100,500
Equity		
P&L	0	0

Source: own elaboration

TABLE 2.3 Alternative approach for hedging of lifetime mortgages.

Balance sheet category	Day 1	After 1 month
Assets		
Mortgage (principal)	100,000	100,000
Fixed interest accrual	0	500
Liabilities		
Variable rate funding	−100,000	−100,000
Equity		
Fixed interest accrual is offset by equity	0	−500

Source: own elaboration

An alternative approach would be to assume that the interest roll-up is not funded by variable rate liabilities. This is because the interest roll-up does not explicitly require to be funded by variable rate funding. Only the initial advance requires funding.

In this option the swap will have a fixed notional equal to the initial advance for the expected term of the lifetime mortgage.

This approach would see the fixed interest accrual asset, representing the interest roll-up, being netted with the credit reserves for this interest roll-up before executing the required balance sheet hedging.

In other words, it assumes that the expected term of the interest accrual and the investment term for capital are the same.

Table 2.3 sets out a numerical example for illustrative purposes.

REVERSIONS

Similar to the options explained for the lifetime mortgages, Bank C has two options for the hedging of this product.

Option 1   If we apply a similar approach to reversions, on a fair value basis, as for lifetime mortgages, then the movement in the asset value is funded by variable rate funding. Table 2.4 shows a numerical example of this hedging option.

TABLE 2.4 Example of reversions funded by variable rate liabilities.

Balance sheet category	Day 1	After 1 year
Assets		
Investment in property	100,000	110,000
Liabilities		
Variable rate funding	−100,000	−110,000
Equity		
P&L	0	0

Source: own elaboration

TABLE 2.5   Alternative option for hedging of reversion products.

Balance sheet category	Day 1	After 1 month
Assets		
Investment in property	100,000	110,000
Liabilities		
Variable rate funding	−100,000	−100,000
Equity		
The increase in value is offset by equity	0	−10,000

Source: own elaboration

In this example, the notional of the hedging would need to increase at each revaluation, such that the notional of the swap matched the asset revaluation. This would mean that on day 1 Bank C would need to execute a swap that matches the expected revaluation of the asset, requiring an assessment of the movement in House Price Inflation (HPI) over the expected life of the product and execute an accreting swap with this profile, or accept that it would need to potentially execute new interest rate swaps as the investment is revalued. In this example, the notional of the hedging would need to increase at each revaluation, such that the notional of the swap matched the asset revaluation.

Option 2   However, as with the alternative approach for hedging of lifetime mortgages, it is possible to assume that the movement in fair value of the "Investment in Property" asset is funded through non-interest-bearing balances. Table 2.5 illustrates the case.

As with lifetime mortgages, this would see the movement in fair value of the "investment in property" asset being offset against the P&L reserves credit generated by the revaluation of the asset. This would mean that the original swap executed for the initial "investment in property" asset would not need to be revised following a revaluation of the asset. This would additionally mean that the P&L generated from this revaluation would effectively be hedged over the expected life of the reversion product.

BRIEF EXAMPLE OF P&L MOVEMENTS FOR REVERSION PRODUCTS

Let's imagine that the investment in the property goes up by £10,000 after 1 year. The initial investment is funded by variable rate funding with the total cost of funding equal to £3,000 in a year. After a year the net P&L movement is equal to £10,000 − £3,000 = £7,000.

In option 1, the higher value of the property is assumed to be funded by liabilities; therefore, the notional of the hedging would need to increase as a result of revaluation, such that the notional of the swap matched the asset revaluation.

Alternatively, the movement in fair value of the property asset could be offset against the net P&L reserves credit generated by the revaluation of the asset. In this case the original swap will not need to be revised following a revaluation of the asset.

CASE STUDY 4: Enhancement of the IRRBB framework

The banking book of Bank D is composed of 5-year duration assets and it is funded mainly by customer deposits. The deposit base is composed of term deposits (with a residual maturity of between 12 and 24 months), notice accounts and savings accounts. Given the significant extent of the duration gap (5-year repricing assets are funded by 0.9-year repricing liabilities) the Bank has entered into payer swaps. These swaps receive the SONIA rate on a quarterly basis and pay a fixed rate annually.

The IRRBB exposure is mostly driven by long-term fixed rate assets. This can be clearly seen in Figure 2.13.

Figure 2.14 shows mitigation of the duration gap of Bank D through swaps.

It is important to highlight that the intention of Bank D's treasurer is to close the residual exposure to IRRBB in order to respect the limits mandated by ALCO. This is why the notional of swaps is lower than the notional of mortgages. There is already partial natural offsetting through fixed rate deposits therefore the treasurer undertakes partial hedging through payer swaps.

Additionally, the intention of Bank D's treasurer is to limit the impact of any significant fluctuations in earnings as a result of future movements in interest rates which would affect its long-term viability. Therefore, the strategy, mandated by the Board of Directors and delegated to ALCO, consists in providing stability of earnings. The liquidity portfolio of Bank D is composed of a central bank reserve and short-term HQLA.

The Board approves the risk appetite for interest rate risk and delegates to ALCO the responsibility for reviewing risk exposure and establishes the direction and strategy for the treasury.

Bank D has the following limit to measure the earnings sensitivity which is approved by the Board and documented in the IRRBB policy.

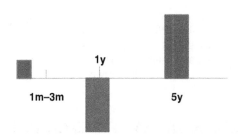

FIGURE 2.13 Exposure to the duration gap in Bank D (without swaps).
Source: own elaboration

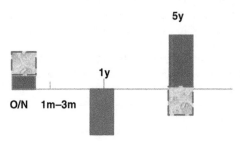

FIGURE 2.14 Mitigated exposure to the duration gap in Bank D (with swaps).
Source: own elaboration

■ Earnings sensitivity under −100 bps parallel shift scenario. This limit is expressed in absolute terms and is equal to £1m.

Bank D does not perform an upward interest rate curve scenario with the scope to analyse the impact on earnings.

Along with earnings sensitivity, the treasury of Bank D performs the analysis of the net present value under a +/−200 bps shock scenario. The limit is expressed as a ratio: *ΔNPV/capital resources* and is equal to 5%. It also monitors the basis risk given the number of swaps.

It is worth highlighting that Bank D is a small bank which needs further improvements related to the IRRBB framework.

It approaches an advisory firm specialising in treasury matters asking for advice on potential enhancements in the existing framework. The analysis provides clear areas for improvement; these are summarised in Table 2.6.

TABLE 2.6 Enhancement of IRRBB framework for Bank D.

Area of improvement	The existing framework	The suggested improvement
Earnings sensitivity (ΔNII)	It is measured under a −100 bps parallel shift scenario. This limit is expressed in absolute terms and is equal to £1m.	Introduce +100 bps shock as the position of the bank in terms of directional gap can change over time driven by items in repricing or in maturity and therefore affect the earnings of the bank. The impact on earnings is better expressed as a ratio: ΔNII/expected NII under 1 year's time horizon (known as the gapping period) as the size of the Balance Sheet can change in the future and consequently the limit will need to be adjusted as well.
Delta Net Present Value (ΔNPV)	It is measured under +/−200 bps shock scenario. The limit is expressed as a ratio: ΔNPV/Capital resources and is equal to 5%.	It is recommended to put in place additional interest rate curve scenarios, for example: – Steepener – Flattener – Short up – Short down – 94 crisis bond shock (historical shock) – Bank specific scenario
PV01	Bank D does not measure PV01 for time bucket	Introduce PV01 analysis both by time bucket and for the whole banking book. It is an important metric which indicates what the interest rate tenor is that Bank D is most sensitive to. Based on the sensitivity of specific tenors the hedging activity is decided by the treasurer.
Basis risk	Bank D does not measure the basis risk exposure	Introduce basis risk metric which measures the effect of an immediate 100 bps rise or fall in the spread Bank rate – SONIA on the NII

(Continued)

TABLE 2.6 *(Continued)*

Area of improvement	The existing framework	The suggested improvement
Behaviouralisation of CASA	There is no modelling in place for CASA	Modelling CASA is recommended through the creation of a target replicating portfolio (for example, a rolling 5-year balance) or application of regression techniques in order to determine the volatile/core part of these positions and their rate sensitivity. Where there is an absence of modelling practice banks have to allocate items to an O/N time bucket and consequently they do not benefit from the possibility of natural offset for the fixed rate assets and over-estimate or underestimate the real risk picture of the banking book
Behavioralisation of assets	There is no modelling in place for the early prepayment of fixed rate assets	It is recommended to build the model based on the historical external market and internal data in order to calculate the rate of financial prepayment. It is especially important in the process of design of the hedging strategy for the bank

Source: own elaboration

THE DUAL NATURE OF IRRBB

As already mentioned in the previous chapter, interest rate risk in the banking book is measured from two different perspectives: the earnings approach and the economic value approach. The first approach concentrates on the effects of interest rates movements on a bank's NII over short time horizons that could span from one to two or even three years. However, the earnings perspective fails to indicate the long-term impacts of interest rate movements, as mismatches might be hidden beyond the horizon of the analysis.

Figure 2.15 shows a situation where the bank analyses only the short end of the interest rate curve and does not look at the medium-to-long-term mismatches. The medium-to-long-term mismatches are not captured through a NII sensitivity metric. There is a potential loss embedded in the banking book where rates move adversely.

In order to have a comprehensive view of the long-term effects of changes in rates, banks must adopt the economic value approach, which is based on the change in the present value of all cash flows under prescribed interest rate shocks. This is known as the *dual view* in the IRRBB world. These metrics are complementary in nature and institutions should monitor both. Both economic value and earnings measures are required because hedging one can have an impact on the other. There is significant negative correlation between the economic value approach versus earnings approach. Reduction in one quite often leads to an increase in the other. The earnings approach

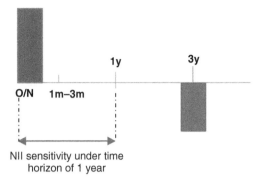

FIGURE 2.15 NII sensitivity time horizon and medium-term balance sheet mismatch.
Source: own elaboration

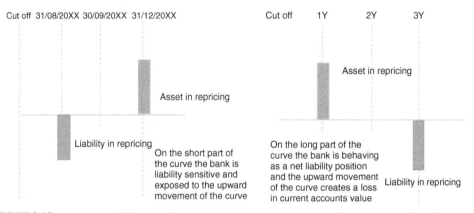

FIGURE 2.16 CASA modelling and impact on earning sensitivity and economic value of equity.
Source: own elaboration

will tend to drive the free reserves and Non-Interest-Bearing Current Account (NIBCA) longer, and smooth the earning but increase the banking book duration. On the other hand, an economic value approach will drive it shorter and increase earnings sensitivity. This phenomenon is shown in Figure 2.16.

EXPOSURE TO SHORT-TERM INTEREST RATE RISK – MATURITY GAP ANALYSIS

Current financial regulation requires banks to have interest rate risk methods in place which are commensurate with the size and complexity of the bank. This is known as the proportionality approach. The bigger the bank in terms of size of Risk Sensitive Assets (RSA) the more sophisticated methods should be applied for the measurement

Earnings perspective

NII simulation	Measures impact on NII for a given period under a variety of interest rate curve scenarios – parallel shift, steepener, flattener etc. Typically based on the bank's current position as well as risk due to future new business (under simulation).
Earnings at Risk (EAR)	
Gap analysis	Comparison of asset and liability repricing cash flows. Gap equals to rate sensitive assets less rate sensitive liabilities.

Economic perspective

EVE	Discounted cash flow analysis of the BS – it is the fair value of the bank's assets and liabilities.
Sensitivity analysis	Effect on the EVE resulting from shocked interest rates curve expressed as a DV01 (parallel shift of 1 bp in rates) or as change in EVE from various curve scenarios: steepener, flattener, etc.

FIGURE 2.17   The two groups of IRRBB measurement methods.
Source: own elaboration

of IRRBB. This chapter is focused on IRRBB measurement methods and contains an interpretation of results obtained through the application of these methods based on practical examples.

Figure 2.17 shows two groups of the IRRBB measurement methods. The first group represents the methods from an earnings perspective, the second one from an economic value perspective. As already highlighted banks should have both methods in place to measure IRRBB effectively.

According to the BCBS Standards, the maturity gap is the simplest technique for measuring a bank's interest rate risk exposure. It distributes interest-sensitive assets, liabilities and off-balance sheet positions into a certain number of predefined time bands according to their maturity (if fixed rate) or time remaining to their next repricing (if floating rate). Those assets and liabilities lacking definitive repricing intervals (e.g., sight deposits or savings accounts) or actual maturities that could vary from contractual maturities (a mortgage with an option for early repayment) are assigned to repricing time bands according to the judgment and the past experience of the bank. There are statistical methods to support the allocation decision for behavioural items. Some of them are described in Chapter 4.

To evaluate earnings exposure, interest rate-sensitive liabilities in each time band are subtracted from the corresponding interest rate-sensitive assets to produce a repricing gap for that time band. This gap can be multiplied by an assumed change in interest rates to provide an approximation of the change in net interest income that would result from such an interest rate movement. The size of the interest rate movement used in the analysis can be based on a variety of factors, including the historical experience of the bank, a simulation of the potential future interest rate movements, and the judgment of the bank's management (Basel Committee on Banking Supervision, 2016). Existing regulatory guidelines, under many jurisdictions, still require that banks apply +/–200 bps parallel shock for this analysis. The application of BCBS Standards introduces an additional 4 shocks for EVE sensitivity analysis.

The application of this method is very simple and can be easily extended to the measurement of the exchange rate risk. The maturity gap is commonly known as the repricing gap, and in this book both terms are used interchangeably.

The static maturity gap method, however, presents significant limitations such as:

- It considers only transactions existing in the banking book at the date of the analysis (there is no new business assumption).
- It disregards different maturities of the transaction within the same time buckets (all transactions falling into the same time bucket have the same risk profile).
- It only allows an estimation of the uniform movements of interest rates.
- It assumes that asset and liabilities in maturity will be reinvested/refinanced within the gapping period (without altering the balance sheet structure) – known as a *like for like* assumption.

Let us analyse some of the above limitations in detail.

RSA and RSL are allocated to time buckets according to their first repricing date (in case the transaction is at a floating rate) or estimated (if a behavioural view is applied) or contractual (if a contractual view is applied) maturity. In practice it means that the asset indexed to the LIBOR 3M and repricing within the next 1 month will be allocated to the O/N to 1-month time bucket. Exactly the same point is valid for an asset indexed to LIBOR 6M and repricing within the next 1 month and to an asset at fixed rate maturing within the next month. These assets will fall into the same time bucket despite the fact they are indexed to different risk factors. This situation is shown in Figure 2.18.

Similarly, assets at fixed rate maturing within the next 62 days will be allocated to the same time bucket as assets maturing within the next 31 days. Both will be allocated to the 1 to 3-months time bucket.

The limits of the static view applied in the maturity gap can be overcome quite easily by application of a simulation module for NII (Figure 2.8) in order to get a more precise picture of the risks run by the bank on the short end of the curve and under a number of interest rate shocks.

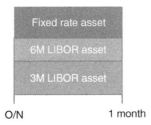

O/N   1 month

FIGURE 2.18   Allocation to the same time bucket assets with different refixing features based on the repricing features.
Source: own elaboration

The impact on the Net Interest Income (ΔNII) resulting from the movements of the interest rates is calculated as a product between the changes in the interest rates and the difference between an interest rate risk sensitive asset and liabilities known as GAP:

$$\Delta NII = \Delta i \times GAP = \Delta i \times (RSA - RSL) \tag{2}$$

where:

   RSA represents assets sensitive to interest rate movements (for example, fixed or floating rate loans);

   RSL represents liabilities sensitive to interest rate movements (for example, wholesale funding or sight deposits);

   GAP is the difference between outstanding RSAs and RSLs over the given time horizon;

   Δi represents the magnitude of the interest rate shock.

Here, it is necessary to introduce the concept of the Gapping Period (GP) which represents the time horizon chosen for this type of analysis, for example 1 year.

Thus, the delta of net interest income is the function of two elements:

- interest rates movements Δi; and
- the difference between RSA and RSL (GAP).

Using the maturity gap method, the bank can manage its position on interest rate risk through:

- The immunisation of interest rate risk keeping the gap close to zero.
- Directional gap, keeping the voluntary mismatching according to the expectation of future movements of the interest rate curve and an analytical understanding of the maturity profile of the balance sheet.

If $GAP > 0$, then the bank is exposed to the reinvestment risk, meaning that in the case of an interest rate increase it will show a profit. On the other hand, in the case of an interest rate decrease it will show a loss.

If $GAP < 0$, then the bank is exposed to the refinancing risk, meaning that in the case of an interest rate increase it will show a loss. On the other hand, in the case of an interest rate decrease it will realise a profit.

In consequence, if $GAP = 0$, the bank is immune to the interest rate risk and movements of the curve. Of course, in this sense the directional gap strategy consists of an adjustment of the sign of GAP (increasing it when there are upward expectations for interest rates and reducing it when there are downward pressures from the market).

EXAMPLE 3

Imagine the following structure of the banking book (in Euro):

Cash 100	Time depo 200
Corporate loans at floating rate 1000	Behavioural liabilities 900
Other assets 200	Wholesale funding 100
Fixed assets 50	Equity 150

The maturity gap for this structure is shown in Figure 2.19.

The repricing gap shows that in the case of a short-term time horizon the bank is *asset sensitive* as the total *GAP* is equal to 500m which means that, with a 12-month time horizon, the NII will increase if the rates go up. On the other hand, the opposite will happen if the rates go down. From the other side – on the medium-to-long part of the curve – the bank behaves as a net liability position, as an increase in rates will have a positive impact on EVE; meanwhile a decrease will have a negative impact. The difference between these two metrics is the time horizon. The first metric looks at the short time period and the immediate impact on NII, the latter measures the change in the present value of the banking book for all items on the balance sheet, including those that haven't matured.

A maturity gap analysis, as described by the Regulator, can be easily performed in an Excel spreadsheet; however, the limitations deriving from its simplistic application cannot be underestimated. This basic method has been enriched through the introduction of the incremental gap method where the incremental gap is obtained by the summation of the subsequent gaps weighted for the time factor (Lusignani, 1996). This time factor represents the time between the central value of the bucket and the end of the gapping period:

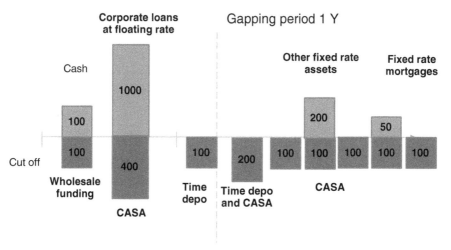

FIGURE 2.19 Repricing gap – IRRBB
Source: own elaboration

(Continued)

$$\Delta NII = \Sigma GAP \times (T - t) \times \Delta i, \tag{3}$$

where:

T is the length of the gapping period;

t represents maturity related to the time bucket;

Δi represents the shock in the interest rate curve.

EXAMPLE 4

Calculation of ΔNII in a gapping period of 12 months under a –200 bps scenario for the EUR currency.

Assumption: a short-term rate in negative territory.

Asset at floating rate repricing (with zero floor) within 1 month's time – EUR 100m.

Liability at floating rate repricing within 3 months' time (no floor) – EUR 300m.

$$\Delta NII = 100 * \frac{11}{12} * 0 - 300 * 9 / 12 * -2\% = 4.5\text{m}$$

There is a positive impact in terms of P&L under a downward movement of the interest rate curve.

Maturity gap analysis according to the advanced approach

As already mentioned, the simple gap technique presented above is static as it is not taking into account the evolution of the interest rate curve and changes in the composition of the balance sheet. However, it should be noted that static methods have evolved over time and have been enriched through the introduction of the advanced approaches applied in ALM models. This methodological progress aims to provide a bank with a clear picture of the underlying forms of IRRBB.

Before entering into details of the methods for measuring IRRBB it is necessary to recall briefly the subtypes of these risk categories and to define them properly.

IRRBB refers to the current or prospective risk to a bank's net economic value, capital and earnings arising from adverse movements in interest rates that affect a bank's banking book positions. The exposure to the interest rate risk derives both from the variation of the interest rate to which the transaction is linked at the fixing date and consequently the impact on the interest flow and the interest margin, and from the positions in maturity which are going to be reinvested or refinanced at the new rate. This first kind of risk exists only in the case of floating rate transactions and only for the component in refixing (as opposed to the component in maturity). The second one refers to transactions at a fixed rate.

The sub-types of IRRBB are as follows:

- **Gap risk** arises from the term structure of banking book instruments, and describes the risk arising from the timing of instruments' rate changes. The risk to the bank arises when the rate of interest paid on liabilities increases before the rate of interest received on assets, or reduces on assets before liabilities. The extent of gap risk depends on whether the changes to term structure of interest rates occur consistently across the whole yield curve (parallel risk) or differently by period (non-parallel risk). Banks measure and control the gap risk through the repricing gap and the analysis of the net mismatch for every time band and by material currency.

- **Basis risk** describes the impact of relative changes in interest rates for financial instruments that have similar tenors but are priced using different interest rate indices (bases). It arises from the imperfect correlation in the adjustment of the rates earned and paid on different instruments with otherwise similar rate change characteristics. Banks measure basis risk by monitoring different benchmarks of assets and liabilities by every time bucket, and shocking them by 1 bp or more to see the potential impact on the P&L (refixing gap analysis). Certain banks, by default, adopt the strategy in terms of the minimisation of the exposure to the basis risk, which consists of an attempt to match the risk factors on the asset and liability side as much as possible.

- **Option risk** arises from option derivative positions explicitly or implicitly embedded in the banking book positions. Those automatic options aim to protect a bank from the decrease/increase in the interest rates and their impact needs to be assessed on the potential change in the EVE (the impact of automatic options on EVE is presented in Example 3). There is also an optional element embedded in banks' customer deposits providing them with a contractual right to withdraw their balance. This phenomenon is known as behavioural optionality embedded in the banking book and is thoroughly examined in Chapter 3.

- **Yield risk** describes the risk arising from unanticipated non-parallel shifts of the yield curve such as steepening, flattening, inverted curve and parallel shifts on the medium-to-long part of the curve.

As already mentioned in Chapter 1, IRRBB has received increasing regulatory attention and it has become one of the hot topics for national and European regulators in recent years. There are clear prescriptions on how this kind of risk needs to be measured, monitored and mitigated. As a result, adequate IRRBB management needs to consider several dimensions, not only in terms of integrated software solutions, but also the revision of metrics and the introduction of a model validation framework. Thus, a simple maturity gap analysis performed in an Excel spreadsheet is not fit for purpose anymore. There is a clear expectation set up in the BCBS Standards to capture all the IRRBB risk subcategories above and to define risk metrics for all of them. In addition, compliance with the enhanced IRRBB framework requires the adoption of simulation tools, especially for NII.

The technical implementation of a NII simulation is needed for the strategic positioning and definition of a steering approach, and this is a major challenge for small banks. This is because the results of an expected NII are required for different purposes and under various views, and therefore requires the flexibility of a calculation tool. For example, the NII simulation required for EBA stress testing in 2018 (wide stress test) implied certain assumptions related to pricing, time horizon and changes in the banking book structure over time.[1] The internal measure which is focused on the pure impact of interest rates on NII within a short time horizon does not include any changes in the composition of the banking book. It is said that the banking book is constant for the purposes of this kind of analysis, i.e., without new business assumption. Expiring items are replaced on a *like for like* basis, i.e., based on the same financial characteristics. Consequently, in order to capture all the above aspects, an integrated and flexible approach is needed, and it requires software solutions that serve the various purposes of NII simulation (not only the static approach). The advanced approach to the measurement of the impact on NII needs to include additional essential features, for example, to provide an indication of which risk factors banking book positions are indexed to in every single time bucket, and if this is a simple (one risk factor) or an average indexation (a number of risk factors). Secondly, there has to be a clear separation through FTP between the interest rate risk component, the liquidity component and the commercial spread in order to allocate the interest income to sales and to the treasury. In conclusion, the compliance with Standards and the enhanced IRRBB framework requires the adoption of an advanced repricing gap view as opposed to the simple maturity gap used, until now, by the regulator to assess a bank's position for IRRBB purposes. This is an important step undertaken by Basel which results in increased complexity in the IRRBB framework.

Brief comparison of two approaches: the basic maturity gap and the advanced repricing gap

Both methods take into consideration the flows related to the underlying transactions, and position them at the date at which they become sensitive to the interest rates. Meanwhile the simple maturity gap classifies them as a function of the time bucket

---

[1]The European Banking Authority (**EBA**) launched in **2018** an EU-**wide stress test**, which involved 48 banks from 15 EU and EEA countries, covering broadly 70% of the total EU banking sector assets.

into which they are expected to fall, and as such the position is weighted by the mid-point of the time bucket, under the advanced repricing gap approach applied by ALM systems, and is expected to position transactions at the exact date of risk. In both cases these flows are used to determine the expected change in the interest margin for a predetermined gapping period given a predetermined shock, for example a parallel shock of 200 bps (obviously it is possible to assign any other magnitude of shock) to the rate curve associated with the transaction. One of the most important limits of simple maturity gap analysis consists in the impossibility of the identification of the parameters (risk factors) to which the transaction is linked. This means that the transaction at floating rate is distributed to the appropriate time bucket according to the time left to its repricing.

Therefore, if the transaction falls into a time bucket of 3–6 months it is not clear to which market parameter it is linked (Figure 2.18). Instead, the advanced repricing gap approach allows an estimation of the impact of each parameter in terms of its contribution to the interest margin for each time bucket (Figure 2.20).

Additionally, using the simple maturity gap approach it is not possible to know if the estimated sensitivity of the expected margin is derived from maturity flows (the transactions which amortise or mature and have to be reinvested or refinanced at the "new" interest rate) or from the flows in refixing. This is an important disadvantage with respect to the advanced repricing gap approach which calculates the NII sensitivity caused by the component in maturity reinvesting (refinancing) it at the forward rate until the end of the gapping period. Figure 2.21 shows the amount in repricing split by component in maturity and refixing.

Finally, the most important thing which gives such a big advantage to the advance repricing gap, calculated by the ALM system, is that it captures the sensitivity deriving from the non-perfect indexation of the transaction. In particular, if the transaction is the floating rate perfectly indexed, the repricing flow is positioned at the first rate reset date for the transaction as a whole. If not, the sensitivity captured from the non-perfect indexation is calculated and shown also for the subsequent refixing dates. Imperfect indexation arises in the following situations:

- A rate fixing period different to the interest payment period.
- The presence of financial spreads.
- The weight of indexation parameter is not equal to 1.
- Average indexation.

It is expected that ALM systems provide the full picture of the underlying IRRBB risk with split by risk factor, component in maturity and refixing and imperfect indexation along with the NII simulation module.

Two different ways of looking at the maturity gap

Besides the differentiation offered by the simple and the advanced repricing gaps there are also two different ways of looking at the maturity gap. These are applied on a daily basis but serve different purposes.

Counterparty type	External counterparty												
Amount type													
Fixing	Fixing bucket date	Fixing bucket label											
	30/09/2020	31/10/2020	30/11/2020	31/12/2020	31/01/2021	28/02/2021	31/03/2021	30/04/2021	31/05/2021	30/06/2021	31/07/2021	31/08/2021
Fixing amount	1M	2M	3M	4M	5M	6M	7M	8M	9M	10M	11M	12M
Market parameter													
EURIBOR 1 M	-218.46	-203.27	-188.41	-174.40	-160.87	-147.75	-134.84	-122.28	-110.43	-98.88	-87.91	-77.66
EURIBOR 3 M	564.85	654.45	548.35	544.25	592.82	492.41	488.42	529.91	512.07	521.34	493.38	487.32
Total	346.40	451.18	359.94	369.85	431.95	344.67	353.57	407.63	401.64	422.46	405.47	409.67

FIGURE 2.20 Repricing gap with split by risk factor.
Source: own elaboration

Bank Code

Repricing

Phase

Cash

Flow Model

Counterparty Type — External Counterparty

AMOUNT

		Bucket Date	Bucket Label					
		01/11/2012	30/11/2012	31/12/2012	31/01/2013	28/02/2013	31/03/2013	30/04/2013
Index Class	Amount Type	1D	1M	2M	3M	4M	5M	6M
EU01	Maturity	−15.80	−33.78	−4.13	−14.36	−13.87	−13.33	−9.50
	Refixing	5.31	−83.26	−178.75	14.89	14.43	14.48	10.30
EU01 Total		−10.50	−117.04	−182.88	0.53	0.55	1.15	0.80
EU03	Maturity	4.25	16.40	21.40	19.04	−464.58	−2.25	19.74
	Refixing	0.09	−36.69	−192.38	−42.38	705.82	4.01	−19.23
EU03 Total		4.34	−20.29	−170.98	−23.34	241.24	1.76	0.51
EU06	Maturity	0.00	5.89	105.21	15.93	0.74	30.95	20.67
	Refixing	0.05	62.40	−81.02	−18.54	69.74	82.44	49.94
EU06 Total		0.05	68.29	24.19	−2.62	70.48	113.39	70.61
EU12	Maturity			5.80				
	Refixing			0.00				
				5.80				
EU12 Total				11.60				

FIGURE 2.21 Amount in repricing split by component in maturity and refixing.

Source: own elaboration

The first view is known as the *flows approach* and designs the maturity gap in terms of cash flows (for the fixed rate items) and outstanding at repricing (items at floating rate). This approach is commonly used for the calculation of the ΔNII for a certain gapping period and shock magnitude. Figure 2.22 shows the calculation of NII sensitivity under +100 bps according to the *flows approach*. The asset repricing flow is positioned by the end of quarter 3, therefore time to the end of gapping period of the asset is equal to 0.25Y. The liability repricing flow is positioned by the end of quarter 2, thus time to the end of GP is equal to 0.5Y. The calculation of NII sensitivity is performed as per equation 3. Overall, Figure 2.22 shows the *liability sensitive* position driven by the liability repricing before the asset. The closer the repricing date of the position the riskier it is. This is due to the time factor. In our example the asset is weighted by a time factor equal to 0.25, and the liability by 0.5.

The second view is known as *stock analysis* and designs the maturity gap in terms of the outstanding for every item rather than repricing or maturing flow. The residual gap creates NII sensitivity and indicates the extent of the exposure to interest rate risk. This approach is usually used for calculation of the bucket exposure and hedging. Figure 2.23 shows the NII sensitivity calculated under +100 bps applying a repricing stocks approach.

It should be highlighted that both approaches produce the same result in terms of NII sensitivity. However, both methodologies aim to answer different questions. The *flows approach* indicates the velocity of repricing of the banking book and, consequently, the exposure to the gap risk. The *stocks approach* indicates the bucket exposure and extent of mismatching to be potentially hedged. It is widely used in NII simulations under a number of interest rate shocks, for example under forward interest rate curve and the simulated composition of the balance sheet.

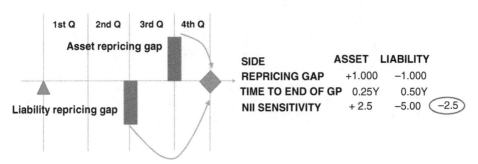

TRADITIONAL APPROACH – REPRICING FLOWS
NII sensitivity calculated with the traditional repricing gap methodology

SIDE	ASSET	LIABILITY
REPRICING GAP	+1.000	−1.000
TIME TO END OF GP	0.25Y	0.50Y
NII SENSITIVITY	+ 2.5	−5.00 −2.5

FIGURE 2.22   Repricing gap analysis – flows approach
Source: own elaboration

REPRICING STOCKS
NII sensitivity calculated as differential change in funding costs for unmatched position

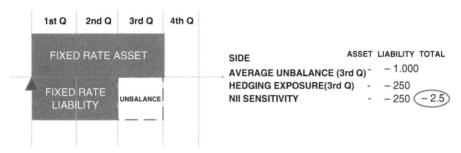

FIGURE 2.23 Repricing gap – stocks approach
Source: own elaboration

Figure 2.24 illustrates an example of a stocks approach produced by the ALM system.

This kind of analysis is important information provided by the treasury to ALCO on at least a monthly basis. Figure 2.25 illustrates a simple example of NII simulation commentary provided to ALCO.

Repricing gap analysis and refixing gap analysis

The repricing gap here refers to the advanced derivation of the maturity gap which was described above. In this stage, the purpose is to focus on its application and the difference with respect to the refixing gap which shows all flows in refixing (not only the first refixing date but also the subsequent dates). The refixing gap is used to monitor the exposure to basis risk and the extent of mismatching between asset and liability side. As such it shows all risk factors a bank is exposed to. Figure 2.26 shows an example of basis risk analysis in a bank.

The repricing gap usually shows the picture of the exposure to the interest rate risk within a short time period (12 months). It captures the positions both at the fixed rate which mature and need to be reinvested (if assets) or refinanced (if liabilities) and the floating rate which will reset its rate, generating in this way the interest rate risk exposure. The gapping period (usually 12 months) is split into monthly time buckets which give more precise information about the time when the risk is present. The more precise information about the timing related to the presence of risk, the more accurate the measure of the exposure to the interest rate risk. It is worth highlighting at this point that even if it delivers the fast overview from the interest rate risk perspective, it does not consider the structure and the positions of the subsequent repricing gaps related to the given position. Instead, it "sees" only the first risk date of the position in the fixation. For example, imagine that a bank has an amount of liabilities which reprice in January 2019, April 2019, July 2019 and October 2019 (it is indexed to EURIBOR 3M). Under the repricing gap approach we

	01/11/2020 1D	30/11/2021 1M	31/12/2021 2M	31/01/2021 3M	28/02/2021 4M	31/03/2021 5M	30/04/2021 6M	31/05/2021 7M	30/06/2021 8M
Assets									
Corporate loans	2,701.64	2,700.01	2,673.54	2,546.99	2,523.04	2,504.83	2,456.51	2,429.94	2,380.88
AVERAGE AMOUNT									
INTEREST	0.19	5.36	5.64	5.16	4.68	5.19	4.97	5.07	4.81
Demand &	121.71	31.54	1.02						
Term deposits									
AVERAGE AMOUNT									
INTEREST	0.00	0.00	0.00						
Other financ-	119.78	119.41	116.14	111.94	109.86	108.67	107.27	105.92	104.08
ing products									
AVERAGE AMOUNT									
INTEREST	0.00	0.14	0.14	0.11	0.10	0.11	0.10	0.09	0.08
Securities	60.66	59.90	57.49	57.49	57.49	57.49	57.49	57.49	57.49
AVERAGE AMOUNT									
INTEREST	0.01	0.16	0.16	0.05	0.05	0.05	0.05	0.05	0.05
Assets	**3,003.80**	**2,910.86**	**2,848.19**	**2,716.43**	**2,690.38**	**2,670.98**	**2,621.26**	**2,593.35**	**2,542.45**
AVERAGE AMOUNT									
Assets INTEREST	*0.20*	*5.66*	*5.94*	*5.32*	*4.84*	*5.34*	*5.11*	*5.20*	*4.93*
Liabilities									
Borrowed interbank	−15.12	−4.64	−4.64	−4.64	−2.65				
AVERAGE AMOUNT									
INTEREST	0.00	0.00	0.00	0.00	0.00				
Corporate deposits	−99.75	−54.96	−15.78	−10.45	−10.33	−10.33	−10.33	−10.33	−10.33
AVERAGE AMOUNT									
INTEREST	0.00	−0.05	−0.02	−0.01	−0.01	−0.01	−0.01	−0.01	−0.01
Funding	−2,745.68	−2,740.91	−2,739.01	−2,737.27	−2,736.89	−2,727.32	−2,707.92	−2,707.37	−2,706.50
AVERAGE AMOUNT									
INTEREST	−0.07	−2.02	−2.18	−1.93	−1.78	−2.07	−2.57	−2.66	−2.53

Liabilities AVERAGE AMOUNT	-2,860.54	-2,800.51	-2,759.43	-2,752.36	-2,749.86	-2,737.64	-2,718.25	-2,717.70	-2,716.82
Liabilities INTEREST	-0.07	-2.07	-2.20	-1.95	-1.80	-2.08	-2.58	-2.67	-2.54
Off-balance sheet Derivatives AVERAGE AMOUNT	0.00	0.00	0.00	0.00	0.00	0.00	0.00		
Derivatives INTEREST	0.00	0.02	0.02	0.02	0.02	0.02	0.01		
Off-balance sheet AVERAGE AMOUNT	*0.00*	*0.00*	*0.00*	*0.00*	*0.00*	*0.00*	*0.00*		
Off-balance sheet INTEREST	*0.00*	*0.02*	*0.02*	*0.02*	*0.02*	*0.02*	*0.01*		
AVERAGE AMOUNT total	143.26	110.35	88.75	-35.93	-59.48	-66.66	-96.99	-124.35	-174.37
INTEREST total	0.12	3.61	3.76	3.39	3.06	3.28	2.54	2.53	2.39

FIGURE 2.24 Time bucket exposure and NII simulation analysis under stocks approach.

Source: own elaboration

Profitability analysis – Net Interest Income projection

Only a forward scenario has been applied. The analysis needs to be extended to multiple scenarios.

Comments

- No new volumes produced after the cut-off date taken into consideration
- The items maturing in the next 12 months will be reinvested or refinanced at the forward rate until the end of the gapping period.

> The analysis shows the NII under the forward curve equal to **Euro33m**.

	01/11/2020 1D	30/11/2021 1M	31/12/2021 2M	31/01/2021 3M	28/02/2021 4M	31/03/2021 5M	30/04/2021 6M	31/05/2021 7M	30/06/2021 8M
Assets									
Corporate loans									
AVERAGE AMOUNT	2,701.64	2,700.01	2,673.54	2,546.99	2,523.04	2,504.83	2,456.51	2,429.94	2,380.88
INTEREST	0.19	5.36	5.64	5.16	4.68	5.19	4.97	5.07	4.81
Demand & Term deposits									
AVERAGE AMOUNT	121.71	31.54	1.02						
INTEREST	0.00	0.00	0.00						
Other financing products									
AVERAGE AMOUNT	119.78	119.41	116.14	111.94	109.86	108.67	107.27	105.92	104.08
INTEREST	0.00	0.14	0.14	0.11	0.10	0.11	0.10	0.09	0.08
Securities									
AVERAGE AMOUNT	60.66	59.90	57.49	57.49	57.49	57.49	57.49	57.49	57.49
INTEREST	0.01	0.16	0.16	0.05	0.05	0.05	0.05	0.05	0.05
Assets AVERAGE AMOUNT	3,003.80	2,910.86	2,848.19	2,716.43	2,690.38	2,670.98	2,621.26	2,593.35	2,542.45
Assets INTEREST	0.20	5.66	5.94	5.32	4.84	5.34	5.11	5.20	4.93
Liabilities									
Borrowed interbank									
AVERAGE AMOUNT	-15.12	-4.64	-4.64	-4.64	-2.65				
INTEREST	0.00	0.00	0.00	0.00	0.00				
Corporate deposits									
AVERAGE AMOUNT	-99.75	-54.96	-15.78	-10.45	-10.33	-10.33	-10.33	-10.33	-10.33
INTEREST	0.00	-0.05	-0.02	-0.01	-0.01	-0.01	-0.01	-0.01	-0.01
Funding									
AVERAGE AMOUNT	-2,745.68	-2,740.91	-2,739.01	-2,737.27	-2,736.89	-2,727.32	-2,707.92	-2,707.37	-2,706.50
INTEREST	-0.07	-2.02	-2.18	-1.93	-1.78	-2.07	-2.57	-2.66	-2.53
Liabilities AVERAGE AMOUNT	-2,860.54	-2,800.51	-2,769.43	-2,752.36	-2,749.86	-2,737.64	-2718.25	-2,717.70	-2,716.82
Liabilities INTEREST	-0.07	-2.07	-2.20	-1.95	-1.80	-2.08	-2.58	-2.67	-2.54
Off balance sheet									
Derivatives									
AVERAGE AMOUNT	0.00	0.00	0.00	0.00	0.00	0.00	0.00		
INTEREST	0.00	0.02	0.02	0.02	0.02	0.02	0.01		
Off balance sheet AVERAGE AMOUNT	0.00	0.00	0.00	0.00	0.00	0.00	0.00		
Off balance sheet INTEREST	0.00	0.02	0.02	0.02	0.02	0.02	0.01		
AVERAGE AMOUNT total	143.26	110.35	88.75	-35.93	-59.48	-66.66	-96.99	-124.35	-174.37
INTEREST total	0.12	3.61	3.76	3.39	3.06	3.28	2.54	2.53	2.39

FIGURE 2.25 NII simulation – example of commentary for ALCO.

Source: own elaboration

The structure of gaps in repricing – basis risk

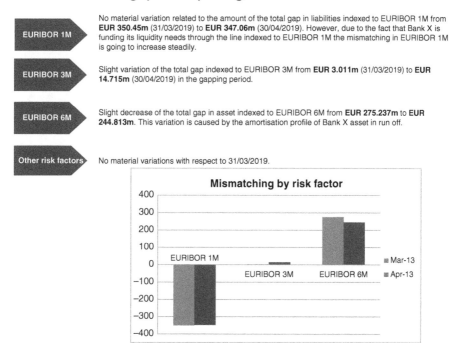

EURIBOR 1M

No material variation related to the amount of the total gap in liabilities indexed to EURIBOR 1M from **EUR 350.45m** (31/03/2019) to **EUR 347.06m** (30/04/2019). However, due to the fact that Bank X is funding its liquidity needs through the line indexed to EURIBOR 1M the mismatching in EURIBOR 1M is going to increase steadily.

EURIBOR 3M

Slight variation of the total gap indexed to EURIBOR 3M from **EUR 3.011m** (31/03/2019) to **EUR 14.715m** (30/04/2019) in the gapping period.

EURIBOR 6M

Slight decrease of the total gap in asset indexed to EURIBOR 6M from **EUR 275.237m** to **EUR 244.813m**. This variation is caused by the amortisation profile of Bank X asset in run off.

Other risk factors

No material variations with respect to 31/03/2019.

FIGURE 2.26 Illustrative example of basis risk analysis by risk factor.
Source: own elaboration

will see only the repricing in January 2019 if analysed in December 2018 (the cut-off date). Under this approach, the positions in maturity and in refixing are separated, which very much facilitates interpretation of the results. The bank is aware when the risk derives from the expiration of the position and when it is caused by refixing (Figure 2.21). In order to calculate the sensitivity of the interest income, flows in refixing and in maturity are summed up. Let us analyse the repricing gap of the bank as shown in Figure 2.27.

Figure 2.27 shows a significant negative gap in January which refers to the liabilities in refixing (circled in grey). From the IRR perspective, this net amount of liabilities will reset its rate and consequently expose the bank to the upward movement of the curve. Furthermore, positive gaps in refixing can be noticed in the successive months. On the other hand, they expose the bank to the downward movement of the curve. The subsequent presence of both negative and positive gaps in refixing partially offsets the exposure to the fluctuations of interest rates.

The refixing gap analysis enriches the details provided by the repricing gap. It gives information about the existing mismatching between assets and liabilities at the

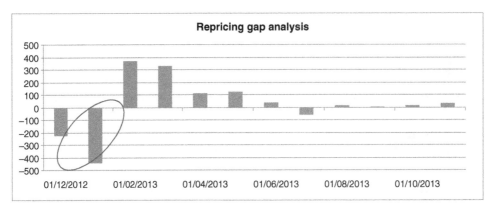

FIGURE 2.27   Repricing gap analysis (numbers are in millions of Euro).
Source: own elaboration

floating rate indexed to the different risk factors (EURIBOR 3M, LIBOR 1M, etc.) grouped in monthly or bi-weekly time buckets (or even daily) within the predetermined time horizon (for example 12 months). The simplest form of the refixing gap approach does not incorporate the projection of the new volumes which the bank is going to disburse under the examination period. Instead, the positions are inertial (in a run-off). Unlike the repricing gap, the refixing analysis takes into consideration all the refixing dates of accounts related to the assets and liabilities under the gapping period. This is important information for the bank in order to contain the risk of mismatching and the high sensitivity driven by the interest rates fluctuations. It is an important tool for setting the hedging strategy to mitigate the basis risk of a bank and to contain the negative impact on the interest income of a bank. Figure 2.28 shows an example of the refixing gap of a bank.

Figure 2.28 shows negative mismatching, i.e., due to liabilities in refixing, in October 2010 and April 2011 caused by a EUR 1bn net position in liabilities. This position is linked to EURIBOR 6M. Instead, from the asset side the numerous net positions in assets are distributed steadily over time (in this case 12 months) linked mainly to EURIBOR 6M and 3M. The bank is significantly exposed to the upward movements in the level of the EURIBOR 6M while approaching the refixing date in October. Furthermore, this risk is concentrated in a one-month time period. Suppose that in October 2010 following some important and sudden event, the market responded with a hike in the interest rate level. This bank incurs losses due to the negative gap in refixing. Subsequently, the market adjusts interest rates to pre-October levels. The bank has positive mismatching in November and again incurs losses. As can be seen, not only the magnitude of the single gap is important but also their distribution over time. The hedging strategy consists in entering into the Forward Rate Agreement (FRA). The bank, in this case, buys FRA, locking the rate on the negative mismatched position in October.

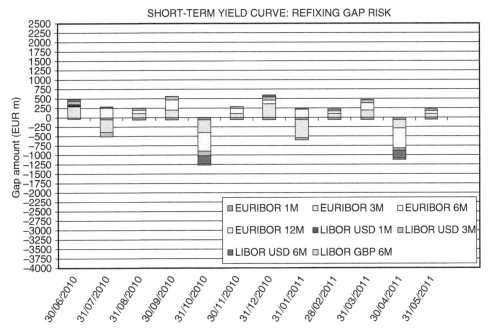

FIGURE 2.28 Refixing gap analysis.
Source: own elaboration

The method presented above is a static one. That is, the evolution of the balance sheet from the perspective of new business production, customers' behaviour with reference to the items with embedded options, and the future evolution of the interest rates, are not taken into consideration. Instead, the positions of the balance sheet are in a run-off or under constant balance sheet, and the impact on NII is calculated under a forward curve scenario or spot interest rates.

MATURITY GAP ANALYSIS FROM THE ECONOMIC VALUE PERSPECTIVE

The delta Economic Value of Equity (ΔEVE) measures the theoretical change in the net present value of the balance sheet excluding equity, i.e., NPV of *Risk Sensitive Assets* – NPV of *Risk Sensitive Liabilities*. The measure therefore depicts the change in equity value resulting from an interest rate shock. Under this method, the value of equity under alternative stress scenarios is compared with the value under a base scenario. This base interest rate scenario is the present value of assets less liabilities under the prevailing interest rate environment. All cash flows from on-balance sheet and off-balance sheet interest rate-sensitive items in the banking book should be included in the computation. The market value of equity is computed as the present value of assets cash flows, less the present value of liabilities cash flows, without including assumptions on the interest rate sensitivity of equity (the equity position is excluded from this approach). The balance sheet is then revalued under the alternative interest rate scenarios and the difference between the value of equity under the base scenario and the alternative scenario is calculated. The accuracy of the valuation of the balance sheet positions is extremely dependent upon the cash flows calculated and the discount rate used. The discounting rates used should match the duration and risk of the cash flows (the category of the instrument which is discounted). In the BCBS Standards, there is an assumption that the cash flows in certain time buckets are discounted with the rates at the mid-point of the time bucket with the risk-free rate (internal view) or adjusted rates if the cash flows include commercial margins (external view). Figure 2.29 shows the external view versus internal view practice.

Banks have the choice of whether to deduct commercial margin and other spread components from the notional repricing cash flows through the FTP methodology. Consequently, the discounting factor must be consistent with the view chosen for the EVE cash flow calculation.

With a static approach there is an additional assumption related to the fact that the timing of the cash flows and their size do not differ under the various scenarios as a result of customer behaviour. This is known as *unconditional cash flows*. In reality, there is a specific relationship between the interest rate scenario and the extent of prepayment and growth of deposits. For example, if the rates go down the prepayment rate tends to go up as clients shop for cheaper borrowing

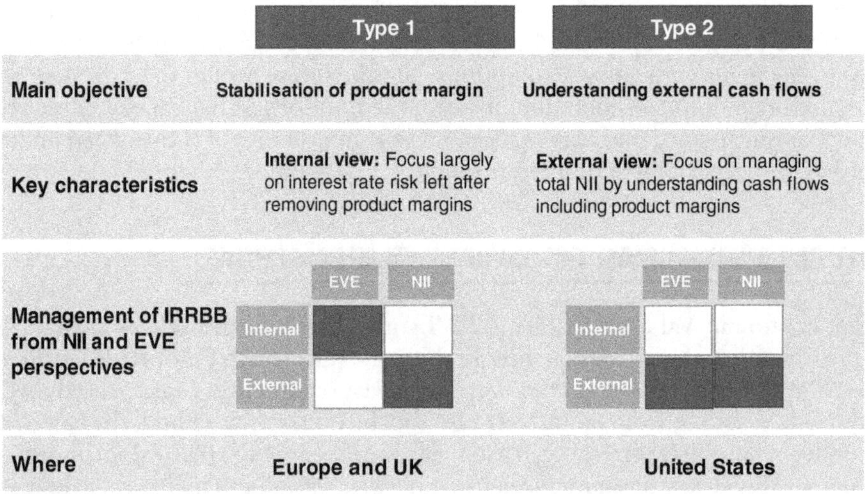

	Type 1	Type 2
Main objective	Stabilisation of product margin	Understanding external cash flows
Key characteristics	**Internal view:** Focus largely on interest rate risk left after removing product margins	**External view:** Focus on managing total NII by understanding cash flows including product margins
Management of IRRBB from NII and EVE perspectives		
Where	Europe and UK	United States

FIGURE 2.29 Management of the EVE under internal and external view.
Source: own elaboration

opportunities. On the other hand, on the liability side, savers tend to search for new investment opportunities and the volatility of this product could increase. Cash flows which are adjusted by potential changes in the behaviour of clients are known as *conditional cash flows* and represent the best practice of the EVE calculation.

The new regulatory framework in Europe (the EBA Final Report on IRRBB issued on 19 July 2018) and in the UK (BCBS, 2016) represents a clear attempt to standardise the IRRBB methodologies across countries and financial institutions demanding the application of the standardised approach (prescribed by the regulator) along with the internal methodology banks already might adopt (for example *Value at Risk*). The EBA Final Report does not claim to replace existing methodologies. Instead, it is an additional analysis which banks must perform in order to comply. For smaller institutions the standardised framework could be used as a platform on which to set up the whole IRRBB framework of the bank.

Under the standardised approach, for the calculation of impact on EVE, institutions are expected to apply six regulatory shocks with prescribed movements in interest rates. These are as follows:

- parallel up (the shift of the whole curve up)
- parallel down (the shift of the whole curve down)
- short up
- short down
- steepener (short rates go down and long rates go up)
- flattener (short rates go up and long rates go down)

The above shocks are calibrated by currency, i.e., the magnitude of the shock differs for EUR, GBP, USD, etc.

Even though this approach is simple and easy to interpret, it has its own pros and cons. The main benefits of the EVE model are the ability to capture the convexity embedded in the banking book, i.e., the extent of the difference between the linear approximation and the full valuation under certain interest rate shock scenarios. Figure 2.30 shows the impact of convexity in the banking book. Under linear approximation the result differs from the calculations under full valuation by each interest rate shock.

Additionally, the objective variable in this approach is the economic value of the banking book and as such the risk is measured in terms of economic value.

Under the static view, the ΔEVE approach shows a snapshot in time of the risk based upon the current portfolio or balance sheet composition; however, it is possible to "simulate" the potential impact of the future business based on the assumption coming from forecast growth or cannibalisation of certain products. The impact of such a simulated position is made at the wide time interval, for example on an annual basis, and reflects the situation at that specific point of time

Scenarios in 000 EUR	∑ PV01 × shock	ΔEVE without options	Difference
94 crash	44,613	43,086	1,527
Parallel up	40,600	39,383	1,218
Parallel down	−40,600	−41,888	1,287
Short up	24,230	23,836	394
Short down	−24,230	−24,640	410
Flattener	13,020	12,903	116
Steepener	−6,203	−6,243	40

FIGURE 2.30   Convexity embedded in the banking book – linear approximation versus full valuation.
Source: own elaboration

taking into account the new composition of the banking book. Thus, it is still a static approach but the assumption about growth is taken into account. On the contrary, the dynamic approach simulates the position of the banking book based on a number of external and internal factors and the simulated curve at a certain point of time.

CASE STUDY 5

Let's imagine that the change in EVE metric under six regulatory shocks of Bank XX looks as in Table 2.7.

We want to analyse how the bank is positioned from the IRRBB perspective under economic view.

It clearly appears that there are no losses under any of the interest rate shock scenarios. This is because the loss in the banking book value is compensated by the change in the economic value of the automatic options under all downward scenarios (parallel down, short down and steepener). Instead, under all upward scenario (parallel up, short up and flattener) Bank XX shows a gain embedded in the banking book but the automatic options become *out of the money* (under upwards interest rate shocks the difference in the economic value of automatic options under shocked scenario and base scenario is negative). This picture indicates that this illustrative financial institution has medium-to-long-term liabilities (for example *behaviouralised* liabilities) which fund the short-term repricing assets. This is because, under upward scenarios, Bank XX behaves as the net liability position and the increase in rates results in the increase of the economic value of its banking book. Overall, it is clear that Bank XX is not exposed to any IRRBB risk on the medium-to-long part of the curve. Neither is it riding the yield curve at this particular point of time.

The importance of automatic options is highlighted in the BCBS Standards and, consequently, reflected in the EBA Final Report on IRRBB. Below is an extract from the BCBS Standards published in 2016 and related to the calculation of the EVE measure.

TABLE 2.7 Delta EVE analysis for Bank XX.

	Economic value analysis – behavioural		
	ΔEVE	**ΔOptions**	**ΔEVE + Options**
2010 scenario	31.724	(6.692)	25.032
Parallel up	39.615	(6.787)	32.828
Parallel down	(42.065)	131.558	89.493
Short up	24.539	(6.238)	18.301
Short down	(25.349)	38.499	13.150
Flattener	13.571	(180)	13.391
Steepener	(6.866)	9.074	2.208
Worse	(42.065)	(6.787)	2.208

Source: own elaboration

CALCULATION OF THE EVE MEASURE

The gain or loss in economic value of equity $\Delta EVE_{i,c}$ under scenario i and currency c is calculated as follows:

1. Under each scenario i, all notional repricing cash flows are slotted to the respective time bucket $k \in \{1, 2, \ldots, K\}$. Within a given time bucket k, all positive and negative notional repricing cash flows are netted to form a single long or short position, with the cancelled parts removed from the calculation. Following this process across all time buckets leads to a set of notional repricing cash flows $CF_{i,(k)}$, $k \in \{1, 2, \ldots, K\}$.
2. Net notional repricing cash flows in each time bucket k are weighted by a continuously compounded discount factor: $DF_{i,c(tk)} = \exp(-R_{i,c}(t_k) \cdot t_k)$ that reflects the interest rate shock scenario i in currency c and where t_k is the midpoint of time bucket k. This results in a weighted net position, which may be positive or negative for each time bucket. The discount factors represent the risk-free rate.
3. These risk-weighted net positions are summed to determine the EVE in currency c under scenario i (excluding automatic interest rate option positions which the bank might have):

$$EVC_{i,c} = \sum_{k=1}^{K} CF_{i,c}(k) * DF_{i,c}(t_k) \qquad (4)$$

The EVE in currency c under base scenario is calculated as:

$$EVE_{0,c} = \sum_{k=1}^{K} CF_{0,c}(k) * DF_{0,c}(t_k) \qquad (5)$$

Finally, the full change in EVE in currency c associated with scenario i is obtained by subtracting $EVE_{0,c}$ from the EVE under shocked interest rate term structure $EVE_{i,c}$ and by adding the total measure for automatic interest rate option risk $KAO_{i,c}$ as follows:

$$\Delta EVE_{i,c} = \sum_{k=1}^{K} CF_{i,c}(k) * DF_{i,c}(t_k) - \sum_{k=1}^{K} CF_{0,c}(k) * DF_{0,c}(t_k) + KAO_{i,c} \qquad (6)$$

In this case, if $EVE_{i,c} > 0$ then the economic value of the banking book is going to increase; whereas if $EVE_{i,c} < 0$ the bank faces the reduction in its economic value. $KAO_{i,c}$ is an add-on for the calculation of the change in value of the automatic interest rate options, whether explicit or embedded.

As an example of the risk-free curve, as specified in the BCBS Standards or ECB IRRBB stress test performed in 2017, could be a secured interest rate swap or Overnight Index Swap (OIS) curve.

TIME BUCKET SENSITIVITY ANALYSIS – PV01

While dealing with IRRBB the usage of the term *IRRBB sensitivity* or *PV01* is essential.

Sensitivity analysis is a method for calculating the change in the present values of items due to a 1 bp shift in the interest rates curve for a given currency. The sensitivity (PV01) of the transaction is calculated as the difference between its Present Value (PV) determined with the current market rates and its PV under the curve shocked with 1 bp (PV*):

$$PV01 = PV^* - PV \tag{7}$$

The traditional approach consists in positioning cash flows at the date (time bucket) at which the flow is expected to occur (according to its contractual or modelled maturity) and calculation of its present value with the discount factor corresponding to the mid-point of the time bucket (in the simplified approach) or to the exact risk date of the transaction (in the ALM system). This representation has crucial importance in hedging or monitoring of the IRRBB structural exposure (usually related to the items at fixed rate) as it allows identification of the points on the term structure of interest rates which are excessively sensitive to interest rates and to "close" them with hedging or natural hedging. The total time bucket sensitivity is a sum of sensitivities by time bucket.

Figure 2.31 shows the PV01 sensitivity by time bucket of a financial institution.

Figure 2.31 clearly shows that the sensitivity of this bank falls into the time buckets between 1 and 5Y and it is due to the liability position. An increase in rates by

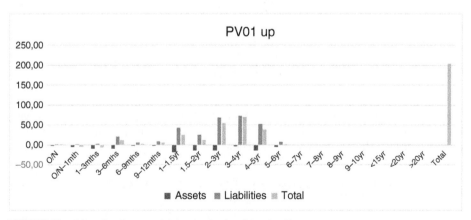

FIGURE 2.31   Time bucket sensitivity in the banking book.
Source: own elaboration

1 bp, in those time buckets, results in a gain for the institution. Overall, the increase in rates will lead to a positive impact.

DURATION GAP ANALYSIS

Duration is a measure of the average life of the security. It represents the speed of payment of a security, and consequently the price risk relative to other securities with the same maturity. Duration is calculated as the weighted average time until the receipt of all cash flows from the security, where the weights are the present values of the cash flows, to the total present value of the security:

$$D = \sum_{t=1}^{n} \frac{t \times PVCF_t}{\sum_{t=1}^{n} PVCF_t} \tag{8}$$

where:

D is the duration of the security; t is the length (number of months, years, etc.) to the date of payment; and $PVCF_t$ is the present value of the payment CF made at t, calculated as $\dfrac{CF_t}{(1+r)^t}$, where the summation Σ is taken from the first to the last payment n; and r is yield to maturity. Duration can be measured in two forms.

The primary application of this metric is to measure the interest rate risk in the market and is known as the *Modified Duration* (MD). This interpretation of duration represents the price volatility of the security and, consequently, its interest rate risk. Mathematically, duration is an approximation acceptable only for very small interest rate movements and it becomes imprecise in cases of significant shift in the term structure.

As mentioned earlier, duration relates changes in interest rates and percentage changes in security prices linearly as follows:

$$\frac{\Delta S}{S} = -MD \times \frac{\Delta r}{1+r} \approx -MD \times \Delta r \tag{9}$$

where:

MD is the modified duration of the security; S is the price of the security; r is the yield to maturity; and Δ is the change from the previous value (shock).

The second form of duration is measured in units of time, e.g., months or years, and is referred to as Macaulay's duration. The two forms are strictly related and can be tranformed through the relation:

$$MD = \frac{Macaulay's\ Duration}{\left(1 + \dfrac{YTM}{n}\right)} \tag{10}$$

where:

YTM is the yield to maturity; and n is the number of coupon periods per year.

Duration is very often used to monitor the value of capital of the financial institution in case of fluctuations of the curve. The assumption of a particular degree of risk exposure is the function of the bank's senior management risk appetite ("risk appetite" of the institution is usually formalised in the ALCO policy). The choice of selecting the capital value as a target position is dictated by the fact that this is a primary concern to the shareholders of the bank. While the interest rate sensitivity or risk of individual position is related to its modified duration, the interest rate risk of the target position is related to the difference, or gap, between the average duration of the assets of the institution and the average duration of the liabilities. The duration gap ($DGAP$) is:

$$DGAP = D_A - w \times D_L, \tag{11}$$

where:

D_A and D_L are the average duration of assets and liabilities, respectively; and w is the weight defined as L/A (market value of liabilities to the market value of assets).

Duration gap analysis belongs to the ALM models which use the impact on net present value as an objective variable. It measures the magnitude and sensitivity of the fair value of BS items resulting from the interest rate curve movements.

When the duration of asset (DA) is higher than the duration of liabilities (DL) weighted by the L/A ratio of the bank, the exposure is called asset sensitive and $DGAP > 0$, meaning that the increase in the interest rate structure leads to the decrease of the market value of assets more rapidly than liabilities.

EXAMPLE 5

Assume Bank YY has the following duration of assets and liabilities and the market value of liabilities to the market value of assets as follows:

DA and DL = 0.619 Y

DL = 0.539 Y

L/A = 0.88

thus: $0.619 - 0.539 \times 0.88 = 0.145$ Y

Assets are slightly more sensitive to the interest rate curve movements than liabilities and the NPV of BS items will increase ahead of an interest rate curve decrease. On the other hand, it will diminish when the interest rate curve increases.

If Bank YY wishes to undertake its immunisation perfectly the duration of asset should decrease by 0.145 Y.

When the $DGAP$ of the banking book items of a financial institution is positive it has a net asset position. Consequently, when the interest rates increase the value of capital will diminish accordingly. On the other hand, where interest rates decrease the capital value will increase as a function of the magnitude of the $DGAP$, the shock in the interest rates movement and the dimension of the assets of the financial institution. Exactly the opposite will happen in the case of the $DGAP < 0$. An institution can change the degree of interest rate exposure to any extent it wishes by changing the composition of the balance sheet in such a way as to obtain the desired duration gap for its target position. The greater the duration gap, the greater is that institution's risk exposure for a particular target position and, conversely, the smaller the gap, the smaller its exposure. The elimination of this risk consists of putting into place the immunisation strategy and setting the duration gap to zero. The financial institution, however, attempts to maximise its profits and profit maximisation presumes a desired level of risk exposure. The desired risk-return trade-off for a financial institution is determined by its ALCO policy and may be different from bank to bank. Managing the interest rate risk consists in determination of both the direction and size of its gap on the basis of its interest rates forecast. A bank may pursue two interest rate risk strategies: a passive (immunisation) strategy or an active strategy. The example below shows the immunisation strategy of a bank. It should be underlined that through the immunisation strategy a bank may reduce or even lose the income gained if it had managed the interest rate risk correctly. On the other hand, immunising the bank also decreases its chances of suffering losses if the risk is mismanaged. Let us consider that the initial value of capital is equal to 100 Euro. The average duration of assets is equal to 4.17 years, meanwhile the average duration of liabilities (deposits P for example) is equal to 1 year and P/A = 0.9. This yields a duration gap: $4.17 - 0.9 \times 1 = 3.27$ years. The immunisation condition is not maintained. The bank can reduce the gap to zero through:

- shortening the duration of its assets by 3.27 years to 0.9 years,
- lengthening the duration of its deposits to 4.63 years so that $0.9 \times 4.63 = 4.17$

Let us suppose that the bank prefers to go through with the second possibility (lengthening the duration of deposits). It can do so by reducing the volume of liabilities with a shorter duration and increasing the volumes of liabilities with a longer duration. Consequently, the immunisation condition is satisfied. An interest rates increase by, say, 200 bps, will decrease the value of assets exactly in the same way as before, changing the composition of the balance sheet (the assets side has been not changed). Instead, the composition of liabilities has been changed by reducing the proportion of the shorter-term deposits. Through the immunisation strategy, the bank protects its capital level as the change in the asset market value is offset by the change in the market value of deposits (Kaufman, 1984). It has to be noted that lengthening of the duration of liabilities in order to pursue immunisation comes with an increase in funding costs for a bank. This point is important from the treasury perspective (and NII of a bank overall). The *trade off* between hedging through synthetic instruments such as derivatives or lengthening duration on the liability side should take into account hedging costs against the increase in the cost of funding. In some cases, the treasury may decide not to hedge the open exposure subject to the extent of the risk appetite of the financial institution. However, in order to undertake the active strategy for the interest rate risk management, the treasurer has to be able to forecast interest rate movements and, more importantly, to be right.

In practice, an immunisation strategy is not the best solution and is not applied frequently. This is because in the developed market hedging through derivatives is easier and often less expensive than lengthening the duration of liabilities, resulting in an increased cost of funds. Also, the treasury is supposed to run healthy *maturity* and *rate transformation* which is well within the limits decided by ALCO.

In some cases, the *match funding* strategy is applied. This is a frequent strategy in situations where the Parent company provides funding to another entity (not necessarily a bank), within the Group, which does not have access to external markets and, therefore, cannot actively manage the exposure to IRRBB. The funding structure of a subsidiary mirrors its asset base and its amortisation profile. A subsidiary is charged the funding cost and the process is agreed between two counterparties in a funding agreement document. Intragroup funding is discussed in Chapter 6. Another example of intragroup funding is between the Parent company and its subsidiary with the banking licence. The subsidiary has all the necessary tools to manage the IRRBB exposure, therefore the funding structure between entities can be more flexible, for example through a number of revolving credit agreements. The subsidiary decides which line to draw to fund the growth of the balance sheet and manages risk arising from the structure according to its own limits and appetite. In analysing the intragroup funding structure and, consequently, the resulting picture in terms of exposure to IRRBB, the regulatory aspects are taken into account. This decides whether there is only a consolidated report needed for the whole Group, or whether each entity has to report the exposure on a separate basis.

Limits of duration gap analysis

The *DGAP* tool is theoretically appealing but requires the complete information of a data set related to items of the balance sheet (such as the maturity and the repricing frequency of every single position). Moreover, the early redemption of loans or other options included in the transactions are not taken into account. From the mathematical standpoint, a duration gap analysis works well only for small interest rate changes and it assumes that when the level of interest rates changes, interest rates on all maturities change by exactly the same amount (parallel shift). However, despite all above-mentioned limits it is still commonly used in banking practice (Lubinska, 2014).

IRRBB METRICS

This section focuses on the main metrics used for the measurement of IRRBB. It provides a summary of metrics and a brief description of the IRRBB risk subcategory captured by each metric.

There are two main approaches (views) which are applied to measure IRRBB exposure. The first group refers to static models which provide a snapshot, in terms of the risk position, at a certain point in time (cut-off date). The interest rate curve is deterministically defined, and the balance sheet is not growing. This is common practice, often used by smaller and less complex financial institutions. The static view is also applied in regulatory reporting, for example FSA017[2] or, in general, in the standardised approach recommended by BCBS Standards.

The dynamic approach, also known as simulation, allows a simulation of the IRRBB position under the stochastically defined interest rate curve scenarios and with changes in the balance sheet structure over time. This requires a system infrastructure in place that is capable of simulating future NII for different purposes and under an integrated and flexible approach. A simulation of NII has been also required by the regulator on several occasions such as in EBA stress tests, ECB IRRBB stress tests, and Short-Term Exercises (STE). The advanced ALM system provides a simulation module which allows a change to the balance sheet structure of a financial institution (growth assumptions) and simulates the movements of the terms structure of interest rates.

Figure 2.32 summarises the main IRRBB metrics, both dynamic and static, and links the risk subcategory captured by the respective metric.

Earnings at Risk (EaR)

EaR measures the potential loss of net interest income which results from upward/ downward interest rate movements over a certain time horizon, which is usually

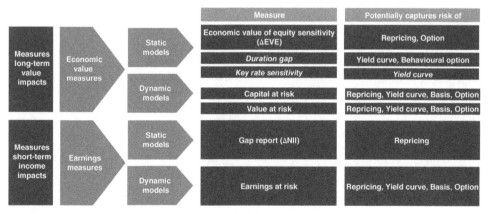

FIGURE 2.32 IRRBB metrics under static and dynamic models.
Source: own elaboration

---

[2]FSA 017 is the regulatory tool for monitoring IRRBB across banks in the UK.

12 months. It belongs to a category of dynamic models and evaluates the risk exposure taking into account the projected changes in maturities, the repricing relationship and the size of the banking book. The important characteristic of this method is that the cash flows are changing based on the underlying stress scenario (changes in the interest rate curve). This is known under the term *conditional cash flows* because the size and timing of flows are driven by the movement in the interest rates. Examples of conditional cash flows are: changes driven by early prepayment, and behavioural characteristics of CASA. Falling interest rates increase cash flows on the asset side due to early redemption of assets at a fixed rate and, at the same time, reduce CASA volatility on the liability side. The reduction in balance volatility and the growing stock of CASA is observed in a low rates environment because customers prefer to "park" their funds in the banks' accounts awaiting the opportunity to invest in more attractive instruments. The "surge" deposits provide a cheap and stable funding source for banks. However, when rates start moving up it is very likely that these funds will migrate towards other products.

Under the dynamic approach, the NII of financial institutions is calculated under a base interest rate scenario which is defined under the prevailing interest rate environment and certain assumptions related to the behaviour of deposits' customers and balance sheet volumes. The result of the alternative (stressed) scenario is then compared against the result under the base scenario. Figure 2.33 shows an example of an EaR calculation under a number of parallel interest rate shocks.

In some cases, banks simulate NII under defined interest rate scenarios and calculate its sensitivity as the difference between the highest and lowest result. The focus of the analysis is to interpret changes in the sensitivity number reported on a periodical basis. Where there is no structural change in the balance sheet structure, sensitivity is driven by the "movement" of gaps in repricing and the impact of the time factor (equation 3).

Interest rate scenario (in bps)	NII (in 000 GBP)	Change relative to base scenario (in 000 GBP)	% change
+300	5,670	−205	−3.49
+200	5,739	−136	−2.31
+100	5,807	−68	−1.16
0	5,875	−	−
−100	5,942	67	1.14
−200	6,008	133	2.26
−300	6,075	200	3.40

FIGURE 2.33 Illustrative calculation of EaR.
Source: own elaboration

EXAMPLE 6 *Calculation of NII sensitivity under the dynamic approach.*

The ALM system performs a simulation of NII under the following scenario and with the assumption of growth in new business.

Based on the ALM modelling techniques NII was calculated by the following scenarios (in Euro):

1. Forward curve scenario   12.8m
2. Constant scenario   11.3m
3. Upward trend scenario   18.4m
4. Downward trend scenario 10.3m
5. Run-off model under forward curve scenario 10.7m

The above results indicate the NII sensitivity equal to EUR 8.1m which is the difference between the highest and the lowest simulated NII, i.e., EUR 18.4m, –10.3m. Additionally, NII sensitivity in the previous month is higher and equals EUR 10.1m.

Based on the above information an ALM manager provides the following analysis:

This slight decrease in NII sensitivity is due to the different repricing dates between assets and liabilities and the fact that the next repricing date of liabilities is expected in October. The bank is heading towards this repricing date lowering the impact of time factor between assets and liabilities. The highest positive NII impact is related to the upward scenario (18.4m) due to the presence of the positive mismatching gaps which reprice before negative mismatching gaps.

An important advantage of this method is the dynamic approach for the calculation of NII of a financial institution. It reflects potential changes in the banking book structure providing management with a complete picture of the risk a bank is running. The changes in customer behaviour, both on the asset and liability side impact NII significantly and, through EaR, this impact is captured. Therefore, it is a meaningful method.

The limitation is characterised by the fact that it can be complex and non-transparent because of changing behavioural assumptions and conditional cash flows. For this reason, EaR is calculated by advanced ALM systems.

Net Interest Income sensitivity – delta NII

Delta NII is a static method for the calculation of potential losses incurred by a financial institution where rates move up or down under the constant balance sheet assumption. The constant balance sheet assumption means that maturing balance sheet items will be replaced by items with exactly the same characteristics until the end of the time period of the analysis which is usually 12 months. Delta NII sensitivity and other static methods were discussed in detail in Chapter 2.

As already shown in Figures 2.22 and 2.23 there are two approaches for the calculation of NII sensitivity. The traditional approach used in the repricing gap of a bank shows the flows on the asset and liability side positioned at the date of their repricing. In Figure 2.22 liability reprices before the asset.

NII sensitivity is calculated through equation 3 which is composed of three elements: Gap, magnitude of the shock and time factor $(T - t)$.

Assuming that repricing asset and liability have the same amount of £1,000 and the interest rate curve shifts up by 100 bps, the NII sensitivity equals –£2.5.

The same result is achieved by calculations through the stock approach where NII sensitivity is calculated as a change in the interest rate for an unmatched position. The potential increase in interest rates, by the end of the second quarter in Figure 2.23, means the increased cost of funding for a bank will be translated into a negative P&L impact.

Under assumption of £1,000 of unbalanced position, the time factor equal to 0.25 and 100 bps shock up, the IRRBB exposure is equal to:

$$-1,000 * 0.25 = -£250$$

Subsequently, the NII sensitivity is calculated as follows:

$$-£250 * 100 \text{ bps} = -£2.5$$

The repricing stocks approach allows the integration of interest rate risk analysis with balance sheet and NII simulation which is a well-known strategy of *yield enhancement* and *optimisation* of balance sheet structure in the medium-to-long term. This is because the NII simulation allows financial institutions to understand the scenario, in terms of curve movement, under which a bank faces the highest adverse impact on its profitability. Based on this analysis the treasurer defines target hedging strategy to mitigate this impact.

Figure 2.34 shows illustrative results of NII simulation for a bank.

CHANGE IN THE ECONOMIC VALUE OF EQUITY (ΔEVE)

The ΔEVE measures the change in the market value of equity resulting from upward or downward interest rate shocks, taking into account the automatic options embedded in the banking book. Therefore, the value of equity under alternative (shocked) interest rate scenarios is compared with the value under a base scenario.

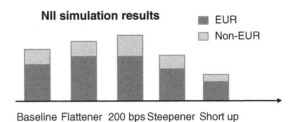

FIGURE 2.34   The results of NII simulation (in millions of Euro) of a bank under different interest rate scenarios.
Source: own elaboration

This base interest rate scenario is the present value of the assets less the present value of liabilities under the prevailing or forecasted interest rate environment. Under the shocked (alternative) scenario the balance sheet is revalued and the difference between shocked and base scenario indicated as ΔEVE. The accuracy of the valuation of the balance sheet positions is extremely dependent upon the cash flows calculated and the discount rates used. As with the NII calculations, under a dynamic approach the size and time of cash flow is dependent upon the underlying interest rate scenarios, i.e., the cash flows are conditional. The movement of market curve impacts the behaviour of the clients both on the asset and liability side. Therefore, an increase in rates has a direct impact on the behaviour of saving accounts holders. Their expectation is to receive higher rates paid by the financial institution as a result of the increase in market rates. Consequently, the stable part of the deposit base can be reduced, which impacts the banking book structure and its risk position. From the asset side there is an impact on the early prepayments rate. The interest rate increase translates into a lower prepayment rate compared to the base scenario. On the other hand, the decrease in interest rates leads to a higher prepayment rate. Under the static approach, the cash flows are unconditional, i.e., their size and timing are assumed to be unchanged under different shocks. The change in EVE is driven by both the change in discount factor under base and shocked scenario, and the change in the value of automatic options which can be either *in the money* or *out of the money* as a function of the underlying interest rates scenarios.

It is important to highlight that ΔEVE can be impacted significantly by both behavioural and automatic options due to *convexity* in the banking book. In the simple explanation convexity means that the change in the banking book value, as a function of interest rates, shows nonlinearity and, consequently, there can be embedded loss/gain under both upward and downward movement interest rate scenarios. Figure 2.35 shows an example of negative convexity in the banking book of a bank. Due to this convexity the EVE reduces regardless of the direction of the interest rate shocks. For illustrative purposes it has been assumed that Tier 1 capital is equal to £263m.

Interest rate scenario	EVE	Change relative to base scenario	Change related to base scenario/ Tier 1
+200 bps	14,669	−3,425	−1.3%
+100 bps	17,005	−1,089	−0.4%
0	18,094		
−100 bps	17,864	−230	−0.08%
−200 bps	17,645	−449	−0.17%

FIGURE 2.35   Change in the EVE under a number of interest rate scenarios.
Source: own elaboration

EXAMPLE 7   *Calculation of delta EVE under a run-off scenario and under an assumption of unconditional cash flows*

Net mismatching in O/N–1-month time bucket = EUR −78.398m
   Discount factor under base scenario: $e^{(-0.05\%*15/365)} = 0.9999$
   PV of net mismatching position in time bucket O/N–1 month under base scenario = −78.398*0.9999 = −78.397m
   Discount factor under shocked scenario (+200 bps): $e^{(-2.05\%*15/365)} = 0.9991$
   PV of net mismatching position in time bucket O/N–1 month under +200 bps scenario = −78.398*0.9991 = −78.331m
   ΔPV in time bucket O/N–1 month = PV under +200 bps − PV under base scenario = −78.331m − (−78.397m) = 0.066m
   The ΔEVE under the shocked scenario is the summation of ΔPV for all time buckets.
   Interpretation of the result: with upward movement of the curve there is embedded gain for the bank as the net mismatching position is the liability.

Present Value under + 1 bp parallel curve shift (PV01)

PV01 is an important IRRBB metric which calculates the change in the PV of the banking book under instantaneous parallel interest rate curve shift by 1 bp.

   PV01 is calculated by every time bucket, and it indicates the sensitivity of every time bucket to the movement in interest rates. The higher absolute number in terms of PV01 of the time bucket the higher its sensitivity is. This is common practice to see limits by time bucket expressed in PV01 terms. Exceeding the limit triggers the need for hedging. The most sensitive time bucket is also known as a *key rate* as it indicates the tenor of the interest rate curve the bank is sensitive to the most.

In many cases banks set up limits in terms of the PV01 number which is a sum of PV01 by every time bucket.

$$Total\,PV01 = \sum_{1}^{19}PV01 \tag{12}$$

Similarly to ΔEVE, the PV01 is calculated as the difference between the present value of the banking book, with an instantaneous and parallel interest rate curve shift up by 1 bp, and the present value under a base scenario.

$$PV01 = PV_{+1bp} - PV_{base} \tag{13}$$

Where PV01 > 0, it means the present value of the banking book increases under a parallel up shift of the curve by 1 bp. Whereas PV01 < 0 means that the PV of the banking book is going to decrease as a result of the parallel shock up by 1 bp.

The limit in terms of the PV01 is set up as a ratio between the total PV01 to Tier 1 equity.

Value at Risk (VaR)

VaR is an estimate of the loss from a fixed set of data over a fixed time horizon that would be equal or exceeded with a given probability. Consequently, from the mathematical standpoint we can define VaR as:

$$P\left(V_T - V_0 \le VaR\right) = 1 - \alpha \tag{14}$$

where α is the confidence level; and V_T and V_0 are values *Mark to Market* (MTM) of the portfolio at time T and 0 respectively.

T is the time horizon under consideration known as the *holding period*.

VaR belongs to the type of simulation methods used to measure value changes as a result of changes in market prices. It models a series of potential changes to the yield curve, based on which the distribution of possible profits and loss outcomes is created. Out of these outcomes the most adverse is taken based on the selected confidence level, i.e., α. The calculation of interest rate changes, for VaR purposes, is based on different approaches. One of them, known as *historical simulation*, is based on the observed history of actual interest rate changes over a certain period of time, usually more than 2 years. The details of the calculations, in a historical simulation, consists in the calculation of value changes over a period of 2 years based on the current structure of the balance sheet or portfolio. Subsequently, the results are ordered by magnitude ranging from the largest loss to the largest gain. The VaR number would be fifth in the rankings, assuming a 95% confidence level. The important underlying assumption of the VaR model is that interest rate changes follow a normal distribution, i.e., a particular form of statistical distribution. Another approach is known as variance/covariance or the parametric method. The calculation of value at risk, according to this method, consists of the determination of portfolio composition from the risk factors perspective. In the case of a calculation of the exposure to IRRBB, the risk factors represent the particular tenors of the yield curve the portfolio is exposed to. The first step is to take daily log return $r_{i,t}$ for all risk factors, where $i = 1,..., n$ indexes the risk factors, and $t = 1,...m$ is the historical scenario number (time sequence) in the observation window. The next step consists of a calculation of risk factor volatility (standard deviation) and correlation matrix from the return data, and subsequently the first-order sensitivities to the risk factor are computed for each asset in the portfolio and summed across assets to the portfolio level. The P&L volatility regarding the i-th risk factor is calculated as the product of the level of the i-th risk factor at the date of analysis, its volatility and sensitivity of the portfolio to this risk factor. In this way, the vector of P&L volatilities is obtained for the portfolio. Due to the diversification effect among risk factors, P&L volatilities must be aggregated through a correlation matrix to yield the total P&L volatility of the whole portfolio.

Given the assumption of normality VaR relates to the volatility by a factor. For example, 1-day VaR at confidence level α is calculated as: total P&L volatility of portfolio σ_p and $\varphi^{-1}(1-\alpha)$ where φ^{-1} is the inverse cumulative density function of standard normal distribution. The square root of the time rule applies to derive the 10-day VaR, i.e. $\text{VaR}_{1\text{-day}} * \sqrt{10}$.

Driven by strict assumption on the distribution of the risk factor returns it is limited to what kind of instruments it can treat. An alternative is the Monte Carlo simulation where, in principle, any risk distribution can be simulated. However, this method is calculation intensive because it uses a large number of simulated scenarios. There is also a need to specify a model for the stochastic process, for example the assumption that the risk factors follow the geometric Brownian motion process.

Most banks disclose their VaR method report using historical simulation, which has gained popularity in recent years. This is probably because this method is based on samples from historical data and, therefore, avoids the need to make any distribution assumption. This overcomes problems with fat tails and skewness.

EXAMPLE 8   *Interpretation of VaR result for the treasury book.*

The treasury book has a VaR of £5m under 99% confidence level and a 10-day holding period. The £5m should be read as a 1% probability (100% − 99%) that the portfolio might lose £5m or more over the next 10 days.

CREDIT SPREAD RISK IN THE BANKING BOOK (CSRBB)

Another risk category which is managed in ALM is the credit spread risk. The credit spread is the yield difference of a bond compared to a risk-free interest rate. The importance of this risk category is also driven by the fact that the new regulatory requirements within the ICAAP framework demand a separate and explicit measurement of the credit spread risk for the adequate calculation of the required own funds for the ICAAP risks. The credit spread risk represents the risk of a value loss which is caused by changes in credit spreads while the counterparty's rating remains the same. For all the bank's assets which are valued with market prices in the balance sheet, the bank will have the risk of changing credit spreads and it should be calculated additionally. Initially, banks had to measure their spread risk just for their trading books. In recent years, however, the regulator has been demanding the measurement of the spread risk for both trading and banking books (Enthofer and Haas, 2016).

The importance of the credit spread risk has grown since the financial crisis as the spread volatility in the market has significantly increased. On one side are the new regulatory Basel III requirements demanding the stock of liquidity portfolio, mainly composed of bonds and, on the other, market volatility and uncertainty have pushed regulatory bodies to demand credit spread risk evaluations from banks, both for the trading and banking books. Credit spread risk is seen as a market risk and, for this reason, the common market risk measurement techniques apply also here. The VaR is the methodological approach followed to quantify the credit spread risk. However, from a practical standpoint it is difficult to gather all the information needed for calculating the volatilities and correlations of the credit spreads. In such cases the benchmark approaches are followed, i.e., groups of bonds for each asset class/credit rating. The credit spread history of each group can be defined and the evaluated average can be used for further calculation. Credit spreads can be also derived from CDS or indices. Until recently, most banks have calculated the risks and results measured for the bond portfolio as one figure with no differentiation of their origin. Currently this situation is changing as the regulator, and the transparency principle within ALM results, forced banks to split the total bond portfolio result into a separate credit spread and interest risk result. In fact, this trend is reflected in the revised IRRBB principle launched by BCBS and EBA in 2016 and 2017 respectively.

The CSRBB has been explicitly allocated as a subcategory of IRRBB in BCBS Standards in 2016 and, thereafter, in the EBA Final Guidelines published in 2018. Since then, there has been a requirement to build appropriate methodology to calculate CSRBB and to set up the metric.

The BCBS defines CSRBB as "any kind of asset/liability spread risk of credit-risky instruments that is not explained by IRRBB and by the expected credit/jump to default risk", stating that "CSRBB is a related risk that banks need to monitor and assess in their interest rate risk management framework."

The EBA, in its 2018 Guidelines on the management of interest rate risk arising from non-trading book activities defines CSRBB as "The risk driven by changes in the market perception about the price of credit risk, liquidity premium and potentially other components of credit-risky instruments inducing fluctuations in the price of credit risk, liquidity premium and other potential components, which is not explained by IRRBB or by expected credit/(jump-to-)default risk" and that "Institutions should monitor and assess their CSRBB-affected exposures, by reference to the asset side of the non-trading book, where CSRBB is relevant for the risk profile of the institution."

Banks' exposure to credit spreads observed in the market takes several forms, the meanings of which overlap to some extent with interest rate risk measures. In my view, CSRBB represents the form of risk to capital from the treasury book driven by widening credit spreads and a decline in the price of securities.

Market tradable assets in the banking book may be held (i) in a buy-and-hold business model, i.e., with the intent to hold these assets to their maturity, or (ii) in an available-for-sale business model, i.e., with the intent to potentially sell these assets before maturity, depending on market conditions. The accounting treatment of these assets is usually derived from the business model in which they are held. This is illustrated by reference to the International Financial Reporting Standards (IFRS 9) as follows:

(a) **Held-to-Collect-and-Sell Assets** (HtC&S) refer to assets where management intend to both collect the contractual cash flows and sell the financial asset before maturity. HtC&S assets are accounted for at fair value, and changes in market values are recognised through Other Comprehensive Income (OCI), as these changes may affect future Profit and Loss (P&L) before the maturity of these assets.

(b) **Held-for-Trading Assets** (HfT). There might be circumstances in which market tradable assets, though held by management with an intention to sell them in the short-term horizon, are nevertheless classified in the Regulatory Banking Book. HfT assets are accounted for at their fair value, and changes in the market value of HfT items are recognised directly through P&L.

(c) **Held-to-Collect Assets** (HtC) refer to assets expected to be held to their maturity by collecting contractual cash flows. Consequently, HtC assets are accounted for at amortising cost and not at fair value, and changes in the market value of these assets do not affect P&L or OCI.

Under this definition, CSRBB is related to the first two categories of assets, i.e., HtC&S and HfT.

HtC assets are held at amortised cost and include potential expected credit/(jump to-) default risk which is beyond the scope of CSRBB.

The EBA Guidelines do not specify how CSRBB should be monitored and assessed. However, considering the fact that the price of these assets is sensitive to the risk factor which relates neither to IRRBB nor to the expected credit/jump-to default risks, the sensitivity approach looks the most appropriate. This typically could take the form of price sensitivity to a change in market credit spread that does not relate to IRRBB (e.g., sensitivity to asset swap spread). Banks should develop their own methodology and metrics for assessing and monitoring CSRBB. In any case, the principle of proportionality should be applied.

Approaches based on full revaluation should not be mandatory and simpler methodologies should be considered suitable, as well as very simplified tools for smaller banks (EBF, 2019). Therefore, two metrics could be used in the assessment of the CSRBB:

- CS01 – sensitivity in terms of movements in the asset swap spread by 1 bp.
- VaR – based on the historical time series to be used by the model.

The metrics would allow the bank to monitor and also capitalise credit spread risk (through VaR). The new model is supposed to be integrated into the ICAAP process to ensure that all material risks are covered. In addition, monitoring of credit spread should be used to quantify the riskiness of various investment options.

CHAPTER 3

How to manage IRRBB

HEDGING INSTRUMENTS FOR IRRBB

Forward starting swaps

A forward starting interest rate swap is similar to a traditional interest rate swap in that two parties agree to exchange interest payments over a predetermined time period. The fundamental difference between a traditional swap and forward starting swap is the timing of cash flows exchange. In the case of forward starting swaps the cash flows will be exchanged at an established date in the future, for example starting in the next year. Whereas with a traditional interest rate swap the cash flows are exchanged immediately after the execution date of the transaction. With a forward starting swap, as with a traditional swap, the interest rate risk protection is established immediately at the execution date of the transaction. This is because the fixed rate paid under the swap agreement is known at the date of the transaction execution even though interest payments do not take effect until the future date. A forward starting swap is arranged in advance before there is a real need to hedge and it alters cash flows in anticipation of future movement in interest rates. It is an important tool in management of the duration gap, i.e., the repricing rate mismatch between assets and liabilities on the medium-to-long part of the interest rate curve.

Figure 3.1 shows an open risk position driven by the duration gap between asset repricing over a 4-year period and liability repricing over a 2-year period.

The margin of the bank is fixed over the next two years. However, there is a risk of interest rates moving up. This risk can be removed through forward starting swaps.

After two years the bank starts exchanging the cash flows (paying fixed rate and receiving floating) over a period of two years.

Figure 3.2 shows IRRBB management through forward starting swaps. This is a situation where an asset is repricing within the next 2 years and is funded by shorter term repricing liability (for example 1-year time deposit). The interest rate margin is closed for the first year but after 1 year there is an open gap which is managed through a forward starting swap executed today but starting in 1 year's time and with

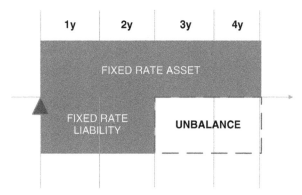

FIGURE 3.1 IRRBB exposure driven by long-term repricing assets funded by shorter-term repricing liabilities.
Source: own elaboration

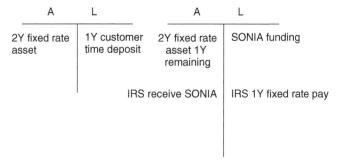

FIGURE 3.2 Illustrative representation of a forward starting swap starting in 1 year's time with a 1-year maturity.
Source: own elaboration

a 1-year maturity. Through entering this transaction the treasurer knows in advance the interest rate margin from year 1 to 2.

It is worth highlighting that a 1-year swap starting 1 year forward is considered as a swap with a 2-year tenor from the counterparty credit exposure perspective and the capital absorption. On the same basis a 5-year swap out of spot, and a 4-year swap starting 1 year forward have the same treatment from the counterparty risk perspective and capital requirements.

Another technique to manage the duration gap is to enter traditional interest rate swaps on the asset and liability side. It is a common practice applied by financial institutions and consists of swapping both sides of the balance sheet, e.g., pay a fixed 7-year swap rate and, at the same time, receive a 2-year swap rate. This strategy consists in entering payer and receiver traditional swaps (not forward starting) to transform both sides of the balance sheet into floating market rate. Figure 3.3 illustrates the management of the duration gap through traditional payer and receiver swaps.

Assets	Liabilities	Assets	Liabilities	Assets	Liabilities
7y fixed rate mortgages	2y customer time deposits	7y fixed rate mortgages	2y customer time deposits		
		2y fixed leg of the swap	SONIA linked floating leg	SONIA linked floating leg	SONIA linked floating leg
		SONIA linked floating leg	7y fixed leg		

FIGURE 3.3 Management of the duration gap through receiver and payer spot swaps.
Source: own elaboration

Hedge accounting considerations In order to pursue the most suitable hedging strategy for a bank it is important to consider the implications on hedge accounting driven by the strategy. Decisions related to the identification of a hedged item is key to determining hedge accounting designation. In the banking book we observe *fair value* hedging and *cash flow* hedging designations. If the hedged item is a floating rate product and the intention is to hedge the variability of the interest rate, then cash flow hedging is applied. For fixed rate items, where the intention is to hedge the fair value of the cash flows (so, long-term assets or liabilities) fair value hedging is applied.

EXAMPLE 9   *Hedge accounting considerations for forward starting swaps*

The hedging strategy of Bank ABC is as follows:

Bank ABC is considering entering forward starting swaps, whereby Bank ABC will pay a fixed rate to an external counterparty and will receive a variable SONIA rate, starting in the future (for example, a swap 2×3, starting in 2 years, settling periodically for 3 years). The swaps will be entered into to mitigate the fair value/duration risk of fixed rate loans to clients (assets) for those time buckets where the future funding will be not of a fixed rate but of a variable/floating nature (in the future, mostly borrowing based on daily repricing). These loans/fixed rate assets being hedged will be mostly maintained till their contractual maturity (except full prepayment), collecting their cash flows, and under IFRS 9[1] rules they will be classified as "assets at amortised cost".

---

[1] IFRS 9 is an International Financial Reporting Standard published by the International Accounting Standards Board.

Fair value hedge accounting could be applied to forward starting swaps, whereby the change in Mark to Market (MTM) of the hedges, since their trade date will be recorded into P&L and largely (if not completely) offset by an adjustment against the book value of the assets. In this type of hedge accounting designation, the asset's "MTM" would be "partially" hedged, for the fixed rate cash flows value in the period when the swap produces cash flows, i.e., in a 2×3 swap, from year 2 to year 5. Bank ABC will be hedging the changes in fair value of the cash flows of the asset from year 2 to 5.

It is worth mentioning that, in the past, under IAS 39,[2] there were some questions on whether an "*asset held to maturity*" could be hedged for interest rate risk that could preclude from applying hedge accounting to swaps hedging it. This should not be the case under IFRS 9. Otherwise, the swaps could be potentially designated as "cash flow hedges" of the future highly probable forecast drawings/funding at variable rates from, in our example, years 2 to 5. In this scenario, the change in MTM of the hedges will be recorded into a *Cash Flow* hedge reserve, Other Comprehensive Income (OCI), and reclassified into P&L via accruals and swap settlements when recording interest expense in P&L due to the funding exposures. It should be noted that the hedging decisions of Bank ABC are based on the risk management of fixed rate assets, meanwhile the cash flow hedging considerations means that the hedging decisions are based on managing variable rate funding exposures/liabilities, not assets.

There are potential sources of ineffectiveness in both cases above which could include mismatches in the timing of the cash flows (i.e., loans/funding being monthly, while the swaps quarterly) and credit risk pricing of swaps.

The above has the same approach and consequences whether the swaps are spot starting or forward starting. The only consideration with the latter is that the more forward starting a swap is, in the case of cash flow hedge alternative, the more questionable could be the "highly probable" criteria of occurring for the hedged future variable rate liabilities.

Interest rate options – caps, floors and swaptions

Caps   A cap is an over-the-counter contract by which the seller agrees to pay a positive amount to the option buyer in case the reference rate, for example EURIBOR, exceeds a strike, i.e., predetermined level of interest rates. This payment happens on some future dates which are defined by the cap contract.

---

[2] Financial Instruments: Recognition and Measurement was an international accounting standard which outlined the requirements for the recognition and measurement of financial assets, financial liabilities, and some contracts to buy or sell non-financial items. It was released by the International Accounting Standards Board in 2003, and was replaced in 2014 by IFRS 9, which became effective in 2018.

The cap contract is composed of the number underlying *caplets*. A typical cap contract has the following features:

1. Notional amount: it defines the volume of the transaction.
2. Reference rate: the rate the contract is linked to, for example EURIBOR.
3. Strike rate: a predetermined level of interest rate which triggers the exercise of the option.
4. Starting date: the date on which the contract is effective.
5. Maturity: the length of the cap contract.
6. Tenor: it is related to the rate reset frequency, for example if the reference rate is EURIBOR with 6M reset then the tenor is 6M. Also, it indicates how many caplets are in the contract (see example below).
7. Day count: Actual/360.

The buyer of the contract pays the Premium to the seller which is equal to the percentage of the cap notional, prorated to the period.

EXAMPLE 10   *Cash flows of the cap contract – caplets*

Notional: 1,000,000 Euro

Start date of the cap: 30 April 2021

Cap maturity: 2 years

Cap strike: 1%

Reference rate: EURIBOR 6M

The premium: 0.1% of the notional paid on semi-annual basis

TABLE 3.1   Cash flows related to the cap contract.

Refixing date	Cash flows
30 April 2021	Starting date of cap
30 October 2021	$10^6 * (184/360) * ((R_{i-1} - 1\%) - 0.1\%)$
30 April 2022	$10^6 * (181/360) * ((R_{i-1} - 1\%) - 0.1\%)$
30 October 2022	$10^6 * (184/360) * ((R_{i-1} - 1\%) - 0.1\%))$
30 April 2023	$10^6 * (181/360) * ((R_{i-1} - 1\%) - 0.1\%)$

Source: Elaboration based on *PRMIA, Volume 1, Book 2, Financial Instruments, 2015*, I.B.8.2.1

R_{i-1} is the value of the reference rate, in this case EURIBOR 6M on the date of the fixing period, i.e., on 30 October 2022, the fixing date is 30 April 2022.

Where, in each period, the EURIBOR 6M is higher than 1% (strike) then the cap buyer receives the difference between EURIBOR 6M and 1%. Otherwise, it receives zero.

Economic value of cap

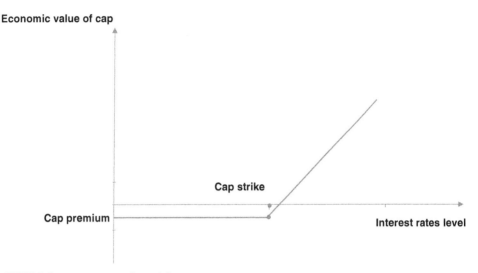

FIGURE 3.4   Economic value of the cap option.
Source: own elaboration

Buying the cap provides the opportunity to set up the limit on funding costs for the institution which is equal to the strike plus the cap premium. In Example 10 it is 1.1%. If EURIBOR 6M stays below the strike level the cap buyer enjoys the lower cost of funding.

Cap is an option which means it is a nonlinear instrument. During the life of the option its value is determined by the volatility of interest rates and time. The total option value, during the contract life is a sum of its intrinsic value and time value. Time value gets smaller as the call option gets closer to its expiration date.

The option is exercised where a certain level of reference rate is realised. Otherwise, it is not exercised, and its economic value is equal to zero.

The payoff of the cap contract at maturity is shown in Figure 3.4.

Structure of cap contract   Let's consider a cap with a nominal amount of EUR 1,000,000, strike at S, based on EURIBOR with δ-month maturity denoted Reference Rate (RR) at date t and maturity δ. If the option is *in the money*, i.e., the level of EURIBOR with δ-maturity is higher than the strike level, then the cap's cash flows are as follows:

TABLE 3.2   Structure of the cap contract.

Time T_i	Cash flows C_i
T_0	
T_1	$C_1 = 1,000,000 * \delta * (RR\ (T_0, \delta) - S)$
T_2	$C_2 = 1,000,000 * \delta * (RR\ (T_1, \delta) - S)$
...	
T_n	$C_n = 1,000,000 * \delta * (RR\ (T_{n-1}, \delta) - S)$

Source: Based on *PRMIA, Volume 1, Book 2, Financial Instruments, 2015,* I.B.8.2.1

We can notice that the cap is composed of a number of C_i call options with payoff occurring on date T_i. The call options of the cap are known as *caplets* (see equation 15).

Pricing of cap contract   Pricing of the cap contract, in the positive interest rates environment, is done by application of the Black (1976) model which is considered the reference for the pricing of caps, floors and swaptions despite its assumption of constant volatility of the forward curve. This is clear model simplification, as the forward curve becomes more sensitive to changes in the spot rate as maturity approaches.

$$Cap(t) = \sum_{i=1}^{n} Caplet_i(t) \tag{15}$$

$$Cap(t) = \sum_{i=1}^{n} N\delta B(t,T_i)\left[F(t,T_{i-1},T_i)\phi(d_i) - E\phi\left(d_i - \sigma_i\sqrt{T_{i-1}-t}\right)\right] \tag{16}$$

where Φ is cumulative standard distribution function; $F(t,T_{i-1},T_i)$ is the forward rate at the date t, beginning at date T_{i-1} and finishing at date T_i; $B(t,T_i)$ is the discount rate from T_i to t; d_i is calculated as follows:

$$d_i = \frac{\ln\left(\dfrac{F(t,T_{i-1},T_i)}{E}\right) + 0.5\sigma_i^2(T_{i-1}-t)}{\sigma_i\sqrt{T_{i-1}-t}} \tag{17}$$

and σ_i is the volatility of the underlying rate $F(t,T_{i-1},T_i)$.

The volatility referred to the single caplet is called caplet volatility.

The discount factor in equation 16 is calculated as follows:

$$B(t,T_i) = \frac{1}{1+\delta F(t,T_{i-1},T_i)} \tag{18}$$

Floors   A floor is an over-the-counter contract by which the buyer of the floor contract has the right to receive from the option seller, for the predetermined period of time (length of the option) and, at the future dates predefined by the contract, the difference between the strike rate and the reference rate, for example EURIBOR. If the difference between the strike and reference rate set at the fixing date is negative, then the contract buyer receives zero. Otherwise, the contract buyer receives the positive amount. Obviously, similarly to the cap contract, the buyer has to pay, to the contract seller, the premium, i.e., the cost of the option.

The floor contract is composed of the number of underlying *floorlets*. A typical floor contract has the following features:

1. <u>Notional amount</u>: it defines the volume of the transaction.
2. <u>Reference rate</u>: the rate the contract is linked to, for example EURIBOR.
3. <u>Strike rate</u>: a predetermined level of interest rate which triggers the exercise of the option.
4. <u>Starting date</u>: the date on which the contract is effective.
5. <u>Maturity</u>: the length of the floor contract.
6. <u>Tenor</u>: it is related to the rate reset frequency, for example if the reference rate is EURIBOR with 6M reset then the tenor is 6M. Also, it indicates how many floorlets are in the contract (see Example 11).
7. <u>Day count</u>: Actual/360.

EXAMPLE 11   *Cash flows of the floor contract – floorlets*

Notional amount: 1,000,000 Euro

Reference rate: EURIBOR 3M

Strike rate: 0%

Starting date of the contract: 1 February 2021

Maturity: 1 year

Tenor: 3 months

Day count: Actual/360

The premium paid by the buyer of the floor is equal to 0.1%

TABLE 3.3   Cash flows related to the floor contract.

Refixing date	Cash flows
1 February 2021	Starting date of the floor
1 May 2021	$10^6 * (89/360) * ((0\% - RR_{i-1}) - 0.1\%)$
1 August 2021	$10^6 * (92/360) * ((0\% - RR_{i-1}) - 0.1\%)$
1 November 2021	$10^6 * (92/360) * ((0\% - RR_{i-1}) - 0.1\%)$
1 February 2022	$10^6 * (92/360) * ((0\% - RR_{i-1}) - 0.1\%)$

Source: Based on PRMIA, Volume 1, Book 2, Financial Instruments, 2015, I.B.8.2.1

(Continued)

(Continued)

> *RR* is the reference rate, in our example EURIBOR 3M.
>
> If the EURIBOR 3M is higher than 0% then the floor is *out of the money* and the option is not exercised. Otherwise, if the EURIBOR 3M is lower than 0% (it is in negative territory) then the floor is exercised, and it is *in the money*. The lower the value of interest rates the higher the economic value of the option is. The economic value of the option is calculated as a difference between 0% and the EURIBOR 3M. By buying this floor the bank will guarantee a minimum rate of return while benefiting from the positive rates environment.

Let's consider a floor with the same characteristics. The floor holder gets on each date T_i cash flow C_i given by:

$$C_i = 10^6 * \delta * \left(S - RR\left(T_{i-1}, \delta\right) \right) \tag{19}$$

where RR (T_{i-1}, δ) is the reference rate at δ tenor and S is the option strike.

The floor is the put option on the reference rate, for example the EURIBOR rate, observed on date T_{i-1} with a payoff occurring on date T_i. The floor is composed of a number of such options. The single option is known as a *floorlet*. Figure 3.5 shows the floor contract composed of four floorlets reflecting the example in Table 3.3.

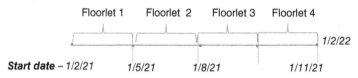

FIGURE 3.5   Floor contract composed of four floorlets.
Source: own elaboration

It is worth noting that the only rate which is known (and fixed) is as of 1 February 2021. The subsequent refixing of EURIBOR 3M is not known at the start date of the contract.

Pricing of floor contract As with the pricing of the cap contract, a floor is priced using the Black 76 model.

$$Floor(t) = \sum_{i=1}^{n} Floorlet_i(t) \tag{20}$$

$$Floor(t) = \sum_{i=1}^{n} N\delta B(t, T_i) \left[-F(t, T_{i-1}, T_i)\phi(-d_i) - E\phi\left(-d_i + \sigma_i\sqrt{T_{i-1} - t}\right) \right] \tag{21}$$

where Φ is cumulative standard distribution function; $F(t, T_{i-1}, T_i)$ is forward rate at the date t, beginning at date T_{i-1} and finishing at date T_i; $B(t, T_i)$ is the discount rate from T_i to t; d_i is calculated as per equation 17; σ_i is the volatility of the underlying rate $F(t, T_{i-1}, T_i)$. The discount factor is calculated as per equation 18.

EXAMPLE 12   *Calculation of the value of the caplet*

The caplet is designed to cap the interest on a loan of £0.5m. It protects a 3-month interest period and starts in 6 months from now. Assuming the 3-month forward rate starting in 6 months is 4.8%, the strike 5% and the 3-month rate volatility is 18%.
   Thus:

N = 0.5m

δ = 0.25 (3 months)

Forward rate F = 4.8%

E = 5%

σ = 18%

Let's calculate the discount factor first:

$$B = \frac{1}{1 + (0.25 \times 0.048)} = 0.98$$

$$d = \frac{\ln\frac{0.048}{0.05} + (0.5 \times 0.18^2 \times 0.5)}{0.18\sqrt{0.5}} = -0.257$$

(Continued)

(Continued)

$$\text{Caplet} = 0.5m * 0.25 * 0.988 * \left[0.048\varphi(-0.257) - 0.05\varphi(-0.257) - 0.18 * \sqrt{0.5} \right]$$

$$= £199.23$$

The value for $\varphi(-0.257)$ is taken from Table of the Standard Normal Cumulative Distribution Function $\Phi(z)$.
Source: PRMIA, Volume 1, Book 2, Financial Instruments, 2015, I.B.8.2.1

Caps and floors are designated to hedge interest rate risk. In particular, the buyer of a cap contract aims to hedge the increase in the cost of funds and, in general, is hedged against an increase in interest rates. Instead, the buyer of a floor aims to secure the minimum return on the assets side in case the rates go down. Floors are commonly executed in the low and negative rates environment. They protect the margin compression resulting from the downward movement of the curve. Additionally, floors represent an important tool in the low rate environment and under downward market pressure on the interest rate curve.

Swaptions   Swaptions are *over the counter* options. They are an important part of the IRO family. The underlying asset of a swaption is a plain vanilla swap and its maturity can vary from 1 to 30 years. Consequently, a swaption is an option on a swap which gives the swaption buyer the right to enter the underlying swap contract at a certain predefined swap rate. If the buyer of the swaption receives the fixed rate it is said that the swaption is a receiver swaption. The payer swaption, instead, gives the buyer the right to enter the swap, paying the fixed rate and receiving the floating rate.

EXAMPLE 13   *Illustrative representation of the swaption*

Let's imagine the payer swaption where its buyer has the right to enter the underlying fixed rate payer swap. The start of the swap contract is T_0, which is the date of the swaption maturity.
    The expected cash flow schedule is as follows:

T_0	T_1	T_2	T_n
Fixed leg	$-F_1$	$-F_2$	$-F_n$
Floating leg	V_1	V_2	V_n

where F_n represent cash flows on the fixed rate leg of the swap and is calculated as follows:

$$F_n = N * \delta * r_{swap} \tag{22}$$

> N is swap notional, r_{swap} is the swap rate and δ is the cash flow payment frequency (in years).
>
> $$V_n = N * \delta * RR \tag{23}$$
>
> RR is the reference rate, for example EURIBOR 3M.
>
> The buyer of swaption has the right to enter a payer swap on date T_0 with the fixed rate at r_{swap}.
>
> We assume the bank funds itself through floating rate liability indexed to EURIBOR 3M.

At the time of the analysis the swap rate for EURIBOR 3M with 5-year maturity is 6% and the treasurer of the bank fears an increase in the interest rates. He or she has the option to enter the payer swap over the 5-year period immediately. In this way the bank will be hedged against an interest rate increase. Figure 3.6 shows the situation where the treasurer executed the swaption and entered the payer swap.

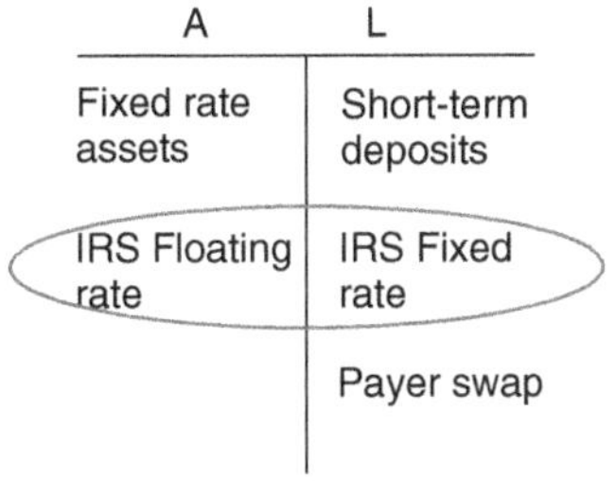

FIGURE 3.6 Hedging the exposure of a bank through a payer swap.
Source: own elaboration

However, there is uncertainty when this increase is going to happen. Consequently, the bank's treasurer decides to buy a protection against interest rate increase in the near future, say, in 6 months' time. She/he buys the payer swaption with the strike 6%. If, in 6 months, the swap rate with 4.5-year maturity is higher than 6% the option is exercised as the underlying swap rate is lower than the market rate. Otherwise, she/he enters a swap under the new market condition (the market swap rate is lower than the strike of the swaption).

The receiver swaption enables the bank to transform its fixed rate debt into a floating rate in the context of a decrease in interest rates. If executed, it allows the entry of a receiver swap as shown in Figure 3.7.

The swaption will be executed if the swap rate in the market is lower than the strike of the swaption, in our example 6%.

The other application of swaption is to protect the floating rate investment in the downward movement of the curve.

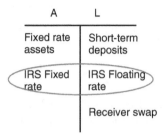

FIGURE 3.7   Hedging the exposure of a bank through a receiver swap.
Source: own elaboration

Interest Rate Swaps   Interest Rate Swaps (IRSs) represent the most widely used swap category. This is because swaps are a very broad instrument category defined, in general, as any sequence of cash flows exchanged between two parties. Thus, there are equity swaps which consist of exchange of return from an equity or equity index against the return of another asset, often against LIBOR based cash flows.

Another category of swaps is represented by commodity swaps. There are two major types of commodity swap. Swap parties can either exchange fixed to floating payments based on commodity price index or exchange payments when one payment is based on an index and the other based on the money market rate, often the LIBOR rate.

Currency swaps are similar to interest rate swaps but there are some differences. First, exchanged cash flows are in different currencies which means that there are two interest rate curves involved instead of just the one as in the case of IRS. Secondly, a floating rate is exchanged against another floating rate. Finally, an important difference is the fact that principals are exchanged at the beginning of the swap life and at maturity. Currency swaps are an example of the basis swap category. However, in the instance of a basis swap the same currency is involved.

The basis swap is the derivative instrument whereby the floating rate is exchanged to another floating rate, for example USD LIBOR is exchanged to USD government curve rate.

IRSs involve exchanging cash flows generated by different interest rates. The fixed swap rate is paid against the receipt of a floating rate, for example LIBOR or overnight rate, in the same currency. As opposed to currency swaps the notional is not exchanged. The most common example of an IRS is the plain vanilla IRS. It is a commitment to exchange interest payments associated with a notional amount N settled at predefined settlement dates $(t_1, t_2, \ldots t_n)$ and initiated at time t_0. The buyer of the payer swap makes fixed payments at size $r^* N^* \delta$ where r is the swap rate and δ the payment frequency in years. It receives floating rate payments of size $L_{t_i}^* N^* \delta$ where L_{t_i} is the LIBOR or overnight rate determined at the set dates $t_0, t_1, \ldots, t_{n-1}$, whereas the buyer of the receiver swap receives fixed rate payments at size $r^* N^* \delta$ and pays variable rate cash flows. It is important to emphasise that the LIBOR benchmark is undergoing reform and the objective is to replace it by the end of 2021. Thus, many banks do not enter the LIBOR indexed swap anymore. Instead, they are moving towards the overnight index swap that uses a benchmark index of overnight interest rates for the floating leg. The floating rate is computed as the geometric average of the relevant overnight index rate over every day of the payment period and paid at settlement dates in exchange for the fixed rate.

The below example shows the IRS indexed to SONIA.

SWAP TICKET EXAMPLE

The terms of the particular Transaction to which this Confirmation relates are as follows:

Notional Amount:	GBP 5,000,000.00
Trade Date	30 April 2020 (time of trade is available upon request)
Effective Date	30 April 2020
Termination Date:	30 April 2021, subject to adjustment in accordance with the Modified Following Business Day Convention
Fixed Rate Payer Payment Date(s):	30 April 2021, subject to adjustment in accordance with the Modified Following Business Day Convention
Fixed Rate	0.064 per cent
Fixed Rate Day Count Fraction:	Actual/365(Fixed)
Business Days for Fixed Amounts:	London
Floating Amounts	
Floating Rate Payer	Counterparty
Floating Rate Payer Payment Date(s):	The last Business Day of July 2020, October 2020, January 2021 and April 2021, subject to adjustment in accordance with the Modified Following Business Day Convention
Floating Rate Option:	GBP-SONIA-COMPOUND
Spread	None
Floating Rate Day Count Fraction:	Actual/365(Fixed)
Compounding:	Inapplicable
Reset Dates	The last day of the Calculation Period

Balance sheet management of interest exposure is a reason for the high liquidity of swaps. The asset and liability interest rate exposure of a financial institution can be adjusted using interest rate swaps and swaptions. If funding is obtained in floating rates and lent at a fixed rate, then an interest rate swap can be entered into and exposure can be efficiently managed. Swap market liquidity is further supported by the needs of mortgage-based hedging activity. It appears that a significant portion of plain vanilla swaps trading is due to the requirements of the mortgage industry.

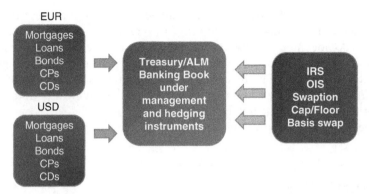

FIGURE 3.8   Components of the banking book.
Note: Commercial Papers (CPs) and Certificate of Deposit (CDs)
Source: own elaboration

WHY CONSIDER INTEREST RATE SWAPS?

There are a number of reasons to consider entering IRS. The most common need for swaps is to lock in a fixed interest rate and to remove interest rate risk. Entering payer swaps in a low rates environment for a longer period, with an expectation of interest rates increase, provides an opportunity to lock in cheaper funding costs. On the other hand, in the situation where there are more fixed rate liabilities than assets on the medium-to-long part of the curve (the bank is net liability position) entering into a receiver swap contributes to the reduction of interest rate expense without the need to refinance a loan and pay the associated costs.

The most frequent reason for entering interest rates swaps is for risk management purposes, i.e., to match *RSA* with *RSL*. Partial hedging allows the diversification of financial risks of the banking book by converting a part of the assets or liabilities portfolio from fixed to floating and therefore to change the interest rate composition without facing the expenses associated with refinancing or issuing new debt.

It is worth highlighting that the banking book is what is not managed in the trading book. It is composed of all single items belonging to the specific category (such as mortgages, bonds, sight deposits) which flow into it under management. The resulting portfolio is a sum of open portfolios managed as a single unit by treasury/ALM via portfolio of hedging instruments. Figure 3.8 shows the components of the banking book.

NATURAL HEDGING AND HEDGING THROUGH DERIVATIVES

Manging the banking book exposure to IRRBB through derivatives is a well-known practice and the most common instrument used for the hedging of the banking book is the plain vanilla interest rate swap.

Figure 3.9 shows an exchange of cash flows where the counterparty receives the cash flow at a fixed rate and pays the cash flows at a variable rate. The counterparty, on the "other side" of the deal will do the reverse. If the cash flows are in the same

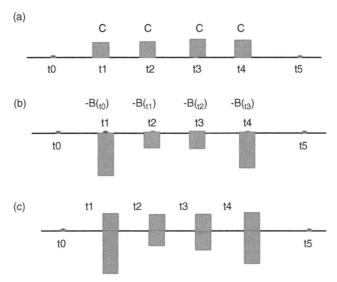

FIGURE 3.9   Interest rate swap structure.
Source: Based on PRMIA, Volume 1, Book 2, Financial Instruments, 2015, I.B.8.2.1

currency, then there is no need to make two different payments at each period *t*. One counterparty will simply pay the other the net amount.

The bank with the net asset position on the medium-to-long part of the curve may want to hedge against the potential increase in interest rates. Through entering the payer swap it will transform the fixed rate asset into the floating rate instrument (Figure 3.10).

Otherwise, the bank may consider redesigning its funding base to achieve natural hedging objectives and, at the same time, to reduce the cost of funding. It is important to highlight that, in order to do so, it is not necessary to launch new products on the liabilities side. In most cases it is sufficient to recalibrate the proportions of the existing funding sources. The concept of optimisation and the setup of the funding and hedging strategy under a holistic and proactive approach, is the main topic of Chapter 5. At this point the intention is to show that there is another way of hedging

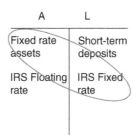

FIGURE 3.10   The mechanics of payer swap.
Source: own elaboration

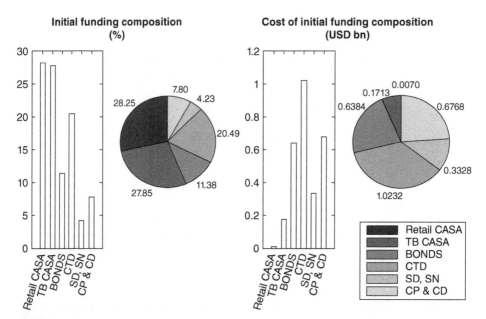

FIGURE 3.11   Natural hedging – funding structure before natural hedging optimisation.
Note: Transactional Banking (TB); Commercial Time Depo (CTD); Senior Debt (SD);
Senior Note (SN).
Source: own elaboration

the banking book, i.e., through a natural hedging strategy which does not necessarily mean a perfect matching between asset and liability side and the achievement of immunisation. Proactive management of IRRBB consists of a healthy equilibrium between risk and return of the banking book driven by the adoption of certain IRRBB strategies, for example funding long repricing mortgages through short repricing liabilities. This strategy is known as *riding the yield curve* (assuming a normal interest rate curve shape) and supposes that a certain level of risk is involved. The magnitude of the risk run by a financial institution is limited by IRRBB limits and the risk appetite is clearly stated in the RAS.

Figure 3.11 shows an example of the optimisation of the funding base through a recalibration of proportions between different funding sources with the objective of reducing the number of derivatives, i.e., applying the natural hedging strategy.

The optimisation exercise not only allows the "avoidance" of derivatives, as far as it is possible, but also to close the IRRBB exposure through natural hedging. It aims to reduce the overall cost of funding for financial institutions. The recalibrated funding base and the reduced cost of funds are shown in Figure 3.12 and Figure 3.13.

The employment of a natural hedging strategy does not mean that I am suggesting that you avoid synthetic hedges in general. Derivatives are an extremely important tool for IRRBB and should be used where there is a need. There is always residual exposure which a financial institution may want to reduce. It can be done only through synthetic hedges.

However, there are clear risks associated with derivatives. First of all, there is an opportunity cost, as locking in a fixed rate through swap may result in a higher

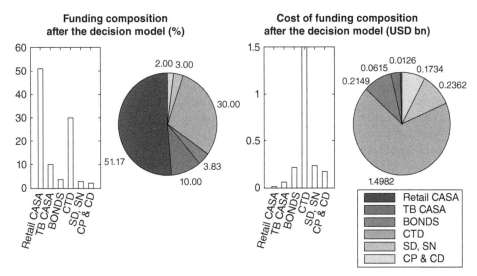

FIGURE 3.12 Natural hedging – funding structure after natural hedging optimisation.
Source: own elaboration

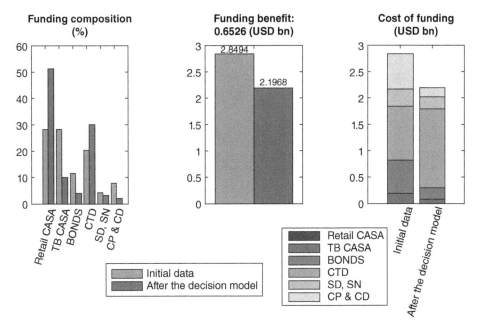

FIGURE 3.13 Natural hedging – application of the optimisation technique and minimisation of funding costs.
Source: own elaboration

interest expense than the average of the floating rate over the same period, i.e., without hedging. This is exactly the decision which a treasurer has to take regarding the expectation over the interest rate movement and position of the banking book of a bank. Where the expectation is that the curve movement will benefit NII and/or EVE then locking in the margin through swap results is missing an opportunity to boost profitability and increase ALM margin. It is important to highlight that this has nothing to do with trading or betting against the market. It is simply the consideration of the opportunity cost and proactive IRRBB management. The IRRBB appetite and, therefore, limits imposed should always be the main driver for a treasurer in her/his daily management of the risk positions.

Another important issue related to derivatives is the impact on short-term liquidity due to the potential variation margin. Swaps cleared through Central Counterparty Clearing (CCP) are subject to mark to market on a daily basis and losses have to be settled with CCP. In the case of bilateral agreement between parties, for swap trading, there is the counterparty credit risk exposure, associated with derivatives, which has to be calculated and monitored on a regular basis. The standard methodology known as the mark to market method, in line with Article 274 of the Capital Requirement Regulation (CRR), requires the determination of the replacement cost (MTM) together with the future credit exposure.

The calculation of the counterparty credit risk exposure of Bank A associated with the swap book is shown in Example 14. The replacement cost only considers positive values of swaps MTM and negative MTMs cannot be netted.

The future credit exposure is dependent upon both product types and maturities. In the case of one-year interest rate swaps, a weighting of 0% is applied to the notional value of the contracts. For contracts with maturity longer than 12 months the notional is multiplied by 0.5% (not exceeding 5 years).

EXAMPLE 14   *Calculation of the counterparty risk for derivatives portfolio*

Bank A has the portfolio of receiver swaps and performs a periodic valuation of the interest rate swap portfolio at a certain point in time. Bank A calculates the counterpart risk exposure through the *mark to market* method.

The notional of the portfolio is £63m. The portfolio has a 2-year residual maturity. At a certain point in time Bank A calculates the value of the swap book at the transactional level. Only one swap contract has a positive value, at the date of valuation and it is £2,774. Bank A has adopted the mark to market method in order to calculate the counterparty risk exposure it is running on the swap portfolio.

Under the methodological choice adopted by Bank A, it has to calculate the *replacement cost* and *future credit exposure.*

The *replacement cost* represents the amount which Bank A would lose where the counterparty fails or does not respect the contractual obligations.

The replacement cost is augmented by a potential *future credit exposure* which is dependent on swap maturity.

In this example, the swap book contains £63m of transactions with a 2-year residual maturity. In order to determine the potential future credit exposure Bank A shall multiply the notional by the respective weightings allocated to each maturity of the swap. For example, for a 1-year swap the weighting is 0% and for a 2-year swap it is 0.5%.

The resulting exposure of Bank A is, therefore, £317,773.

$$0.5\% * 63m + 2772 = 317,773.$$

Another implication of hedging through derivatives is the need to apply for hedge accounting designation. In order to obtain the hedge accounting designation, and to avoid the P&L volatility, it is necessary to identify the hedged and hedging items. The objective of hedge accounting designation is to prove that the derivative has been used exclusively for the banking book's item hedging purposes, for example for hedging of the portfolio of fixed rate assets. Hedge accounting designation requires underlying valuation models and detailed documentation along with the assessment of hedge effectiveness on a regular basis. Any ineffective parts of hedging will cause P&L volatility.

Finally, there is a basis risk associated with derivatives transactions which cannot be underestimated. The index of the variable leg of the swap transactions often does not match with the indexation of the underlying asset or liabilities. For example, the variable leg of GBP Overnight Index Swap (OIS) swap is indexed to SONIA; meanwhile most variable loans in the UK are indexed to the BoE base rate (BoE trackers). The basis risk arises because these two indexes are not perfectly correlated, i.e., the SONIA rate fluctuates on a daily basis. Meanwhile the BoE base rate is decided by the Monetary Committee Policy (MCP) on a monthly basis.

HEDGING STRATEGIES

Interest rate swaps, natural hedging strategies and other hedging strategies provide a way to manage the potential impact on the banking book driven by changes in the interest rate environment. Every hedging strategy applied has its own objectives. For example, if the objective is to reduce interest expenses and the bank has a net liability position on the medium-to-long term then entering a receiver swap meets the objective. Another example of a clearly defined hedging strategy is entering the payer swap when a bank has the net asset position on the medium-to-long part of the banking book, and it fears an increase in interest rates. In this case the ALM margin can be locked in by swapping shorter-term repricing liabilities and locking the interest rate for the swap duration.

FIGURE 3.14 Unhedged open position driven by the expectation of a reduction in interest rates. *Source:* own elaboration

The most important factor which needs to be analysed before undertaking any strategies is the expectation of interest rate movements, and the interest rate environment in general. For example, the expectation of a downward movement of interest rates, for a bank with a net asset position on the medium-to-long part of the curve and staying well within the IRRBB limit, may lead the treasurer to decide to leave the open position unhedged as shown in Figure 3.14.

However, it is important to highlight that interest rate trends are very difficult to predict, and historic trends can only prove this statement. It can be easily realised how quickly rates can rise or fall in certain environments. In recent years interest rates have reached near historic low levels.

In 2014 the ECB employed negative rates as an unprecedented measure to combat recession and foster recovery. The idea of being charged for lending is counter-intuitive and puts into question the concept of the time value of money. Such a move is viewed as controversial by economists as there is a clear impact on the economy and banking system. However, the lesson from the past shows that a dramatic rise in interest rates can occur over a short period of time. Interest rate spikes can happen in a short time and without much notice.

The employment of negative interest rates has an important impact on pricing automatic options and the typically applied Black 76 method does not work under the assumption of negative rates (Appendix 1 includes the description of an alternative model used for IROs pricing under negative rates assumption).

The section below summarises common hedging strategies employed in the IRRBB management.

Blended rate strategy (also known as partial hedge)

In order to describe this strategy, let's assume that a bank needs to raise £100m of funding in order to cover the new business growth which is mainly composed of fixed rate assets. The treasurer does not intend to apply full hedging as it is a costly strategy and, as regards the banking book, it is the overall exposure which matters, i.e., rather than hedging on the portfolio basis only the residual gap is closed.

Consequently, the treasurer will consider applying a blended rate strategy, which consists of locking in the interest rate for only a portion of liabilities while the rest is placed in the variable rate loan. The objective is to obtain the blended rate that is lower than the fixed rate, and to reduce interest expense for a period of the loan. Depending on the interest rate environment a bank may realise significant savings by using this strategy.

Interest rate cap and floor

This is a very common strategy which consists of removing interest rate uncertainty using the variable loan through caps, floors or collars. The interest rate ceiling locks in the maximum rate which needs to be paid should there be an interest rate increase. The applicable interest rate, which fluctuates, is subject to the cap and a bank avoids payment of higher interest expenses. The main benefit of this strategy is that the borrower retains the benefit for the rate decrease but, at the same time, won't pay interest charges higher than the ceiling. Obviously, this protection comes at a price (premium). The interest floor strategy is extremely important for banks in low and downward moving interest rates environments. It protects the interest income which a financial institution earns on floating rate assets.

Forward rate lock

This strategy is used to lock the predetermined interest rate over a certain period of time. The driver for undertaking this strategy is the expectation of a sharp increase in interest rates occurring during the lock-in period. The *locked-in* rate is higher than the current market rate due to the market expectation of a rate increase. Under this strategy the treasurer believes that the actual rates increase will be higher than is predicted by the market through the forward curve.

Figure 3.15 summarises the hedging strategies applied by banks.

Name of strategy	Description of strategy	Strategy objective
Partial hedge (blended rate strategy)	Combination of swapped fixed rate and variable rate loans	To obtain a blended rate that is lower than the fixed rate reducing interest expense for the period of the loan
Interest rate cap strategy	Eliminates interest rate uncertainty using a variable rate structure through set up of a ceiling	The applicable interest rate which fluctuates is capped – hedging against a significant increase in rates
Forward rate lock	Series of loans over a number of years at a predetermined interest rate	Hedging against a significant increase in rates
Blend and extend strategy	Extension of existing interest rate pay-fixed swap over a longer period of time than its original term at a lower interest rate (if liability) or higher (if assets). The overall value of the swap remains the same	Protection from raising rates for longer (if liability) and decreasing the cash flows from the liability

FIGURE 3.15 Examples of hedging strategies of the banking book of a financial institution.
Source: own elaboration

There are a number of financial instruments to undertake hedging strategy. Figure 3.16 describes some of them for the benefit of the reader.

Tools	Description
Swaps	Hedge floating interest rate risk by creating a set of cash flows that result in a fixed borrowing rate
Bullet swap	Swap with a constant outstanding balance
Step-up swap	Swap with a notional amount that increases over time
Forward start amortising swap	Swap that begins in the future with an outstanding amount that decreases over time. No cash flows until the loan begins
Forward start cancellable swap	Swap that begins in the future and offers the ability to terminate the swap contract at or after specified dates at known or zero cost
LIBOR cap	Creates a maximum interest rate per period. Allows participation in current low LIBORs with a known worst case
LIBOR collar	Creates a maximum interest rate per period in exchange for giving up ability to participate in current low LIBORs
Variable rate forward swap	Forward starting swap, no cash flows until loan begins. Rate is set at a later date between an upper and lower boundary
Swaption	Borrower purchases the right to pay a fixed rate at a certain level at the start of the loan. Offers ability to fix rate at a lower level if available

FIGURE 3.16 Interest rate hedging tools in the banking book.
Source: own elaboration

EXAMPLE 15   *The key sections of ALCO report focused on IRRBB*

This example provides the reader with practical examples of key sections of an ALCO report related to IRRBB. It shows the analysis of two European banks, i.e., examples (a) and (b).

SECTION 1. EXECUTIVE SUMMARY

This section introduces the funding structure of a financial institution, describes the characteristics of the main funding sources and the impact it might have on the IRRBB and liquidity position of the financial institution. It could be as follows:

(a) *The following analysis is based on the numbers as of Date provided by the ALM system.*

The total amount of Risk Sensitive Assets of the Bank amounts to Euro 5bln which are funded by Euro 3.8bln of Risk Sensitive Liabilities. 70% of debt is provided by depositors in the form of current and saving accounts (CASA) and time deposits. The residual portion of funding is provided by interbank borrowing (10%), sub debt (2%) and current/savings accounts (CASA) which amounts to 900m. The CASA product provides good quality funding for the Bank. The share of this product in the funding base is growing at a speed of around 30m a month. The Bank currently pays 0.5% for this product.

The Bank has Non-Performing Loans and undrawn commitments included in the IRRBB analysis.

(b) *The following analysis is based on the data at the end of Date provided by the internal ALM system. The data are reported on a statutory basis – for IFRS purposes.*

It is referring to the XXX (called "Banking Group" for the purpose of the following analysis) which includes the following members:

- XXX1
- XXX2
- XXX3

The total amount of asset amounts to Euro XXXbln in which Euro XXXbln is interest rate risk sensitive funded by Euro XXbln of risk sensitive liabilities. Y% of debt is provided by the Parent Company in terms of Revolving Credit lines at floating rate and fixed rate credit lines.

The Banking Group has Euro XXXm of assets classified as Non-Performing Loans.

SECTION 2. SUMMARY OF EXPOSURE TO FINANCIAL RISKS

The second part of the Executive summary contains the main points related to the exposure to all financial risks run by the bank and managed by the ALM department. The section could be structured as follows:

(a) *The financial risk position of the Bank is considered **stable** within the ALCO policy limits for the interest rate risk, liquidity risk and FX risk as of Date. However, the Bank has quite recently changed its IRRBB strategy, in the sense that it has started riding the yield curve, i.e., funding long-term repricing assets with short (or shorter) term repricing liabilities. This means*

(Continued)

(Continued)

that the previously endorsed IRRBB framework needs to be enhanced in order to reflect the new commercial strategy of the Bank. Moreover, the main points of attention related to the hedging of new product originated by the asset side are highlighted on page X.

As of Date, **the Bank breaches the Net Interest Income sensitivity metric** *(herein Delta NII) facing potential losses, in case of the instantaneous shock of –200 bps, equal to Ym.*

The liquidity position is stable due to the high amount of treasury portfolio (XXm) which contains high quality liquid bonds. Additionally, the Group has the possibility to repo those bonds in the market securing new funding, if necessary. The ALM report analyses the short-term liquidity position (known as the tactical position) and the long-term liquidity position (known as the structural position). The structural liquidity ratio monitors the maturity transformation run by the Bank in light of the new long-term maturity product origination (the extent of the maturity transformation run by the Bank after origination of this new product).

The FX position is within the limits defined in the treasury policy and is mainly related to the exchange rate between EUR and GBP currencies. The Banking Book of the Bank is denominated in EUR currency. The GBP currency is considered material for the Bank and therefore the GBP exposure is measured separately (for example for IRRBB analysis).

(b) The financial risk position of the Banking Group is stable and within the ALCO policy limits as regards the interest rate risk exposure. However, the Group breaches the limit related to the structural liquidity ratio which is below the limit established in the Liquidity policy of the Banking Group. This is mainly caused by the fact that 100% of XXX funding at floating rate at the cutoff date is considered as volatile (maturing within 1-year time period). Consequently, it needs to roll over beyond 1 year in order to restore the liquidity ratio.

SECTION 3. DETAILED ANALYSIS OF FINANCIAL RISKS EXPOSURE

(a) The Bank performs the analysis of the exposure to the Interest Rate Risk through the following metrics:

- Delta Net Interest Income impact under +/–200 bps parallel shock scenario – focus on the short-term part of the curve
- ΔEVE under 7 interest interest rates shocks
- PV01
- DGAP
- Time bucket sensitivity
- Refixing gap exposure – the extent of mismatch between market risk factors on assets and liabilities

The Bank, as part of the active strategy, simulates the Net Interest Income under interest rate shocks in order to actively steer the Banking Book towards its most profitable composition.

Gaps in repricing

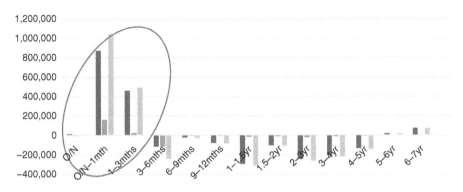

Residual Gaps in repricing of Bank XXX

SHORT TERM INTEREST RATE RISK EXPOSURE: DELTA NET INTEREST INCOME MODEL

*The model is based on the synthetic indicator adopting as the objective variable the **interest margin** and measures the impact of the interest rates movements on it (known as delta NII impact).*

The Repricing Gap analysis of the Bank shows the positive net Gap equal to EUR 245m within the Gapping Period of 12 months.

*This means that the Bank is **reinvestment risk sensitive** realising profits if interest rates increase and facing losses in the case of downward movements of the curve. Thus, in case of –200 bps shock applied to the interest curve as of XXX (the term structure provided by Reuters) the Bank faces losses of **Xm**.*

The above exposure is within the limit dictated by the ALCO policy of the Bank:

DELTA NII UNDER +/–200 BPS / EXPECTED NII >= –13%

Comments – NII sensitivity

*The Bank is expected to originate the new product class and to invest further. This will alleviate tension related to the **excessive cash position** and **negative cost of carry** it is running at the moment.*

Otherwise, the Bank could enter the short-term reverse repo transaction and mitigate the sensitivity.

(Continued)

(Continued)

This temporary (until full deployment of excess cash) strategy would diminish the loss run on cash accounts.

The additional point of attention should be raised in this report once analysing the future hedging strategy of the new product. The floating rate leg of the hedging swaps, if indexed to EURIBOR 3M or 1M will create a constant breach of the NIIS limit. The potential solutions could be to calibrate the risk factor on the floating rate leg of the swap (longer repricing tenor) or to review if the NIIS limit, in its current form, is still fit for purpose.

(b) The Repricing Gap analysis of the Banking Group (composed of entities XXX, YYY and ZZZ) shows the positive Gap equal to Euro 156MM within the Gapping Period of 12 months.

This means that the Group is **reinvestment risk sensitive** realising profits if interest rates increase, and facing losses in the case of downward movements of the curve. Thus, in the case of a –200 bps shock applied to the interest curve as of Date (the term structure provided by Bloomberg) the Group faces losses of **XXm.**

The above exposure is within the limit dictated by the ALCO policy of the Group:

$$Delta\ NII\ /\ Expected\ NII >= -7.5\%$$

Comments NII sensitivity

The Group can evaluate if it is willing to keep this exposure or prefers to diminish it given its profitability impact and current market situation.

It can be partially done through putting in place the credit facility indexed to EURIBOR 1M and EURIBOR 3M with fixing dates in April/July/November/ January provided by the Parent company.

Another solution consists of using the hedging derivative (Forward Rate Agreement) which would close 100% of the exposure if the asset in refixing had the standard indexation. However, most of assets of XXX do not have a perfectly indexed structure.

Fixing Gap Analysis – exposure to basis risk

(a) The basis risk of the Bank stems from the following sources:

- the imperfect correlation between the risk factors on the asset and liability side.
- the imperfect correlation between the government curve, i.e., the treasury bonds and money market curve (EURIBOR and repo rate).
- the imperfect correlation between the money market curve for EUR currency and GBP currency.

■ *the imperfect correlation between adjustment of the rate on CASA and fluctuation of market rate.*

The corporate assets are mainly indexed to EURIBOR 1M and EURIBOR 3M and are funded by administered rate products. The adjustment of rates for administered rate products can be done at the Bank's discretion but it is highly unlikely that if rates move the Bank will reprice all deposit bases by the full extent of the market move.

There is a basis risk stemming from the imperfect correlation for items denominated in the GBP currency. As of Date, the Bank has EUR 900m of corporate loans denominated in GBP which are indexed to GBP LIBOR 1M, 3M and 6M. Consequently, imperfect correlation in movement between GBP LIBOR with different tenors (for example assets indexed to GBP LIBOR 1M can be raised quicker than GBP LIBOR 3M) will have the P&L impact.

(b) *The purpose of the repricing analysis is to provide trend information about the Group's interest margin and, therefore, to generate a series of indicators about both expected value and sensitivity. The analysis takes two different approaches: Flow and Stock. In this report only the Flow Approach is analysed.*

The purpose of the flow approach is to position the transaction principal at the date, or in the time bucket, when the transaction begins to become sensitive to rate changes. The transaction principal comprises:

■ *Maturity flow*
■ *Repricing flow*

These flows are used to determine the expected change in the interest margin for the gapping period of 12 months given a parallel shock of 200 bps.

Repricing gap – underlying assumption:

– *Considering run off schedule, no new business included.*

– *Only parallel shock is applied to the interest term structure.*

– *Assets and liabilities are renewed without changing the maturity structure of the Banking Book, i.e., the amounts in maturity reinvested until the end of Gapping Period.*

The graph below shows the repricing gap of the Group within a gapping period of 12 months as of Date.

(Continued)

(Continued)

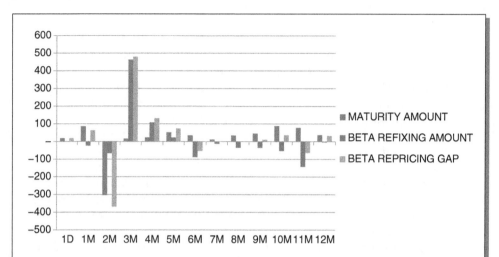

It shows a significant negative gap in October caused by a liability in maturity. From the IRR perspective this net amount of liabilities needs to be refinanced and consequently exposes the bank to the upward movement of the curve. EUR 200m of funding is due to expire and needs to be rolled over. Even if there is no real liquidity risk with reference to this particular position given that it is ensured to be renewed, there is the exposure to the interest rate risk. Furthermore, the positive gap in refixing can be noticed in November. The position is due to EUR 480m assets in refixing and causes an exposure to the downward movement of the curve.

The repricing gap analysis is enriched providing details of the amount in refixing split by the market parameter and appropriate bucket date. For the purpose of this analysis the monthly time buckets have been applied.

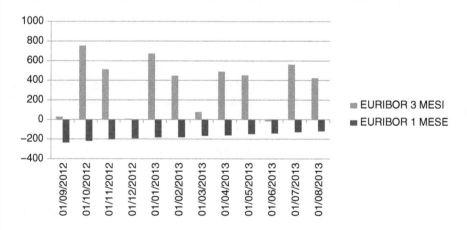

The graph above shows the positive mismatched position between assets and liabilities at floating rate and different refixing gaps between these items. Furthermore, a comprehensive assessment of the basis risk of all assets and liabilities as of Date is analysed.

The Group is significantly exposed to the movements in the level of EURI-BOR 3M and EURIBOR 1M. In particular, there is mismatching in terms of the risk factor as assets are indexed to EURIBOR 3M and liabilities to EURIBOR 1M.

In the current market environment, in case of a drop in the EURIBOR 3M level the Group will face the negative P&L impact. Every 1 bps of down-ward movement in the EURIBOR 3M level will have a negative P&L impact of Euro 75K per year. However, the Group has an opposite exposure (i.e., towards upward movement of the curve) at a level of EURBOR 1M. This partially off-sets potential losses due to the current trend of EURIBOR 3M. Every 1 bps of downward movement in EURIBOR 1M values Euro 50K per year. The net exposure is negative and equal to X.

The impact on value – Economic Value of Equity (EVE) volatility

This kind of analysis belongs to the ALM models which use the impact on net present value as an objective variable. It measures the magnitude and sensitivity of the present value of balance sheet items resulting from the interest rate curve movements.

(a) *The following table shows the impact on the Net Present Value attributable to a number of different interest rate shocks prescribed in the EBA Final Guidelines. The Bank takes into consideration the worst scenario between the behavioral and contractual view. As of Date, the Group shows the fol-lowing exposure to IRRBB in terms of ΔEVE:*

EVE volatility – behavioural

Scenarios	Name	ΔEVE (in 000)	EVE sensitivity
1	Short up	10,731	3.0%
2	Short down	34,763	9.6%
3	Parallel up	17,225	4.8%
4	Parallel down	133,919	37.0%
5	Flattener	20,931	5.8%
6	Steepener	1,309	0.4%
7	94 crisis	20,358	5.6%
	Worst outcome	1,309	0.4%
	Limit		−13%

*On the medium-to-long part of the curve (beyond 1 year) the Bank behaves as a **net liability position**. It means that, under behavioral view, it has more repricing liabilities than assets. Such a structure of the Banking Book exposes the Group to the interest rate decrease.*

The structural exposure for the Bank as of Date can be seen in the Figure below:

(Continued)

Position (cash flows) under baseline scenarios – behavioural

	1–2yr	1.5–2yr	2–3yr	3–4yr	4–5yr	5–6yr	6–7yr	7–8yr	8–9yr	<10yr	<15yr	<20yr	>20yr	Total
Total net mismatch														
Consolidated	−307,922	−110,395	−264,509	−215,643	−140,154	20,550	73,400	0	0	0	0	0	0	236,311
EUR	−292,148	−99,323	−240,290	−201,590	−132,141	20,550	73,400	0	0	0	0	0	0	262,455
GBP	−13,265	−8,834	−19,336	−10,635	−6,203	0	0	0	0	0	0	0	0	−102

Parallel up 100 bps	1–2yr	1.5–2yr	2–3yr	3–4yr	4–5yr	5–6yr	6–7yr	7–8yr	8–9yr	<10yr	<15yr	<20yr	>20yr	Total
EVE														
Consolidated	3,849	1,933	6,613	7,542	6,278	−1,119	−4,692	0	0	0	0	0	0	20,976
EUR	3,652	1,739	6,008	7,051	5,919	−1,119	−4,692	0	0	0	0	0	0	18,683
GBP	163	152	470	357	265	0	0	0	0	0	0	0	0	1,786

Parallel down 100 bps	1–2yr	1.5–2yr	2–3yr	3–4yr	4–5yr	5–6yr	6–7yr	7–8yr	8–9yr	<10yr	<15yr	<20yr	>20yr	Total
EVE														
Consolidated	−3,898	−1,967	−6,781	−7,811	−6,567	1,182	5,007	0	0	0	0	0	0	−21,415
EUR	−3,698	−1,770	−6,160	−7,302	−6,192	1,182	5,007	0	0	0	0	0	0	−19,064
GBP	−166	−154	−482	−370	−277	0	0	0	0	0	0	0	0	−1,829

There is no material exposure in terms of structural risk, consequently no hedges are required as of Date. The Bank is exposed to the downward movement of the curve.

(b) *In a case where the duration of asset (DA) is higher than the duration of liabilities (DL) the exposure is called **asset sensitive** and a Duration Gap (DG) > 0 means that the increase in the interest rate structure leads to the decrease of market value of asset more rapidly than liabilities.*

*In a case where the duration of asset is less than the duration of liabilities the exposure is called **liability sensitive** and a Duration Gap (DG) < 0 means that the increase in the interest term structure leads to the decrease of market value of liabilities more rapidly than assets.*

The duration of asset of the Group is slightly higher than the duration of liabilities (5Y vs. 3.4Y). It means that the above condition of immunisation is not fully maintained.

Consequently, assets are slightly more sensitive to interest rate curve movements than liabilities and NPV of the BS items will increase in front of a decrease in the interest rate curve. On the contrary, it will diminish in case of the increase in interest rates.

The impact on the value of the Group is within the limit required by the ALCO policy.

*In terms of the EVE volatility, the Group is exposed to **upward movements** of the interest rates curve. In particular, in the case of a +200 bps parallel shock the Group will face deterioration in the equity value by Euro 50m. On the contrary, –200 bps parallel shock will have a positive impact on an equity value of Euro21m.*

TIME BUCKET SENSITIVITY

The methodology of bucket sensitivity allows the analysis of variation in terms of present value of cash flows by each time bucket caused by the shock of the interest rate curve.

(a) *The Group performs the time bucket sensitivity analysis under the parallel shock scenario +/–200 bps.*

The table below shows the time bucket sensitivity under the scenario +/–200 bps parallel shock:

(Continued)

(Continued)

Data in Euro								
Time bucket	1M	2–3M	3–6M	6–12M	1–2y	2–3y	3–4y	beyond 4y
Parametric sensitivity +200 bps	–58.285	–1.766.535	–666.560	–803.175	–3.985.468	–4.173.056	3.635.843	–1.857.998
Parametric sensitivity –200 bps	3.847	295.994	215.600	55.646	1.180.727	1.329.631	–1.659.264	2.300.565

There is no significant time bucket sensitivity on the consolidated basis. This is mostly due to the fact that the mismatched position in zero coupon bonds issued are partially matched by the assets at fixed rate.

(b) *The Bank analyses the time bucket sensitivity by shocking the whole term structure of interest rates by 1 bp. The Bank does not have limits in terms of the single time bucket exposure although it is best market practice. Instead, it monitors the overall PV01 and monitors it against the limit defined in the ALCO policy.*

It can be seen that the most sensitive time bucket is 3–4Y and 4–5Y. Every 1 bps DOWN movement of the curve creates losses equal to 50K and 42K respectively.

CHAPTER 4

Behaviouralisation of items without deterministic maturity and their impact on IRRBB

THE SIGNIFICANCE AND IMPACT OF BEHAVIOURAL ISSUES IN THE BANKING BOOK

To analyse behaviour, banks combine statistical information with some assumptions. An interesting characteristic of behaviour assumption is that it does not always follow market conditions. In some cases, clients or counterparties behave contrary to their own interest but in ways that are aligned with their psychological demands. In other cases, behaviour is driven by rumours or loss of confidence in financial institutions. The impact of behavioural issues can be seen in terms of both interest rate and liquidity risk exposure.

One of the biggest challenges of ALM is the management of the interest rate risk associated with customer products with an undefined interest rate commitment. Under recent regulatory developments, the regulator demands a documented and validated approach as to how the interest rate commitments are derived and managed in the bank. Not fully transferred interest rate risk of products with undetermined maturity to ALM/treasury cause significant residual risk left within the business units and therefore earnings and equity volatility which has to be monitored and managed by ALCO. The balance sheet items require behavioural assumptions in order to manage the interest rate risk correctly as raising interest rates may reduce the net interest margin, given a bank's limited ability to raise client rates in line with the market rates, especially when market rates rise to very high levels. Early redemption of assets, if not accounted for in the hedging strategies of the bank, cause over-hedging because the amount of the swap payers is higher than the actual amount of fixed rate assets. Consequently, the bank has to adjust hedging positions and, in the meantime, is left with time bucket sensitivity and negative impact in terms of the PV01 metric. The prepayment pattern will change as a function of the interest rates movements. Where there is a low interest rate environment, i.e., higher differential between the committed interest rate paid by a client and external market rates, the prepayment events tend to increase as clients want to refinance their loans in order to pay lower rates. The early redemption of mortgages (prepayments) and withdrawal of deposits have an important impact on both the repricing gap and refixing gap analysis.

Another important source of the interest rate risk driven by the behavioural assumptions is pipeline risk. It is driven by the time difference between agreement of the mortgage product rate and the draw down of balance and consequent risk of repricing an interest rate move, compressing the margin of the product. To reduce the impact of this risk the pipeline is typically pre-hedged on the basis of expected volumes. Expected volumes are modelled using observed experience with management judgement overlay based factors such as where the product is priced relative to the market. There is a model risk that expected volumes differ due to incorrect assumptions. There is also an option risk that customer behaviour will change due to changes in the interest rate, e.g., take up is higher if rates have risen, or less if rates have fallen.

THE REASON FOR MODELLING CASA UNDER IRRBB

Many banks worldwide are funded with non-maturing deposits, and the way the product is modelled has significant implications in terms of the exposure to the interest rate risk. The whole picture in terms of the NII sensitivity and EVE volatility can change, driven by changes in customer behaviour. Presumably by increasing the rate paid to the customer, an inflow of deposits will in turn increase. On the other hand, a decrease, or low level of interest paid to the customer, increases volatility of deposits balances.

However, there is always some portion of funds, often called *"lazy money"* which will stay within a bank regardless of macroeconomic factors and the level of interest rate paid. A common example of long-term deposits is the transactional account which the client holds for salary, bills payment, mortgage instalment payment, etc. In the IRRBB world these accounts are important because of their natural offset against fixed rate assets. These cheap and sticky funds mitigate time bucket sensitivity (discussed in Chapter 2) and diminish ΔEVE driven by fixed rate assets. Given that the BCBS Standards introduced caps on the average life of Non-Maturing Deposits (NMDs), a quite common practice is to hedge the residual exposure through derivatives. For example, the long repricing tenor of fixed rate assets funded by shorter repricing tenor of NMDs (subject to a regulatory cap) exposes a bank to the upward movement of the interest rate curve (a net asset position on the medium-to-long part of the curve). This residual exposure has to be monitored or hedged in case it becomes excessive.

Table 4.1 shows the caps related to the stability and average life of NMDs as per BCBS Standards.

The incorrect assumption related to the behavioural assumption of NMDs results in an under- or over-hedged IRRBB position. For example, if the NMD product is modelled with too short repricing a bank is exposed to earning sensitivity and, on the short part of the curve, it will show the liability sensitive position as there are more short-term repricing liabilities than assets. From the other side, modelling

TABLE 4.1 Caps as a proportion of core deposits, and as the average life of NMDs as per BCBS Standards.

Category	Cap as a proportion of core deposits (in %)	Cap as average maturity of core deposits (in years)
Retail/transactional	90	5.0
Retail/non-transactional	70	4.5
Wholesale	50	4.0

Source: BCBS, 2016

NMDs with too long repricing will result in a net liability position on the medium-to-long part of the curve and exposure to the downward movement of the curve. Figure 2.16 (p. 45) shows this situation for both the short and medium-to-long part of the curve.

Where NMDs are modelled with short-term repricing (as short-term liabilities) the potential increase in interest rates causes a negative impact on a bank's P&L. This is because, in order to keep customers, banks will pass through the increase in rates (at least to some extent) which will drive the cost of funding higher. It has to be highlighted that the extent to which banks will pass through any rates changes is the commercial decision of the bank and has to be taken by senior management. Once there is a clear understanding of the bank's willingness to pass through rates the earning sensitivity can be calculated accurately. This decision will impact the liquidity position of the bank as a low repricing appetite within a financial institution will encourage depositors to look elsewhere and to find more attractive investment opportunities. This is a typical example where IRRBB risk is strongly interrelated with liquidity risk.

Instead, assuming long repricing of NMDs will expose a bank to the downward movement of the curve as the net present value of liabilities (deposits) is higher and implies the loss embedded in the banking book.

Traditionally, NMDs and free reserves hedging have provided a significant part of the Net Interest Income (NII) for a financial institution. This is because, as already mentioned above, institutions may lock margins by investing in assets (or derivatives) matching the expected behavioural maturity/repricing of NMDs. Low levels of interest rates decrease margins as banks have to reinvest NMDs in assets with lower yield. This phenomenon is known as *margin compression* and is faced by banks operating in low or negative levels of interest rates. A persistent low interest rate environment has driven margins down.

Figure 2.5 (p. 32) shows an example where a bank has administered rate assets funded by NMDs. The characteristic of administered rates is that they are highly correlated with base rates. Therefore, the potential cut in the base rate will have a negative impact on the bank's P&L.

In order to mitigate the margin compression from a low-rate environment institutions may lock margins by investing in assets (or derivatives) matching the expected behavioural maturity/repricing of NIBCA/IBCAs. This is known as margin hedging and correct behavioural assumptions are crucial in this exercise. In order to estimate the period over which margin hedging should operate, institutions need to assess how fast such low-cost balances might decay and have to be replaced. Incorrect assumptions about the behavioural life/repricing may lead to margin loss due to return on locked-in assets being less than the repriced cost of funding.

The BCBS Standards divide NMDs into three different categories: retail/transactional, retail/non-transactional and wholesale.

It defines NMDs behaviouralisation as: "*Behavioral assumptions for deposits that have no specific repricing date which can be a major determinant of IRRBB exposures under the economic value (EVE) and earnings-based (NII) measures. Banks should document, monitor and regularly update key assumptions for NMD balances (how the behavioral part is used for the ALM risk metrics or ratios).*"

In BCBS Standards NMDs are divided into a stable and a non-stable part. The stable part is the portion of the NMD that is unlikely to be withdrawn. The portion of the stable part that will remain undrawn with a high likelihood even during significant changes in interest rate environment is called the core deposit, while the rest of the NMD is called the non-stable portion. These portions should be determined using observed volume changes over the past 10 years according to BCBS Standards.

Figure 4.1 shows the methodological details related to NMDs modelling.

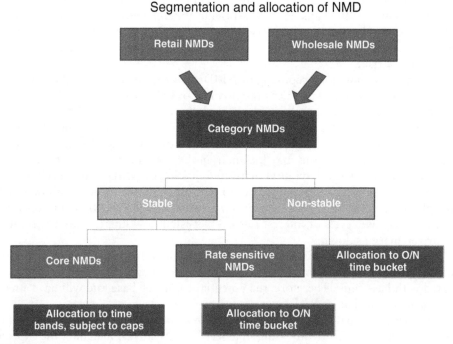

FIGURE 4.1   Behaviouralisation of NMDs based on BCBS Standards.
Source: BCBS, 2016

THE IMPACT OF EARLY REDEMPTION OF FIXED RATE ASSETS ON IRRBB

The common practice of hedging the fixed rate assets is to use their behavioural profile to determine the tenor of hedging. In order to come up with the behavioural schedule of assets it is necessary to take into consideration the prepayment rate which is determined by the willingness of the customer to redeem the loan earlier. The prepayment phenomenon is driven by many factors, i.e., it could be the macroeconomic circumstances and the level of interest rates in the market or changes in the personal situation of the borrower, for example moving to another city or country. The prepayment phenomenon is particularly relevant in the case of fixed rate assets where the main driver is the movement in interest rates. An increase in interest rates translates into a reduction of early redemptions of assets and, on the other hand, a reduction in the interest rates will imply an increase in the prepayment rate. This is driven by the customer's rationale to refinance the loan at a lower cost whenever it is available in the market. A bank's treasurer hedges the exposure to the structural risk based on the behavioural (adjusted) amortisation profile of assets. The accurate behavioural assumption results in effective hedging. However, with respect to the banking book, there is always some residual risk left. In managing IRRBB, it is important to make sure that this exposure is always within a predefined limit and that the ALCO is comfortable with it. There are different ways of hedging the fixed rate asset book. Chapter 3 details hedging instruments and hedging strategies. Therefore, the main point to highlight here is that the treasury has a number of tools to go with. It could apply natural hedging, i.e., where there is a sufficient amount of existing liabilities or to fund itself through longer term liabilities (which would impact on the cost of funds for a bank). The most common way is to use derivatives, such as interest rate swaps (plain vanilla or forward starting).

BASIC APPROACHES FOR THE MODELLING OF NMDs

The way an NMD product is modelled has significant implications in terms of the exposure to the interest rate risk, liquidity risk and funds transfer pricing. The whole picture of risks a bank is running can change driven by changes in the customers' behaviour. For this reason, an understanding of the main underlying factors is of crucial importance. The balance fluctuations are a function of multiple factors, including the macroeconomic environment as well as the product pricing structure. As already mentioned, by increasing the rate paid to the consumer, inflows of deposits will in turn increase. The analysis of the customer–financial institution relationship indicates that there is certainly a positive correlation which may exhibit a linear or even exponential relationship over a particular interest rate interval.

The purpose of this section is to present two different methods which have been used in international banks to determine the structure of the liabilities with undetermined maturity – current and savings accounts. The first, common approach, is based on the application of the regression model that predicts the likelihood of the event happening. The regression model yields a set of parameters variables (and their associated estimates) that would feature the relationship to the dependent variables.

Regardless of the methodology used, the first step in current account modelling is to apply the correct segmentation scheme. The main goal of product segmentation is to preserve the underlying balance and rate characteristics of products/product subdivisions for the full deposit modelling, while also ensuring a minimum threshold of materiality and simplicity. The segmentation process seeks to reach a balance between three dimensions:

- Homogeneity: The balances within each segment should behave in a similar manner with respect to balance volatility, average life, and rate administration.
- Simplicity: The number of segments should be kept as small as possible, while capturing differences in behaviour.
- Materiality: Each segment should represent a significant portion of the portfolio.

It should be noted that, all else being equal, the first criterion calls for more segments while the second and third criteria call for less segments. The "sweet spot" is to divide the portfolio into the fewest number of classes while capturing major differences in behaviour.

In the majority of cases the portfolio can be optimally segmented along three main dimensions:

- Geography: Products from different geographies should not be examined together since the economic and regulatory conditions tend to differ between countries.
- Product type: Only products of the same type should be examined together, i.e., savings products should not be examined together with current accounts.
- Currency: Products with different currencies should not be examined together.

The segmentation process requires information about the product's characteristics, contractual specifications, history, information on whether it is a new product or whether it is a run-off product etc. Along with this information, joint historical evolvement of the balance and interest rate paid data should be considered to come up with the segmentation of the products. Once an intuitive and appropriate segmentation scheme has been defined and established, the modelling process may begin. The overall goal is to forecast the future trajectory of the liabilities so that the volatility of balances may be estimated. One simple way to estimate balance volatility is to model it singularly as a function of time. Balance volatility analysis splits the balances as core balances, which stay with the bank under almost all economic conditions, and non-core balances, which tend to leave the bank either idiosyncratically or with the movements of macroeconomic factors.

The balance volatility model determines what level of balances will remain with the bank in the long term, given a certain level of confidence. As an output, the balance volatility model divides the balances into two portions: core balances, which remain with the bank under almost all market conditions; and non-core balances, which fluctuate over time due to market and idiosyncratic reasons and are typically characterised as short term. There are multiple approaches to modelling the non-maturity deposits, and each bank follows its own approach. Some banks underline the importance of the simplicity of the model, others prefer sophisticated approaches using stochastic interest rates and credit spreads. The complexity of the methodological approach is often commensurate with the size of the financial institution and its business model.

The following section presents two simple methodological approaches followed by sample banks in Europe.

One of the methods of performing an analysis of core versus non-core balances consists of the application of a growth-based regression model (Figure 4.2). In this approach, the model fits the product balances to find both a trend line (exponential, linear or logarithmic), and the variation of actual balances around the trend line. It then sets the trend line at a certain confidence level. The confidence level should be set by management depending on the risk appetite of the bank.

The following part describes the exponential model. Under this model the product balances are modelled to fit balances to an exponential curve of the form:

$$Balance = B_0 e^{rt} \tag{24}$$

where B_0 represents the initial balance and r denotes the fixed growth rate.

Obviously, this simplified approach neglects the fact that, in practice, the growth rate of balances is not constant over time but depends on different factors, both internal and external (for example interest rate and product pricing).

The exponential model can be converted to a linear relation through the log function:

$$\ln(Balance) = \ln(B_0) + rt \tag{25}$$

A regression model is utilised to compute the growth rate of the natural logarithm of the balances, and the standard error of the estimate, σ_{Fit}.

To ensure that the probability of core balances dropping below the actual balances is minimal, the fitted equation is lowered with some multiple of standard deviation; 99.9% approximately corresponds to a 3.1 standard deviation shift in balances for a normal distribution. The growth rate is decreased by $n*\sigma$, or 3.1 times the standard deviation, to decrease the chance of the total balance level falling below the core level to 0.1% of the time, or approximately one month in every 83 years (Figure 4.2). The resulting core balance equation is:

$$Balance_{Core} = B_0 e^{rt - n\sigma_{Fit}} \tag{26}$$

Where the exponential fit function results in a very small R^2, implying that the fit is very poor or the fit for the last 12 months is poor, the usage of a different model should be taken into consideration.

The core percentage for a given fit equation is calculated as the average of the last 12 months:

$$Balance_{Core} / Balance_{Fit} \text{ ratio}$$

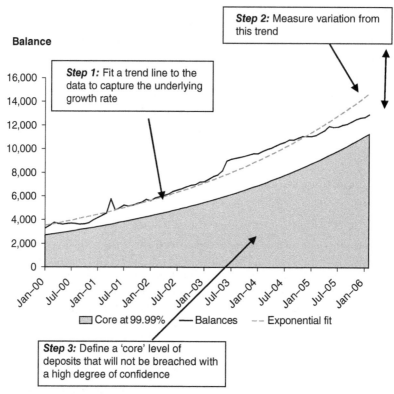

FIGURE 4.2 Exponential fit methodology.
Source: own elaboration based on the methodology applied by 5 banks based in Europe and US

By the virtue of the exponential fit, this core percentage is fixed for every month. The core percentage number is converted to a core amount by considering the balance behaviour of the last 12 months. The core amount is calculated with the following equation:

$$Core = Core\% \times \min\left(Balance_{last\,month},\, Balance_{average\,from\,last\,12\,months}\right) \qquad (27)$$

This equation introduces a level of conservatism to the core amount. If the balances are declining, core percentage is multiplied by the balance of the last month; if the balances are increasing core percentage is multiplied by the average of the balances of the last 12 months. The remaining balances not identified as core are defined as non-core, which are then tested for further decomposition as volatile and sensitive through sensitivity analysis.

$$Balance_{NONCORE} = Balance_{ACTUAL} - Balance_{CORE} \qquad (28)$$

Another approach consists of a calculation of the monthly relative returns for each business day as an equation:

$$M_i = \left(\left(X_i - X_{i-30} \right) / X_{i-30} \right) * 100 \tag{29}$$

where:

M is computed relative change between months (expressed in percentage terms);

X is the product balance for the given reporting date (expressed in absolute terms).

Subsequently, *Monthly Volatility* (MV) is computed. It is done through ordering all monthly returns from the highest percentage balance increase through the highest percentage balance decrease. The 95th percentile worst decline in balance is taken and represents the volume which the bank considers flowing out of the portfolio over 1 month at a 95% confidence level. Obviously, the confidence level is decided by the management team and represents the risk appetite of the bank.

The non-core portion is calculated by annualising the monthly volatility. This is done by multiplying MV by the square root of time (MV is annualised therefore a 12-month time interval is used). The Core% is the difference between 100% of the portfolio and the computed Non-core%.

$$\text{Non-core}\% = 95\text{th percentile of monthly returns} * \text{sqrt}(12) \tag{30}$$

$$\text{Core}\% = 100\% - \text{Non-core}\% \tag{31}$$

In order to obtain the nominal core amount the Core% is multiplied by the lower of the last 1-month average or last 3-month average balance (in absolute terms) in the historical data series of the relevant cohort.

$$\text{Core amount} = \text{Core}\% * \min\begin{pmatrix} 1\text{-month average balance of the cohort,} \\ 3\text{-month average balance of the cohort} \end{pmatrix} \tag{32}$$

Instead, the rate sensitivity analysis captures the repricing behaviour of the product; it explains the changes of the product rate with the changes of the market rates. Characterisation of administered rates for deposit products ascertains the significance of market rate changes on the rates paid by the bank. By modelling the behaviour of interest rates paid relative to market rates, a better understanding of repricing behaviour and the sensitivity of interest expenses to market rates can be gained, i.e., how rates paid to customers vary with market conditions. This determines the effective duration and value of deposits. Rate sensitivity modelling is a key aspect of funds transfer pricing in determining which assets a bank can match with minimal risk.

The interest rate paid to indeterminate maturity products' depositors is generally a combination of one or more market rates, and an idiosyncratic 'fixed' component. The repricing frequency for the market driven component is simply the maturity associated with that rate. The fixed component is assumed to have a repricing frequency equal to the duration, i.e., in line with the observed core/volatile split.

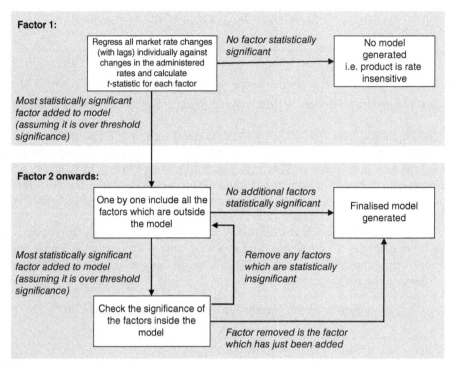

FIGURE 4.3   Assessment of the regression analysis outcome used in the deposit characterisation model.
Source: own elaboration based on the main concepts of the regression methodology (PRMIA, 2015)

For example, if the core part of the balances has the duration of 5 years it is assumed to reprice after 5 years. However, the volatile part, which is assumed to outflow after day 1, is assumed to reprice O/N.

The interest expenses are regressed with key market rates to determine the repricing sensitivity of balances (pass-through rate). Rate sensitivity analysis requires regression of the changes in the administered rates on the changes in the various market rates. It is also possible that administered rates are driven by the market rates with a lag, e.g., changes in 3-month rate in June 2021 might have an effect on changes in the administered rates in August 2021 (a two-month lag). In order to determine which of the market rates explain the changes in the rates paid by the bank, a multiple regression is employed. Regression analysis forms an equation with multiple explanatory variables which jointly explain the changes in the administered rates. In addition, it forces all the independent variables to contribute to this explanatory power beyond some threshold. This threshold is determined by the significance level which can be set to be 95% in the calculations. Mechanics of the regression equation can be explained as shown in Figure 4.3.

It is very likely that more than one significant regression equation can be formed that explains the changes in administered rates with the changes in the market rates.

For most of the products, the most significant equation is the one that captures repricing behaviour.

Coefficients of this regression equation tell us what percentage of the portfolio reprices with the associated market rate.

In order to estimate the economic life of NMD products banks perform the analysis of the decay profile of the portfolio over a certain time horizon (for the sake of statistical significance, a minimum 2 years of data is required). The average life modelling assigns a life of the product by tracking the closing behaviour of the customers' accounts. This can be done through tracking the decaying of the number of accounts or through the decaying of balances. When data is available, tracking the decay of balances is preferred and the one that is calculated by tracking the decaying of the number of accounts is usually used for sanity checking purposes.

The analysis of the decay profile can be done through the following approach:

1. **Collect the account level data and form the "triangle":** "Triangle" is a form of representing the account level data such that the continued presence of the number of accounts (sum of average balances) opened in one month can be tracked through different age buckets. It gives the remaining number of accounts (sum of average balances) for a given age bucket for a given opening month. It has the form of a triangle (an example is given for decaying of the number of accounts).
2. **Calculate the mortality ratio for each age bucket:** Mortality ratio is defined as the number of accounts closed at that age to the number of accounts that were alive at the beginning of that age (or in balance terms it is the ratio of balances that left the bank at that age to the total balances that were available at the beginning of that age). All the mortality rates for each age bucket together tell how fast (or slow) the accounts close.
3. **Compute the average life of accounts:** Once the mortality rates are determined, one can track what percentage of all the accounts remain at each age.

Balance sensitivity modelling

The goal of balance sensitivity analysis is to further decompose the volatile component into two: a rate-sensitive component and a purely volatile component. Rate sensitive balances are those for which the volatility in the balances can be explained by changes in macroeconomic factors.

Balance	Definition
Core	Balances that are stable under all market conditions as long as pricing behaviour remains as it is
Rate sensitive	Balances that fluctuate when interest rates or macroeconomic conditions change
Volatile	Balances fluctuate randomly and independently of time or interest rates

The first step in the process is to carry out single factor regression analysis between the product balances and each of the macroeconomic variables of interest. This is performed through comparison of the changes in the residual component of the balance (non-core) against changes in the variable of interest. Similarly, the change in spreads from rates paid to the market rates is analysed. The market variables examined are:

- Stock Market Index
- Stock Market Volatility Index
- Inflation (CPI)
- 1-month Interbank Offer Rates
- 1-year Interbank Offer Rates
- 10-year swap rate
- Spread between 10-year and 3-month rate
- GDP

Similarly, the spreads between the rates paid and the market rates are analysed:

- Product's spread to 1-month market rate
- Product's spread to 1-year market rate
- Product's spread to 10-year market rate

Moreover, lags between the changes in the macroeconomic factors (and also the changes in spread of rates paid to the market rates) and the changes in the non-core balances should be considered.

Balance sensitivity analysis looks for a strong, structural relationship between the non-core portion and the macroeconomic variables; hence a high R^2 value is set as a threshold. A high threshold for R^2 also prevents any spurious correlation governing the results. For this purpose, a threshold R^2 value of 50% is set.

In summary, rate sensitivity analysis captures the repricing behaviour of the product; it explains the changes of the product rate with the changes of the market rates. Average life analysis finds the average life of the product by making use of the account level data and their mortality characteristics. Balance sensitivity tests whether the non-core portion can be explained with the changes in the macroeconomic factors. In addition to the analyses, benchmarks are incorporated into the decision process. Output of the deposit characterisation is crucial in matched funds transfer pricing, interest rate risk measurement and management, pricing of new deposit products, funding management, cash flows and liquidity needs, valuation of deposit, hedging, ALM risk and economic capital.

Figure 4.4 summarises the process flow of modelling NMDs. The modelling process starts with data gathering and selection. This part of the process shouldn't be underestimated as without availability of proper data deposits modelling is just impossible.

The second part starts with segmentation based on product type, geography and distribution channel (internet accounts versus direct channel). Once the products are

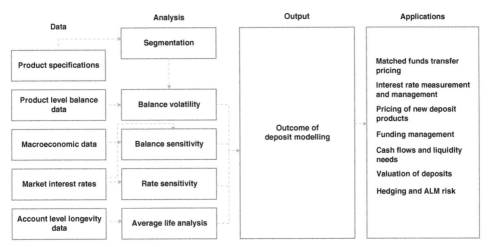

FIGURE 4.4 The process of modelling NMDs.
Source: own elaboration

grouped into cohorts the stability, rate sensitivity and average life of the product are estimated and the application of the model output are: allocation of FTP rate, management of interest rate risk, management of funding risk and daily management of liquidity needs and cash flow analysis.

Figure 4.5 shows the illustrative representation of results obtained by deposits modelling. In this example the balance volatility analysis split the balances between stable and volatile portions (82% are stable balances and 18% are volatile). However, the balance volatility analysis does not answer the question as to how long depositors keep their money within a bank. For this reason, the next step of the analysis consists in the calculation of the average life of the product (one of the possible approaches is through mortality ratio analysis). Having an answer to the questions regarding the stable portion and the average life allows the performance of an analysis from the liquidity standpoint. In the example, 82% of product balances represent the long-term funding for the bank. However, there is a need for additional information about client behaviour, i.e., to identify the rate sensitive portion of the product. This group of customers will react when rates start moving and if there is no rate adjustment on the bank's side the rate sensitive customers will leave the bank and search for other investment opportunities. In the example, 27% are rate sensitive balances. As already mentioned, the further decomposition of the volatile portion could be modelled, i.e., isolation of rate-sensitive component and purely volatile component (in the example 5% versus 13%).

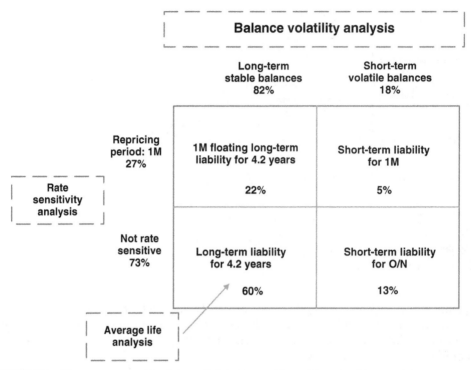

FIGURE 4.5 Illustrative example of the split between stable and rate sensitive portion of NMDs.
Source: own elaboration

BASIC APPROACHES FOR THE MODELLING OF STATISTICAL PREPAYMENT ON THE ASSET SIDE

The prepayment phenomenon has a significant impact on ALM and consequently can alter the exposure of the banking book to the interest rate risk and liquidity risk. This impact should not be underestimated and modelling of the prepayment rate on the asset side is one of the main activities of the ALM manager.

The prepayment event represents a possibility for the client to reimburse or pre-pay the credit outstanding fully or partially during the credit contractual life. Prepayments therefore decrease the outstanding principal so that the interest and cash flow the investor expected to receive in the future decreases.

The ALM manager distinguishes between two types of prepayments:

- Financial prepayments – these prepayments are potentially cyclical and have rational reasons, such as interest rate levels or other macroeconomic conditions. The important task in modelling financial prepayments events consists in understanding the underlying factors driving the model and behaviour of the customers.

■ Statistical prepayments – these prepayments are partially irrational from an economic point of view as statistically there is always a minimum prepayment rate. Financial prepayments will not explain these prepayments.

The statistical prepayments need to be added to the financial prepayments in order to come up with the total prepayment rate (Adam, 2007).

Statistical prepayments

Statistical prepayments are driven by sociological reasons and are not related to the level of interest rates in the market. That kind of prepayment is mostly determined by the loan seniority as the client having already gone through the process of applying for one mortgage would not be immediately looking to remortgage. The change of the financial status of the client also has a significant impact on the statistical prepayments. For example, divorce, inheritance and geographic mobility affect the financial situation of the client and consequently his or her willingness to prepay the mortgage or remortgage in another bank loan (Adam, 2007). Consequently, it is usually modelled through the analysis of the historical data in a simple database.

Below is a walk-through of the method described in the *Handbook of Asset and Liability Management* written by Alexandre Adam on how to build a database to obtain the statistical prepayment rate.

Such a database contains monthly outstanding of mortgages extended to clients over several years of an observation period (for example 4 years). These loans should be grouped according to the year in which they have been disbursed, for example, loans extended to clients in 2014, 2015, 2016 and 2017. Having the total amount of disbursements, residual outstanding at the observation date and the total prepayment amount up to the observation date (clients default and credit restructuring have to be excluded), it is possible to calculate the hypothetical outstanding amount, i.e., the outstanding amount determined by the contractual schedule of the loans. It is important to split loans according to certain criteria, such as the currency in which they are denominated, contract type (mortgages, personal loans) and month of production.

A database such as this is sufficient to come up with the prepayment turnover, i.e., the prepayment amount occuring between one month of observation period and another (effectively it represents the difference between the residual amount at the observation dates, for example between January 2017 and February 2017).

The prepayment rate is calculated for every loan seniority bucket as a ratio of observed statistical prepayments to the hypothetical (scheduled) outstanding amounts multiplied by 12 (in order to obtain the annual prepayment rate). The average prepayment rate is calculated as a ratio between the summations of prepayment amount over all seniority buckets to the sum of hypothetical outstanding amount multiplied by 12.

At the beginning of the life of the loan the prepayment rate is low. This is likely to be explained by the unwillingness of the client to prepay (and remortgage) having already gone through the process of applying for one mortgage. At some point in its life the prepayment event becomes more likely as different sociological factors come into effect. Finally, as time passes the prepayment rate seems to decelerate again.

Financial prepayments

Financial prepayments are linked with the market rates level. The relation between the market rates level and customer rates explains the greater part of those prepayments. This is driven by the fact that a significant rate decrease will incite customers either to find the new loan with a lower interest rate and to prepay the existing loan or to renegotiate the existing loan (Adam, 2007).

Prepayments are very important for a bank and the correct understanding of underlying factors driving the customers' behaviour is an ALM imperative. Otherwise, the hedging strategies put in place will be inefficient or impossible to determine. Macroeconomic variables affect the financial prepayments. These are as follows:

- Unemployment levels which reflect the general "health" of the economy.
- Growth of GDP which indicates the state of the economy.
- House price inflation which leads towards higher prepayment frequency.

There are three crucial variables in modelling of the prepayment rate: interest rate spread, seniority/residual maturity and burnout phenomenon.

The interest rate spread is the difference between the loan initial interest rate and re-employment rate. The higher the spread, the higher the customer interest to prepay. However, when the interest rate spread is negative, the customer interest is to keep the initial loan. The interest rate spread is either the absolute spread or relative spread (Adam, 2007).

The burnout phenomenon measures the likelihood that customers will react to an interest rates decrease. It turns out that there are different activating levels for the prepayment option among clients. The burnout variable tries to capture the different readiness of customers to prepay their mortgage.

It appears that there is strong heterogeneity between customers: their reactivity varies. For example, a "rational" customer prepays as soon as the prepayment is profitable for them, while another customer will wait. The customer's likelihood of reacting to the interest rate decrease is known as the "burnout phenomenon". For example, if there is an interest rate decrease followed by an interest rate rise and then by another decrease it will produce less prepayment than two interest rate decreases followed by a rise. This is driven by the fact that the client needs time to assess the prepayment decision and, in the first case, it gives more time for the decision to be worthwhile.

Theoretically, residual maturity explains both financial prepayment and statistical prepayment. The statistical prepayments are driven by two fundamental reasons:

1. At the beginning of the loan life, the customer has no real reason to prepay.
2. By the end of the loan life, customer wealth has increased, and the customer is more likely to be cash rich so will statistically prepay more (Adam, 2007).

It turns out that modelling prepayments on conventional parametric models often has bad out-of-sample predictive ability. A likely explanation is the highly non-linear nature of prepayment functions. Non-parametric techniques are much better in detecting non-linearity and multivariate interaction.

MODEL RISK

The process of measuring exposure to IRRBB and behavioural optionality embedded in the banking book exposes a financial institution to another important risk category, i.e., model risk. This aspect is growing in importance and has regulatory oversight.

In recent years there has been a trend in financial institutions towards greater use of models in decision making, driven in part by regulation but manifest in all areas of management. In this regard, a high proportion of bank decisions are automated through models (whether statistical algorithms or a set of rules). In part this is encouraged by Basel regulations – for example, the allocation of capital for credit risk is performed through advanced models which estimate the probability of default of the client or develop statistical profiles of delinquent customers in order to apply different recovery strategies. The use of valuation models for products and financial instruments has become widespread in financial institutions, in both the markets and the ALM business. Other examples include models for the quantification of the bank's liquidity position, projected under different scenarios, the projection of the balance sheet and income statement and the use of the stress testing models. The recent BCBS Standard require development of the sophisticated models for the IRRBB and CSRBB.

The term model refers to a quantitative algorithm, system or approach that applies statistical, economic, financial or mathematical theories, techniques, and assumptions to process input data into quantitative estimates (OCC, FED, 2011–2012). There are three components of the model:

- The inputs, which introduce hypothesis and assumptions into the model.
- A method to transform the input into estimates. This method will generally rely on statistics to produce quantitative estimates.
- A reporting component that converts the estimates into useful business information.

The sources of model risk can be classified in three different groups:

- Data deficiencies in terms of both availability and quality, including data errors, lack of historical depth, errors in the feeding of variables or insufficient sample size.
- Estimation uncertainty or model error in the form of simplifications, approximations and flawed assumptions or incorrect model design.
- Model misuse, which includes using the model for purposes other than those for which it was designed and where it has not been recalibrated in a long time.

The use of models brings undoubted benefits such as:

1. Automated decision making which in turn improves efficiency by reducing analysis and the related cost of a manual decision.
2. Objective decision making, ensuring that the estimated results are the same in equal circumstances and that internal and external information is reused, thus leveraging historical experience.
3. Ability to synthetise complex issues such as a bank's aggregate risk.

Model risk is defined as the potential for adverse consequences based on incorrect or misused model output and reports and is considered an important risk, which is only now capturing the attention of regulators and institutions, whose approach ranges from mitigation via model validation to the establishment of a comprehensive framework for an active model risk management. There has been little regulatory activity on model risk until now.

The first guidelines were published in 2011 and 2012 in the *Supervisory Guidance on Model Risk Management* which defines model risk and provides a set of guidelines establishing the need for entities to develop a board-approved framework to identify and manage this risk (though not necessarily quantify it). These guidelines cover all phases of a model life cycle: development and deployment, use, validation, governance policies and documentation as the most important factors in the model validation. The main requirement from this regulatory paper emphasises the need to address the model risk with the same importance as any other risk. Consequently, this risk category can only be mitigated (and not removed) through critical analysis and effective challenge. In addition, models should be continuously improved through expert modelling and robust model validation, which are necessary elements in model mitigation. There is the need to establish a clear distinction between model ownership, control and compliance roles, and the specific framework setup remains an important task for an institution. The ultimate responsibility for approving the model framework for Model Risk Management (MRM) is the Board of Directors. Finally, regulators emphasise that the fundamental principle in model risk management is "effective challenge" – understood as a critical analysis by objective, qualified people with experience in the line of business in which the model is used, who are able to identify model limitations and assumptions and suggest appropriate changes. Model risk can have a very significant quantitative impact that can result in management making poor decisions and underestimating the risks that the bank runs on its books. It is therefore important and desirable to have a MRM framework in place and, where appropriate, develop robust model risk estimation techniques aimed at implementing suitable mitigation techniques. Model validation is a key element in model mitigation and its purpose is an effective and independent challenge of the decisions made under the model development. All models that may involve risks should undergo the model validation process and there is no single standardised validation method for all institutions and models. Each institution needs to set standards using its own criteria and these standards should be commensurate with model risk. The model validation function itself must be reviewed by an internal audit, which needs to analyse its work and implement controls as well as to give its opinion on the degree of actual independence of this unit.

From my experience model validation is usually divided into several parts:

1. Assessment of the outcome of the model with the view that it provides the solution in line with our expectations.
2. Assessment of the assumptions used in the model with the view that they are appropriately applied and aligned with the objective of the model.
3. Assessment of the methodology applied in the model.
4. Assessment of the potential risks related to the model feeding and data gathering process.

Banks are required to develop model risk policies which provide them with a list of crucial models used for the decision-making process. These models have ownership precisely allocated and there is a robust validation process, either provided by an external counterparty or an internal department within the financial institution.

CHAPTER 5

Interest rate risk and asset liability management

MANAGEMENT OF IRRBB UNDER STRATEGIC ALM – PROACTIVE MANAGEMENT OF IRRBB

This section is the most crucial in this book. It focuses on the proactive management of interest rate risk which means optimisation of hedging strategy achieved through the multi-dimensional exercise, and the integrated management of different aspects – such as the liquidity profile of a bank, its IRRBB exposure, position on the interest rate curve, diversification of funding sources and avoidance of maturity cliffs – provides the quantifiable savings in terms of funding cost. This book proposes the adoption of a proactive approach for the funding plan strategy setting. The proportions of funding sources are precisely calibrated in order to reduce hedging expenses (and costs of hedge accounting designation) and, at the same time, to reduce the cost of funding. The funding tenor and proportions are driven by growth on the asset side and its financial characteristics. It means that funding strategy is not a *silo basis* exercise. It is a proactive and sophisticated process which brings both aspects together, i.e., hedging based on the projected growth on the asset side and reduction in the overall funding cost.

Additionally, there is a description of both directional gap strategy on the short end of the interest rate curve (usually up to 12 months), natural hedging strategy and residual gap hedging strategy on the medium-to-long part of the curve.

The second part of this section is dedicated to the strategic Funds Transfer Pricing (strategic FTP) which works as a tool to achieve the *target profile* of the bank. The words "strategic" and "optimised" are heard even more frequently in the aftermath of the financial crisis, the introduction of negative rates and onerous regulatory landscape. At the end of this section there are examples of ALM optimisation, i.e., integrated management of interest rate risk and liquidity risk and the construction of the funding plan.

Introduction to integrated management of interest rate risk and liquidity risk

Ever since the 2008 bank crash, the redefinition of the ALM function in the active management of the banking book is becoming an important challenge for financial institutions. This is driven by the contribution that the ALM function has in the overall profitability of a bank in times of challenges driven by margin compression. It is extremely important to have ALM flexibility and proactivity, since many years of low and negative interest rates resulting from the financial crisis have impacted competitiveness and created considerable challenges in balance sheet management. Consequently, there is a clear need to reset the business model and redefine the priorities for ALM discipline.

The ALM function has two important tools at its disposal in order to be a profitability enhancer: active and integrated management of financial risks, in particular interest rate risk with liquidity risk, and Funds Transfer Pricing (FTP). These tools, if managed correctly, allow for the achievement of a profitable *target profile* of the banking book and significant reduction in funding and hedging costs.

It is very clear that there is a strong interrelation between interest rate risk and liquidity risk and that those risks should be managed under an integrated approach. The interest risk gap, its impact on the ALM margin and, consequently, the net interest income sensitivity deriving from the Interest Rate Risk (IRR) exposure is one side of the coin. Then, there is another one that results from the funding gap, its impact on the ALM margin and its riskiness in terms of margin sensitivity.

Let's consider this concept in a very simple case, in which the banking book of a bank is composed of a fixed rate loan funded by a floating rate note with a 3-month reset. The financial characteristics are as follows:

ASSET – Fixed rate loan at maturity 100
Repayment type: bullet
Next capital payment date: 31/12/2013
Next repricing date: 31/12/2013
Customer rate: 3.5%
FTP IRRBB component: 2%
FTP Term Liquidity Premium: 0.5%
LIABILITY – Floating rate note 3-month reset 100
Repayment type: bullet
Next capital payment date: 31/09/2013
Next repricing date: 31/03/2013
Customer rate: 1.5%
FTP IRRBB component: 1.25%
FTP Term Liquidity Premium: 0.25%

The ALM manager finds its banking book structured as shown in Figure 5.1.

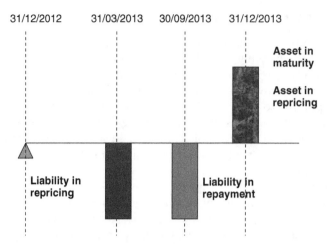

FIGURE 5.1   Exposure to the IRR and liquidity risk according to the *flows* approach.
Source: This example is replicated from Lubinska (2020)

This banking book shows the exposure to the IRR on 31 March 2013, due to the refixing of the floating rate liability. Starting from that date, the refixed asset will be funded by the refixing liability, generating an interest rate gap and, subsequently, NII sensitivity. The profitability of this position, due to the interest rate risk component, is equal to 0.75% in the form of a *locked-in* ALM margin. Instead, the ALM margin at risk is equal to 1% under the assumption of the decrease in LIBOR 3M (under the assumption that liability is indexed to LIBOR 3M) by 25 bps (from 1.25% to 1%).

However, the same situation analysed from the liquidity standpoint looks slightly different. The bank begins to be exposed to the liquidity risk on 30 September 2013 when the liability expires and needs to be rolled over. Starting from that date, the funding gap creates NII sensitivity. The ALM locked-in margin deriving from the funding gap is equal to 0.25% (the difference between liquidity spread of asset and liability). Instead, the ALM margin at risk depends on the new liquidity spread related to the liability that needs to be rolled over. Arriving at the total profitability of the ALM book, we need to sum the NII margin obtained by the positioning of the bank in terms of both interest rate risk and liquidity risk. There is a clear trade-off between the unrealised ALM profit, which depends on:

– new liquidity spread of the liability in maturity
– movement of the LIBOR 3M tenor of the interest rate curve
– NII sensitivity which those positions have created.

Therefore, it is imperative for the ALM function to find this optimal structure. Figure 5.2 summarises the concept of a trade-off between profitability and risk in an ALM analysis.

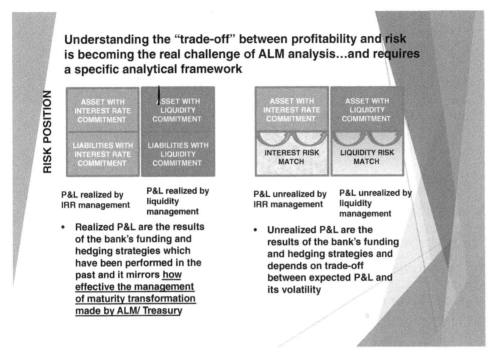

FIGURE 5.2 The trade-off between profitability and risk in ALM analysis.
Source: own elaboration

Introduction to strategic FTP

The second powerful tool that ALM has at its disposal is the FTP process. In a Maturity Matched Funds Transfer Pricing (MMFTP) process, ALM acts as a central unit (bank within a bank) which charges the asset centre the FTP rate for funding and recognises the FTP rate to the liability centre. The central model consists of risk transfer through the FTP rate from the business units to the central unit to be managed. In this way, the business unit remit is to focus on the relationship with the client as opposed to the management of any financial risk which client activity exposes the bank to, in particular interest rate risk and liquidity risk. Under this model ALM is left with the risk exposure which is managed according to the limits established by ALCO. This separation of remits between business units and central unit is a crucial element underlying this model.

Figure 5.3 provides an example of the MMFTP process. In Figure 5.3 ALM is charging the asset centre the FTP rate (1.31%) for 2Y funding. The asset centre passes the FTP rate on to the client with additional mark up, i.e., commercial spread. At the same time, ALM "borrows" 3M funding from the liability centre at the FTP rate (0.32%). It is left with the margin between the FTP charged to the asset side and paid to the liability side, i.e., 0.99% (1.31% − 0.32%); however, there is maturity and rate transformation which needs to be managed at the central level.

Under the MMFTP model, ALM has to be a *"zero sum game"*, which means that its profitability is determined exclusively by the IRR strategies and the extent of the maturity transformation that it is running, and not by charging additional mark up to the FTP rate which is charged to, or recognised by, business units. FTP should be the transparent process that applies the fair (term liquidity) price for funds and

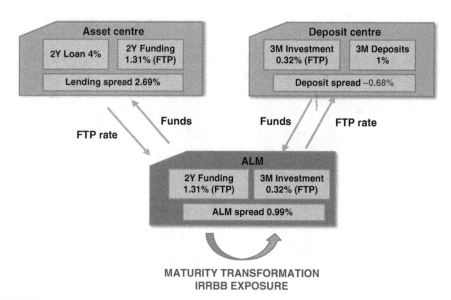

FIGURE 5.3 MMFTP process.
Source: own elaboration

transference of interest rate risk and liquidity risk from business lines to the ALM unit. It must be based on one set of rules described in the FTP policy.

FTP is also a powerful tool in assisting the forward shaping of the banking book. Its steering role consists in the application of techniques, such as FTP curve dampening, incentives premium, and the application of management overlays (shifting whole parts of the FTP curve up or down) in order to arrive at a desirable banking book shape. The importance of this tool, post financial crash, has been recognised across the banking industry. FTP is not, and has never been, simply a "right-pocket, left-pocket" static mechanism solely used for performance reporting.

Thus, the modern, proactive ALM function works in a multi-dimensional world. First, it has to be able to determine the best achievable trade-off between profitability of the ALM book and its riskiness through an integrated approach to the management of financial risks. The *silo* approach, which can still be found in many financial institutions, is sub-optimal and reduces the performance of the ALM unit. In today's world, having an overall picture of risks faced by the financial institution is an imperative. Therefore, the revision of the methodological approach determines the first dimension where a modern ALM operates.

In order to provide a reader with the illustrative example of the active management of the interest rate risk let us consider two situations which the bank's treasurer could potentially face (Figures 5.4 and 5.5). These examples are meant to provide better understanding of directional gap strategy (described in Chapter 2) in order to manage actively the short end of the interest rate curve.

Where the total *GAP* position under a gapping period of 12 months is higher than zero (Figure 5.4), the treasurer is willing to keep the positive directional gap if she/he

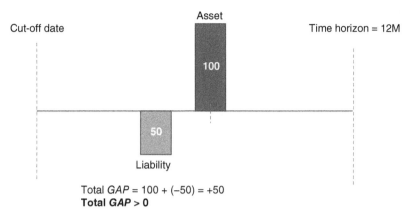

FIGURE 5.4 Total repricing gap of the banking book is higher than zero.
Source: own elaboration

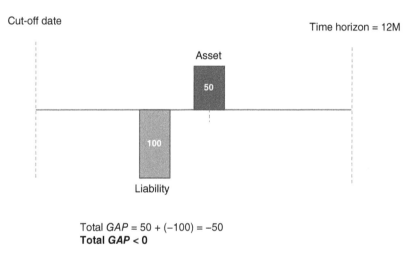

FIGURE 5.5 Total repricing gap of the banking book is lower than zero.
Source: own elaboration

believes that the short-term market rates are about to increase. Obviously, she/he has to be aware of the magnitude of the NII sensitivity caused by this open position and, at the same time, to maximise the profitability of the banking book from the interest rate positioning (risk return trade-off).

In Figure 5.5, she/he is willing to keep the negative directional gap if she/he believes that the short-term market rates are about to decrease. Likewise, she/he has to make sure this open position does not exceed the internal limits for the NII sensitivity.

The liquidity management is another imperative for the treasurer and one of the highest points on the treasury agenda as she/he has to manage it from both a short-term (sufficient amount of the liquidity buffer and the counterbalancing capacity of

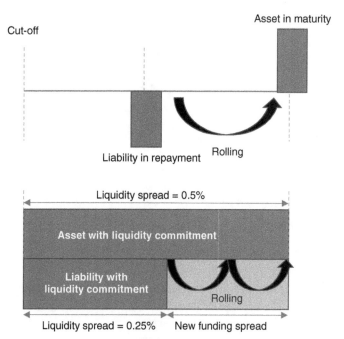

FIGURE 5.6   Liquidity mismatching and potential NII impact.
Source: own elaboration

the bank) and from the medium-to-long term perspective (maturity transformation and structural liquidity position).

Figure 5.6 shows the impact of the maturity transformation resulting from the difference between maturity of asset and liability and the potential impact on NII where there is an increase/decrease in the funding costs of a bank.

Consequently, the understanding of the trade-off between the degree of the maturity transformation of a bank and the P&L impact resulting from the difference between the liquidity spread of assets and liquidity spread of liabilities is the first thing to be assessed and discussed in ALCO based on the liquidity risk appetite of the financial institution.

The integrated management between interest rate risk and liquidity risk can be performed through:

1. An optimisation model which represents the quantitative approach.
2. Setting up the funding strategy for a bank, taking into consideration the hedging requirements.

Meanwhile the first approach consists of building the optimisation model and solving it for objective variables; the second one varies from static quantification of hedging requirements, based on the future business growth and under a forward interest rate curve environment, to a dynamic simulation approach which includes stochastic movements in the interest rate curve.

SETTING UP THE *TARGET PROFILE* AND INTEGRATED MANAGEMENT OF LIQUIDITY AND INTEREST RATE RISK THROUGH THE APPLICATION OF NUMERICAL OPTIMISATION TECHNIQUE

This section only introduces the main concepts of the optimisation exercise which are described in more detail in *Asset Liability Management Optimisation* (Lubinska, 2020). The objective of the application of the optimisation method under the IRRBB view is to come up with a funding structure and funding sources proportions which support the natural hedging strategy (without the need to use synthetic hedges). In order to minimise hedging requirements, funding strategy has to be analysed together with hedging strategy using a holistic approach. It can be done either by a quantitative approach, i.e., the application of a mathematical model (optimisation techniques with objective and constraints functions defined) or a "qualitative" approach set up by the treasurer where the funding strategy is set up in such a way as to minimise the need for derivatives and, at the same time, to reduce the funding cost as much as possible. It is more like a "calibration" exercise, where the funding products available to the treasurer are calibrated to achieve both objectives. This is a multi-dimensional exercise, which provides the bank with the tools to manage treasury risks using a holistic approach as opposed to the silo basis approach. Additionally, the integrated management of different aspects – such as the liquidity profile of the bank, its IRRBB exposure and position on the interest rate curve, diversification of funding sources and avoidance of maturity cliffs – provides quantifiable savings in terms of the funding cost.

Introduction to the optimisation concept

The optimisation problem can be described in the form of mathematical functions, and the solution is obtained by applying optimisation techniques. The functions are built for the objective variables which need to be optimised (for example income on assets and cost of funding); and constraints variables which need to be considered in the optimisation exercise (for example, exposure to the interest rate risk and liquidity risk).

Optimisation modelling is always performed within a certain time horizon and its general structure is as follows:

$$\text{maximise } f(x) \text{ subject to } x \in D \text{ or} \qquad (33a)$$

$$\text{minimise } f(x) \text{ subject to } x \in D \qquad (33b)$$

where:

f is called the *objective function* and D is known as the *constraint set*.

Problems of the first sort are termed *maximisation problems* and those of the second *minimisation problems*. From a mathematical standpoint, optimisation is the process of finding the minimum and maximum value of a function. Given that differential calculus estimates the rate of change of the function, and whether the rate is accelerating, slowing down or stationary, it is used to find the "optimum" points of a function. The first derivative identifies these points, and the second derivative looks at their nature. The local maximum, minimum and the stationary point of inflection are all points where the first derivatives are equal to zero, i.e., $\dfrac{dy}{dx} = 0$. They are all known as stationary points. If at a stationary point the second derivative is negative, then $\dfrac{dy}{dx} = 0$ and $\dfrac{dy}{dx}$ is falling. Therefore, moving from left to right there is a positive gradient followed by a zero gradient, followed by a negative gradient. This characteristic points towards the local maximum. A similar argument shows that if there is a point at which the second derivatives are positive and, moving from left to right the gradient changes from negative to zero and subsequently to positive, then the point represents the local minimum. A stationary point of a function of more than one variable is a point where all partial derivatives are zero. A stationary point, as in the case of the function of one variable only, can be a local minimum, local maximum or a saddle point. The saddle point is a point with a maximum in at least one direction, and a minimum in at least one direction. To discover the type of a stationary point the Hessian matrix of second partial derivatives is examined. Mirroring the situation with one variable, if at the stationary point the Hessian matrix of second derivatives is positive definite then there is a local minimum. If it is negative definite then there is a local maximum. If it is neither then it is necessary to examine the change in gradient to see which point it is.

In finance it is common that the function to be optimised is subject to certain constraints, for example the required expected return. In constrained optimisation, the Lagrange multiplier is used. The Lagrangian is constructed as follows:

$$L(x, y, \lambda) = f(x, y) - \lambda g(x, y) \tag{34}$$

where $L(x, y, \lambda)$ is the Lagrangian function of three variables; $f(x, y)$ is the objective function of two variables; λ is the Lagrange multiplier; and $g(x, y)$ is the constraint function.

In this case, the Lagrangian is a function of three variables, x, y and λ, where λ is constant. The result for the calculation of partial derivatives of the Lagrangian is as follows:

$$\frac{\partial L}{\partial x} = \frac{\partial f}{\partial x} - \lambda \frac{\partial g}{\partial x}; \tag{35a}$$

$$\frac{\partial L}{\partial y} = \frac{\partial f}{\partial y} - \lambda \frac{\partial g}{\partial y}; \tag{35b}$$

$$\frac{\partial L}{\partial \lambda} = g \tag{35c}$$

Setting the first two partial derivatives to zero (35a and 35b) gives a situation where the gradients are in the same direction, i.e. that:

$$\frac{\partial f}{\partial y} \Big/ \frac{\partial f}{\partial x} = \frac{\partial g}{\partial y} \Big/ \frac{\partial g}{\partial x} \tag{36}$$

Setting the third partial derivative (35c) to zero gives the constraints $g(x,y) = 0$. Hence, to solve the constrained optimisation problem it is necessary to look for a stationary point of Lagrangian, i.e., a point where the partial derivatives are all equal to zero. The value of λ is the marginal value of the relaxing of a constraint. So, if the constraint were to be changed by a small amount h, the constrained maximum would change by λh. As already pointed out, the solution to the constrained optimisation problem is given by finding the stationary point of the Lagrangian, and we require that all partial derivatives are equal to zero. By setting all derivatives (for variables and λ) to zero the sequence of simultaneous linear equations is obtained. Those equations can be written out in matrix form by extracting the matrix of coefficients, the vector of variables, and the vector of right-hand sides. The system can be solved using the matrix inverse (PRMIA, 2015).

A different approach has to be followed in order to solve the inequality constrained optimisation problem. For this kind of problem, the Theorem of Kuhn and Tucker is applied. The cookbook procedure for using the Theorem of Kuhn and Tucker to solve an inequality constrained optimisation problem involves essentially the same steps as those used in the Theorem of Lagrange for equality constrained problems. However, there are differences regarding the solving of maximisation and minimisation problems.

Nevertheless, it is important to keep in mind that in any given optimisation problem, a solution may fail to exist (that is, the problem may have no solution at all) and, second, that even if a solution does exist, it does not need necessarily to be unique (that is, there could be more than one solution). For this reason, it is very important to identify a set of conditions on f and D under which the existence of solutions to the optimisation problem is guaranteed.

Summarising the section related to the solution of analytical optimisation problems, the **Lagrange multipliers** method consists in finding out the Lagrange function and the multiplier. Subsequently, the function needs to be differentiated with respect to variables and the partial derivatives have to be equated to zero. Such a constructed sequence of equations (including the constraints) has to be solved for unknowns and multipliers giving all pairs of numbers (x, y) that can possibly solve the problem.

The optimisation exercise for the banking book of the bank almost always involves inequality constraints. For example, the limit related to NII volatility is expressed as an inequality, indicating the range for the acceptable level of NII volatility. The same point is valid for the liquidity ratios, both short term and medium to long term. In such cases, where the constraints are expressed as inequalities, the optimisation problem can be solved applying the Theorem of Kuhn and Tucker.

The problem becomes more complex when it comes to the numerical optimisation problems which are formulated very often, especially in finance. In this case, solving the optimisation problems involve the application of numerical methods which are required to optimise the value of something when it depends on multiple inputs. Whilst analytical optimisation involves finding the maximum and minimum of a function by finding the point at which the function derivatives are zero, numerical optimisation is used when the explicitly defined function to be optimised does not lend itself to analytical techniques, or when the function is not explicitly defined (Parramore and Watsham, 2015). This section addresses the optimisation method known as the *interior-point method*, which gets its name from the fact that the optimal solution is approached from the strict interior of the feasible region. This method is used in the Matlab optimisation toolbox known as *fmincon* to find a minimum of a constrained nonlinear multivariable function. Interior-point (or barrier) methods have proved to be successful for nonlinear optimisation, and they are currently considered the most powerful algorithm for large-scale nonlinear programming. Barrier methods for nonlinear optimisation were developed in the 1960s but fell out of favour for almost two decades. The success of interior-point methods for linear programming stimulated renewed interest in them in nonlinear cases and, by the late 1990s, a new generation of methods and software for nonlinear programming had emerged. The terms "interior-point methods" and "barrier methods" are now used interchangeably (Nocedal and Wright, 2006). The problem under consideration here can be described as follows:

$$\min_{x \in R^n} f(x)$$

$$\text{subject to: } c_i(x) = 0, i \in \varepsilon \tag{37}$$

$$c_i(x) \geq 0, i \in I$$

where $c(x)$ is an m-dimensional vector of nonlinear constraint functions with i-th component $c_i(x)$, $i = 1,...,m$ and ε and I are non-intersecting index sets. It is assumed that f and c are twice-continuously differentiable. Any point x satisfying the constraints above is called a feasible point, and the set of all such points is the feasible region. In order to solve the optimisation problem, the gradient of objective function $f(x)$, denoted by $\nabla f(x)$ or $g(x)$, has to be determined along with the Hessian matrix of second partial derivatives of $\nabla^2 f(x)$. The gradient and Hessian of *constrained functions* $c_i(x)$ are denoted by $\nabla c_i(x)$ and $\nabla^2 c_i(x)$ (Forsgren et al., 2002).

The logarithmic barrier function associated with (37) is defined as follows:

$$B(x,\mu) = f(x) - \mu \sum_{i=1}^{m} \log c_i(x) \tag{38}$$

where μ is a small positive scalar, often called the barrier parameter. As μ converges to zero the minimum of $B(x,\mu)$ should converge to a solution of (38).

The barrier function gradient is:

$$g_b = g - \mu \sum_{i=1}^{m} \frac{1}{c_i(x)} \nabla c_i(x) \qquad (39)$$

where g is the gradient of the objective function $f(x)$ and ∇c_i is the gradient of c_i.

In addition to the original, known as "primal" variable x, the Lagrange multiplier inspired dual variable λ is introduced:

$$\lambda \in R^m \quad \text{and} \quad c_i(x)\lambda_i = \mu, \forall i = 1,...,m \qquad (40)$$

In order to find the solution to the optimisation problem it is necessary to satisfy the Karush–Kuhn–Tucker (KKT) optimality condition. KKT are first-order necessary conditions for a solution in nonlinear programming to be optimal, provided that some regularity conditions are satisfied. Allowing inequality constraints, the KKT approach to nonlinear programming generalises the method of Lagrange multipliers, which allows only equality constraints. The system of equations and inequalities corresponding to the KKT conditions is usually not solved directly, except in the few special cases where a closed-form solution can be derived analytically. In general, many optimisation algorithms can be interpreted as methods for numerically solving the KKT system of equations and inequalities.

One of the methods of solving the optimisation problem in the banking book is called the interior-point algorithm and is based on the Lagrange multipliers method. This method is embedded in the Matlab solver: *fmincom*.

The optimisation problem herein is defined through the construction of the optimisation functions, i.e., the minimisation of the funding costs of the bank subject to constraints. The analysis needs to be performed over a certain time horizon and a predetermined maturity profile for the banking book items – for example, under a constant balance sheet scenario where there is a renewal of assets and liabilities falling under maturity/repricing with items with the same financial features (a *like-for-like* assumption).

The objective function for the liability side aims to minimise the total funding cost of a bank. It is a multivariable equality function which describes the total cost of funding with variables representing the proportions of a different source of funding in the total liabilities structure. The model searches for the minimum value of this function subject to certain constraints.

The minimisation function can be written as follows:

$$f\left(w_A, w_B, w_C, w_j\right) = w_A * L * \sum_{i=1}^{6} c_{A_i} / 12 + w_B * L * \sum_{i=1}^{6} c_{B_i} / 12$$
$$+ w_C * L * \sum_{i=1}^{6} c_{C_i} / 12 + w_j * L * \sum_{i=1}^{6} c_{j_i} / 12 \qquad (41)$$

where:

$w_A, w_B \ldots w_j$ are the proportions of the funding opportunities in the total funding base,

$c_{Ai}, c_{Bi}, \ldots c_{ji}$ represents the annual cost of funding for the respective funding opportunity j in i-th month of the observation period.

The optimisation decision model always has a number of underlying assumptions, for example:

- The analysis is performed over a precise time horizon (for example, a period of 6 months, from t_0 to t_6).
- The maturity profile of assets is determined based on the constant balance sheet scenario, i.e., it is assumed that the amortising or maturing assets and liabilities are renewed as *like for like* (by assets and liabilities with the same financial characteristics).

Finding the proportions which satisfy the objective function addresses the question as to what the target profile of a bank should be when considering the initial structure of the banking book, the assumptions listed above, and with pricing unchanged in the next 6-month period. The shorter the period of the analysis the more precise the model outcome is because there is less uncertainty in external market conditions.

There is a *non-negativity* condition which must be maintained (the model does not allow the proportions to be set at zero). This is driven by the fact that the optimisation model is not meant to change the business model of the financial institution through excluding certain liability classes. Instead, it is meant to change the relative proportions in the funding base with the objective of minimising (for liabilities) the objective function.

The *non-negativity* condition for liabilities is described below:

$$w_A + w_B + w_{C+\ldots+}w_j = 1 \tag{42}$$

$$w_{funding} > 0 \tag{43}$$

The constraints functions are set up in such a way as to reflect the metrics which a financial institution monitors for liquidity and interest rate risk purposes. This is because the aim of the optimisation exercise is to minimise the funding cost under the constraints that metrics are within the required limit.

Given that this is the holistic view for liquidity and interest rate risk management, the constraints are both for liquidity and interest rate risk metrics.

The optimised structure satisfies the following objectives:

1. minimisation of synthetic hedges
2. minimisation of overall funding cost for a bank

SETTING UP THE FUNDING STRATEGY FOR A BANK TAKING INTO CONSIDERATION THE HEDGING REQUIREMENTS

Hedging and funding strategies under holistic view

CASE STUDY 6

The treasurer of Bank Y has to define the funding strategy for the forthcoming months. Funding requirements are based on Bank Y's growth assumptions and the minimum amount of liquidity buffer required to respect the short-term liquidity metrics. It is also necessary to replace existing funding sources which are due to mature. This is a complex exercise because there is always some portion of funding sources which will roll over and, therefore, does not need to be refinanced. Most banks are funded through different types of deposit (time deposits, notice accounts, instant access accounts). Thus, it is necessary to maintain a constant dialogue between the deposit centre and the treasury. The deposit unit has the knowledge of customer behaviour and the sensitivity of the deposit base. Therefore, the role of expert judgment cannot be underestimated in the construction of the Funding Plan. The treasurer has a number of different funding opportunities and it is important to calibrate their proportions in such a way that it is beneficial for the bank's P&L.

In our example, Bank Y has a variety of deposits and has secured long-term funding provided by an external counterparty.

1. Time deposits.
2. Notice accounts.
3. Instant access accounts.
4. Secured long-term funding indexed to the central bank rate.

Table 5.1 illustrates the funding requirements to support the growth of the asset base.

As a next step the treasurer has to design the composition and proportions of available funding sources in order to achieve a number of objectives:

- A reduction in the cost of funding.
- A reduction in the number of synthetic hedges needed to manage growing exposure to the interest rate risk and maintain the adequate size of liquidity buffer to withstand the potential liquidity stress.

The construction of the funding plan cannot be done in isolation, i.e., only from a liquidity risk perspective. This is because the available funding sources have different repricing characteristics, different sensitivity to the changes in interest rates and a different impact on Bank Y's IRRBB exposure. For example, the notice accounts are known to be very sensitive to their price. The higher the rate paid to

TABLE 5.1   Funding requirements of Bank Y.

April 2021	May 2021	June 2021	July 2021	August 2021	September 2021	October 2021	November 2021	December 2021
20m	35m	45m	45m	45m	50m	55m	50m	50m

Source: own elaboration

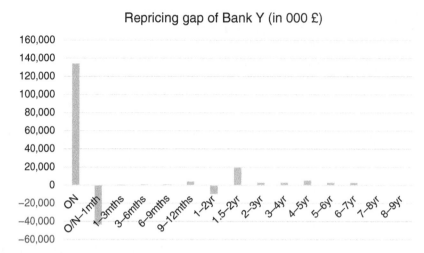

FIGURE 5.7   Repricing gap of Bank Y including new production.
Source: own elaboration

depositors the higher propensity to stay within the bank. On the other hand, the lower the interest rate renumerated to depositors the higher propensity to shop for better rates in the market and, therefore, increased outflow.

The secured long-term funding has the short-term repricing as it is indexed to the base rate. As a secured funding there is a need to pre-position the collateral as a guarantee for the funding provider.

Based on the above information, the next step is to understand the structure of the banking book from the IRRBB perspective, i.e., what Bank Y's sensitivity is to movement in interest rates in terms of ΔNII and ΔEVE.

For this reason, the treasurer analyses the repricing gap of Bank Y simulating (including) the new business assumption, i.e., the growth in the asset base. This is in order to understand the impact of the new business in terms of IRRBB metrics.

Figure 5.7 shows the repricing gap of Bank Y including new volumes on the asset side as of the end of May 2021. However, it does not include funding required to cover the balance sheet growth over the next month. In order to cover growth, Bank Y needs to raise 45m of funding.

Bank Y is asset sensitive both on the short and medium part of the curve which means it is going to benefit from the rates increase as assets will reprice at the higher rate. On the other hand, an interest rate decrease will have immediate negative P&L impact.

On the long part of the curve (from 1.5 years to 7 years) Bank Y shows a net asset position which means that an increase in the interest rates will be reflected in the embedded loss in the banking book value. The net asset position can be seen in two ways, i.e., ALM margin is locked in for the long term and rates increase means the bank loses opportunity to reprice at a higher rate or fixed rate assets are discounted at higher rates which results in their lower present value.

This can be clearly seen analysing the PV01 position of the bank as per Figure 5.8.

Figure 5.8 shows that a parallel increase in interest rates by 1 bp results in an embedded loss in Bank Y's value by £10K.

As already mentioned, Bank Y needs to raise 45m of funding to cover new production over the next month. The treasurer analyses the following funding opportunities as shown in Figure 5.9.

Additionally, Bank Y can raise the secured funding indexed to the base rate.

It is important to note that the definition of funding and hedging strategy is also driven by the treasurer's expectations regarding the direction of the movement of interest rates in the market.

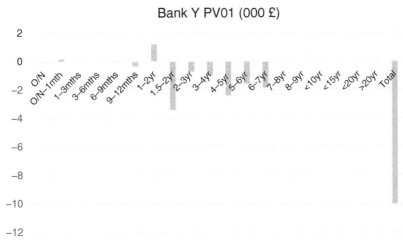

FIGURE 5.8 The PV01 of Bank Y before increasing volumes in short-term repricing liabilities.
Source: own elaboration

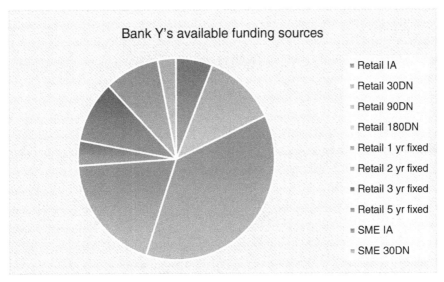

FIGURE 5.9 Funding sources available to Bank Y.
Source: own elaboration

The asset sensitive position, on the short part of the curve, along with the expectation of a downward movement of the interest rate curve, implys a negative impact on P&L. If this position is not hedged the bank will face margin compression as rates start moving.

Bank Y can offset the potential impact through its funding strategy, i.e., finding the mixture between wholesale funding, indexed to the base rate (tracker), and short-term repricing deposits, for example instant access accounts. In expectation of a downward movement of interest rates, Bank Y might decide to keep the open position on the long part of the curve because it would lead to an embedded gain in terms of banking book value (ΔEVE metric). This is obviously on the strict condition that Bank Y will not breach any limit for IRRBB exposure, i.e., ΔEVE, PV01 or DGAP. Otherwise, it could enter the forward starting swaps (hedging strategies are described in Chapter 3).

Funding the balance sheet with short-term repricing products results in a reduction in Bank Y's margin sensitivity as shown in Figure 5.10.

As per Figure 5.10 the introduction of short-term repricing liabilities has not impacted the PV01 of Bank Y. This immaterial impact is driven both by the extremely low level of interest rates in 2021 and the short-term repricing tenor (the impact of increased volumes in the O/N time bucket, in terms of PV01, is immaterial). It does not mean that changing the net gap position in short-term time buckets does not impact the PV01 metric at all. The impact can be seen where the net gap position changes significantly (Figure 5.11).

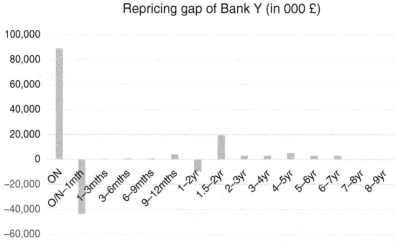

FIGURE 5.10   Reduced margin sensitivity of Bank Y through funding the asset base with short-term repricing liabilities.
Source: own elaboration

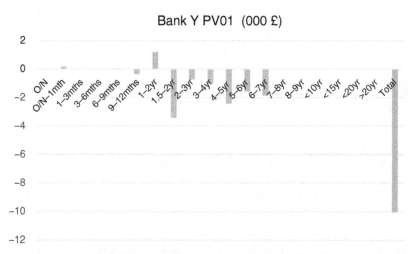

FIGURE 5.11   The PV01 of Bank Y after increasing volumes in short-term repricing liabilities.
Source: own elaboration

As already mentioned, Bank Y shows net asset position on the medium-to-long part of the curve. Although it can be clearly seen in Figure 5.7 (repricing gap of Bank Y), the IRRBB exposure in terms of ΔEVE is limited. However, if the bank continues to originate fixed rate assets this exposure will grow over time and will need to be managed by the treasurer when approaching the management trigger. The exact timing of hedging depends on:

1. The treasurer's expectations as to the direction of future movements of interest rates.
2. The extent to which the bank can fund the new business with long-term repricing products (for example time deposits at a fixed rate) at reasonable cost.
3. The appetite of the senior management of the bank for running the IRRBB exposure which is translated into the IRRBB limits (for example ΔEVE, PV01 and ΔNII)

This illustrative and simple example of Bank Y leads to the following conclusions:

1. Defining funding strategy has a clear impact on the IRRBB position of the bank and, therefore, both the funding plan and the heading strategy should be analysed together in one holistic approach.
2. There is a decision to be taken by the treasurer, i.e., to what extent to hedge the IRRBB position using the natural hedging strategy and/or derivatives and their timing.

IRRBB AND FUNDS TRANSFER PRICING

The following section provides analysis of the FTP landscape, modelling and transfer both of interest rate risk and liquidity risk from the business units to ALM. It introduces the concept of the FTP process as one of the main tools which a bank has at its disposal to transfer those risks from the business units to ALM and to price the banking book items according to their liquidity value. In addition, it provides a brief overview of the balance sheet shaping techniques through FTP. For the sake of completeness transfer of liquidity risk is included in this section.

The FTP process is the sum of policies and methodologies banks apply to charge or credit products for the liquidity consumed or gathered during a bank's activity. Active balance sheet management through FTP should be a key priority for all banks that want to optimise resources such as capital and funding. There are several reasons why active and conscious balance sheet structure management has increased in importance: scarcity of resources and a new regulatory landscape which set minimum levels for funding structure and liquidity buffers. Therefore, the FTP framework is used as a tool to incentivise behaviour that helps to achieve a bank's goals and the fair pricing of interest rate and liquidity costs.

Banks must have a true and fair value of liquidity and the FTP scheme has to be aligned to their strategic objectives through incentivising or subsidising businesses and activities which are aligned with the overall strategy. For this reason, the set-up of the FTP framework needs to be an integrated part of the overall optimisation process.

ALM must steer the banking book through a number of FTP techniques designed to arrive at the target balance sheet profile. If ALM uses FTP as a dynamic tool to incentivise growth or get rid of certain products, then it actively contributes to setting the target profile of the banking book. The active FTP provides another dimension for ALM to operate in.

Successful navigation in the multi-dimensional ALM universe is an important challenge for every bank and requires strong analytical tools to obtain this objective. However, it is crucial to take this step to remain a long-term, viable, and prosperous financial institution.

FTP is an extremely powerful tool which is deeply rooted in any divisional P&L or profit centre calculation. In fact, FTP is the means by which a bank's overall net interest income can be split into originating units and subunits, thus enabling the bank's management to perform an effective planning, monitoring and control cycle (Widowitz et al., 2014). The FTP rate is composed of several components which basically represent the transference of the interest rate and liquidity risk from the business units to the treasury/ALM in order to be managed centrally and keep the business units immune to financial risks.

Figure 5.12 shows the FTP process from the ALM standpoint. ALM acts as a "bank within a bank" as it gathers funds from the liability centre at the FTP rate and lends those funds to the asset centre at FTP rate. As a result of this process, the maturity transformation run by the bank is managed by ALM and generates the profitability for the bank. On the other hand, the profitability of the asset centre and liability centre is assessed through the difference between the external product price and FTP rate.

FTP separates customer from risk business: the application of funds transfer prices for each single transaction assumes that every deal will be hedged against risk.

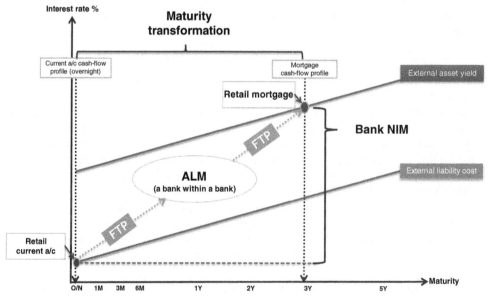

FIGURE 5.12 FTP process and the role of ALM.
Source: own elaboration

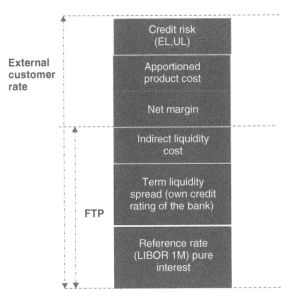

FIGURE 5.13 FTP building blocks.
Source: own elaboration

Thus, one can calculate the customer margin without market risk. Consequently, applying FTP, the customer margin remains constant during the whole product's life, independently from interest movements, higher liquidity cost or changing currency prices. The funds transfer price reflects the (market) price ALM is entering into a transaction. If ALM decides to hedge the risk position immediately it should be able to do so without any profit or loss. This is an approximation because of bid/offer prices and because a bank normally is able to hedge positions only after bundling many customer transactions due to the small size of customer business and the large size in the financial markets.

Figure 5.13 shows the building blocks of the FTP rate. Note that indirect liquidity cost has been included as a part of FTP. This is on the assumption that there is a *behaviouralisation* process in place (explained later in the section) and indirect liquidity is allocated to the product based on its behavioural characteristics.

As already pointed out, FTP separates the NII components arising from client business margins, interest rate positioning and liquidity maturity transformation. Even though the best FTP practices are still under development there is a necessity to include the new Basel III regime into the framework, which leads to a more sophisticated approach for FTP.

The FTP framework should cover the following aspects:

■ The default FTP curves to use and the discretion around the adoption of the default methodology.
■ The interest rate risk profiling for contractual maturity and non-defined maturity products/items such as:

(a) Fixed rate products.
(b) Floating rate products.
(c) Fixed or floating rate loans against committed facilities.
(d) Core, non-core and price sensitivity.
(e) Products with early redemption optionality.
(f) Investment term of equity deployed.

- The liquidity risk profiling for all products.
- The Cost of Liquidity (COL) to transfer indirect liquidity costs, for example LCR and NSFR.

There are at least four elements that need to be included in the integrated FTP framework. The first element consists in the definition of the framework for all products which represent the sources of liquidity cost, both based on the deterministic cash flows (known as term liquidity) and for contingent liquidity arising from the stochastic cash flows. It should include all relevant balance sheet and off-balance sheet positions that need to be considered from a liquidity and interest rate risk perspective. The FTP landscape should include all products which represent sources of liquidity cost, both based on the deterministic cash flows (known as term liquidity) and contingent liquidity arising from the stochastic cash flows. The FTP rate should be allocated to these products based on their financial characteristics, for example both floating and fixed rate loans get charged the liquidity premium which depends on the length of time for those funds to be consumed. The same point is valid for liabilities which are recognised liquidity value based on their liquidity tenor.

The second one – in the view of the author the most important one – is the FTP curve set up. This is driven by the underlying principle that assets get charged by their cost of funds which is credited to the bank's funding units, and the base of this calculation is the FTP curve. The FTP methodology is based on a gross marginal cost approach which reflects the opportunity cost to fund one unit of new asset volume in the market. However, this approach should be adjusted in order to reflect the funding characteristics of the balance sheet. Where a liquid interbank yield curve is available then the choice of that FTP yield curve is clear. The default treatment is to use the benchmark rate identified by a bank. The FTP rate is usually applied both to assets and liabilities and, under this practice, there is no internal spread on a matched position basis in ALM since this is FTP methodology which is based on the Matched Maturity Transfer Pricing methodology (MMFTP). Where there is no practical interbank yield curve, then transactability should drive how the curve is set. In most instances, this will mean the use of Government paper/CD yields, with interpolation.

Table 5.2 shows a number of curve construction methodologies as a function of different scenarios.

The shape of the medium-to-long FTP curve could be determined with reference to a bank's senior debt issuance levels by tenor. However, in some cases, in order to steer the growth of the balance sheet, the FTP curve is dampened, i.e., the medium-to-long-term curve set up is lowered by a factor so that only a certain portion of the bank's funding spread paid in the wholesale market is charged to assets.

TABLE 5.2 FTP curve construction methodologies.

	Curve scenario	Examples of the curve choice
1	Deep, liquid interbank yield curve is available	This curve should be used
2	Interbank yield curves are available, but liquidity may not be consistently available at all required points	This curve should be used with a process of interpolation
3	Only curve available is derived from Government Securities	The Government Securities curve should be used with a process of interpolation
4	Where there is no effective curve at all	In the extreme case that no external reference rates are available, ALCO may apply a simplified methodology of averaging the weighted average customer loan and deposit rates for use as the FTP rate

Source: own elaboration

The proportion of senior debt cost included in the medium-to-long-term FTP benchmark curve is determined by a factor set by ALCOs.

Nevertheless, it has to be noted that the aforementioned approach was developed and implemented at a time when balance sheets were growing, and the growth was funded by additional capital market issuances very easily. Since the 2007–9 crisis, things are different, as banks are shrinking their balance sheets and are trying to reduce their dependence on wholesale funding. In addition, treasurers are more restricted in issuing specific tenures on capital markets (Widowitz et al., 2014). This leads to the necessity of a more sophisticated and tailored FTP curve set-up. For example, having a stable and cheap deposit base is an imperative to maintain competitiveness. This fact has to be reflected in the FTP curve construction. The challenge in the FTP curve set-up is to answer the question: what is the opportunity benefit of investing one unit of new deposit? (Widowitz et al., 2014).

On some occasions a bank's senior management may decide to introduce an Incentive Premium (IP) on specific assets or liabilities with an offsetting charge on specific assets or liabilities to achieve precisely defined, short-term balance sheet objectives. There are very precise rules that need to be followed when introducing the IP scheme. In particular, it should be recognised/charged out to businesses, it should represent only a temporary tool for steering, it should not seek to compensate for regulatory liquidity value, and it should not replace the role of the curve in establishing marginal funding costs. This is because the objective of the IP scheme is to achieve a specific short-term balance sheet objective, i.e., subsidise a specific product to protect the bank's liquidity, or to manage a regulatory ratio. The IP application must be compliant with the FTP policy in terms of the duration and transparency of the funding cost with strong governance process around it.

There are different solutions for the dynamic FTP curve construction, and, in the view of the author, there is no best practice with reference to it. Setting the right curve

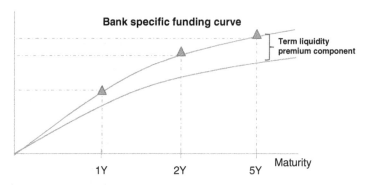

FIGURE 5.14 Example of the specific FTP curve.
Source: own elaboration

is a very bank-specific and individual task. However, the importance of this element in the FTP framework needs to be stressed, as the curve construct should be aligned with the strategic objectives (decided on by the senior management) and support the business model of the institution. The first rule, to achieve this goal, is transparency in the curve setting and deep understanding of the specifics of the balance sheet (target funding base and the extent of maturity transformation run by the bank).

Figure 5.14 shows the underlying concept behind the FTP curve. The bank's specific curve is always composed of two elements, i.e., the risk-free interest rate curve which reflects the IRR component and the Term Liquidity Premium (TLP) which reflects the perception of the bank's creditworthiness in the market. Liquidity spread is usually derived from the difference between the bank's funding curve (the swap curve shifted by the bank's term funding spread) and the swap curve for the tenor which corresponds to the behavioural or contractual life of the product.

The third element in the FTP framework is the methodology. The pricing methodology has to be set up according to precise rules and the principles have to be understood by all FTP process stakeholders. It is based on predetermined principles aligned with the strategic objectives of a financial institution and according to transparent rules and methodologies. The product pricing is always based on the FTP curve which acts as an internal product price benchmark.

For example, the transfer price for the revolving credit facility is calculated according to two approaches. The simplified approach consists in the allocation of the FTP rate to the drawn part of the product, in line with its drawn amount and its tenor. For the undrawn portion, the contingency liquidity costs are allocated. Although simple, this approach represents some limitations, such as the necessity of generating a large number of funding tickets that have to be adjusted upon each change of the drawn amount. Furthermore, the treasury/ALM neglects the fact that many short-term draws are rolled over and are actually drawn until the final maturity of the facility.

In order to overcome the limitations coming from the simplified approach, an alternative is to carry out the behavioural analysis of portfolios of the revolving facility and identify the core and volatile part of the product. The core part, which is supposed to be drawn until the final maturity, is charged by the term liquidity cost equal to the final maturity of the facility. Meanwhile the volatile part is short term with a short-term fluctuating usage. For the uncertainty of the volatile part, the contingent liquidity, for which the costs should be allocated to the product, needs to be held. The behavioural analysis is performed also for other items, such as current or savings accounts.

Pricing of different products on the banking book

One of the central tenets of the FTP framework is to transfer interest rate risk and liquidity risk from the business to ALM to manage. Furthermore, FTP should cover all material business activities, incorporating all relevant liquidity costs, benefits and risks. As such, pricing of products should follow the following rules:

1. FTP should attribute liquidity and funding cost or benefits to the businesses and products to enable appropriate business decisions and to allow ALM to manage the liquidity and funding risks in an effective and consistent manner.
2. Liquidity Transfer Pricing (LTP) should consider both business-as-usual and stressed costs. Hence the liquidity profiling for FTP purposes should consider the liquidity cash flow under normal business conditions and under liquidity stress condition.
3. Cost of maintaining a liquidity reserve (or liquid asset buffer) should be allocated to the source of liquidity risk. The liquidity reserve or liquid asset requirement can be driven by internal or regulatory stress parameters including LCR or internal stress testing (e.g., Survival Horizon).
4. Regular review to ensure the LTP is appropriately calibrated.

The differences between behavioural liquidity tenor and the behavioural interest rate tenor should be captured under the FTP framework. The recent Basel III requirements for liquidity pose significant challenges on banks as it is still an open issue how to integrate the cost to comply with Basel III into the FTP framework. There are clear additional costs resulting from the implementation of the new regulatory requirements which need to be recognised and charged back to businesses in the revised FTP process. Furthermore, there is a need to enhance the FTP framework in order to effectively transfer interest rate risk and liquidity costs to the central unit. An inefficient FTP process can lead to margin compression and loss in competitiveness of a bank. Some banks employ *behaviouralisation* as a tool to manage behavioural aspects both from interest rate risk and liquidity risk perspective. The behavioural profiling provides the methodological overview on how to calculate FTP rate to reflect both interest rate risk and full liquidity costs. In addition, it shows how the liquidity profiling can be structured to include both the contingency costs and liquidity value the product is generating or consuming. This is particularly important for the products which do not have deterministic cash flows, such as current accounts. The FTP rate, in this case, needs to reflect the behaviour of the product cohort both from the interest rate risk and liquidity perspective.

Figure 5.15 shows the behaviouralisation process and its impact on FTP.

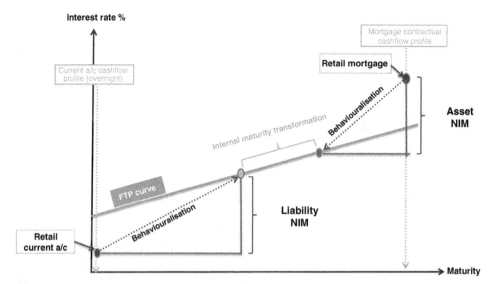

FIGURE 5.15   Behavioralisation process and FTP.
Source: own elaboration

It can be clearly seen that behavioralisation shortens the average maturity of assets and lengthens the average maturity of liabilities. Therefore, the behavioural-ised FTP rate for assets is lower than FTP for assets without behaviouralisation and, similarly, the behavioural FTP rate for liabilities is higher than FTP rate for liabilities without behaviouralisation.

The last element of the FTP framework is the Target Operating Model. One of its main objectives for the FTP is to ensure that transparency is the main principle in the FTP framework. To achieve this transparency, interest rate risk and liquidity risk need to be separated into different portfolios within treasury/ALM. As a basic rule, the banking book results can be split into the following components:

- Result of interest rate positioning and interest rate maturity transformation.
- Result from liquidity maturity transformation.
- Result from the investment book management (credit spread risk management).

Figure 5.16 shows the separation of results from interest rate risk and liquidity risk management through the FTP process. The IRR component of the FTP rate has been transferred from the business unit for central management along with the liquid-ity component which has been split from the IRR component to ensure separate man-agement of these two risk categories. In this way it is possible to understand which risk category is driving the exposure of a bank and to what extent (through sensitivity analysis).

Transparency and simplicity in the FTP framework should be an unques-tionable driver in the definition of the target operating model, as only the clear

			Jan 18	Feb 18	Mar 18	Apr 18	May 18	June 18	July 18	Aug 18
VOLUMES	**ASSETS**	Liquidity run-off	100	100	100	100	100	100	100	100	100
		Repricing run-off	100	100	100	100	100	100	100	100	100
	LIABILITIES	Liquidity run-off	−100	−100	−100	−100	−100	−100	0	0	0
		Repricing run-off	−100	−100	−100	0	0	0	0	0	0

INTEREST RATE RISK EXPOSURE ⟵   LIQUIDITY RISK EXPOSURE ⟵

Interest rate risk	Open interest risk position	0	0	0	−100	−100	−100	−100	−100	−100
	Bucket exposure	0	0	0	−8.2	−8.4	−8.2	−8.4	−8.4	−8.2
Liquidity risk	Open liquidity risk position	0	0	0	0	0	0	−100	−100	−100
	Bucket exposure	0	0	0	0	0	0	−8.4	−8.4	−8.4
Sensitivities	Shock on risk free parameter 0.20%	0	0	0	0.016	0.017	0.016	0.017	0.017	0.017
	Shock on liquidity spread 0.60%	0	0	0	0	0	0	0.05	0.05	0.05

FIGURE 5.16 The separation of results from IRR and liquidity management through the FTP process.
Source: own elaboration

methodology rules shared by every single participant in the FTP process can lead to the achievement of the strategic objectives of a bank and the correct shaping of the balance sheet. Another important aspect in the FTP governance and framework is the oversight of the incentive premium scheme and of the management overlays. A Prudential Regulation Authority (PRA) cross-firm review of the FTP practices at major UK banks revealed important issues in bank's internal transfer pricing policies and framework. One of the major issues, underlined in the PRA's review, was that banks were not separating the management overlays from their funding curve. Some banks were found to be applying different cost of funding curves to new loans and deposits to incentivise loan origination and deposit-gathering simultaneously. The PRA view is that this is a vulnerability in the FTP framework of the bank, as dampening practice skews business incentives and makes it less clear what performance is for individual products before and after any management overlay. An important point has been made, that strategic decisions need to be made acknowledging the true economics of business and not unwittingly, as a result of the inappropriate internal pricing methodologies (Cadamagnani et al., 2015). Given that the internal FTP methodologies play a key part in profit allocation within a bank and influence business lines' activities, a robust FTP regime is a must. If funding costs are underestimated, business lines offer customers cheaper loans and increase funding volumes in the mistaken belief that they are profitable. If funding costs are overestimated, business lines may mistakenly require higher customer rates to be perceived as profitable.

As already mentioned, these tools are powerful and for this reason their implementation and inclusion in the FTP framework should be well governed, documented and transparent.

The product pricing (asset *all in* rate and deposit customer rate) is not a random activity. It is based on the predetermined principles aligned with the strategic objectives of a financial institution and according to the transparent rules and methodologies. The product pricing is always based on the FTP curve, which acts as an internal product price benchmark.

Behaviouralisation concept in FTP

The overall objective of such an exercise is to construct a framework that is better defined, simple to understand, makes internal drivers of the bank's Net Interest Margin (NIM) more transparent and less volatile, and appropriately considers both the interest rate risk component for behaviouralised products and their regulatory liquidity costs. In order to summarise this concept correctly we need to diverge slightly from the IRRBB world and to focus on liquidity aspects. As emphasised by the author many times, the interrelation between those two risk categories is so strong that often it is simply not possible to speak about one risk category (IRRBB) in isolation without mentioning another risk category (liquidity).

The main challenge of the inclusion of Liquidity Coverage Ratio (LCR) and Net Stable Funding Ratio (NSFR) requirements into the FTP framework consists, in the author's view, in the fact that banks already have stress test metrics and scenarios for liquidity which, in many cases, are included in FTP. Consequently, there will be a necessity to align those metrics with LCR in the first place. Stress liquidity assumption (either internal stress liquidity risk view or regulatory view) reflects customer behaviour or product characteristics under a stress scenario(s). The net stress outflow will determine how much liquid assets (or High-Quality Liquid Assets, HQLA) a bank is required to hold in order to survive under the stress conditions. Therefore, holding liquid assets can be costly (for example, where there is a big difference between cost of funding and opportunity cost). ALM is bearing this cost for the bank. Consequently, in principle, through FTP process, this cost should be allocated back to the business in order to reflect the full and true liquidity cost of doing business. Figure 5.17 represents the contingent liquidity cost and *negative cost of carry* driven by holding HQLA. The negative cost of carry arises because the cost of funding HQLA is higher than the weighted average return on a LAB portfolio.

The stress liquidity portion will profile at the short-term stress tenor, for example Overnight, 1-Month or 2-Month, or 30-Day LCR stress outflow horizon (or 30-Day in the name-specific stress) and 60-Day in the market-wise stress horizon. Profiling the stress portion at shorter tenor will reflect a lower liquidity valuation for liability (net) outflow.

Stress liquidity assumption will be adopted from either an internal stress liquidity risk view or a regulatory view. Internal stress liquidity risk view is based on a bank's internal stress testing Survival Horizon, which models a combined (name specific and market wide) stress scenario for a period of, for example, two months. Regulatory

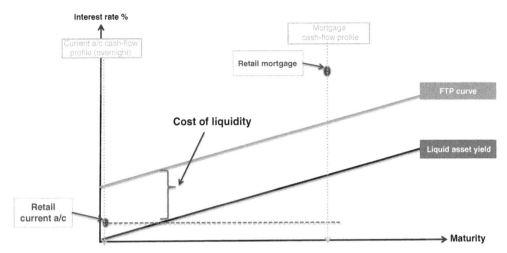

FIGURE 5.17　Contingent liquidity cost and *negative cost of carry*.
Source: own elaboration

view will be referring to Basel III LCR assumption or local regulatory requirement for 30 days stress. The guiding principle, in this approach, is to use the more binding metric between the internal stress liquidity risk view and regulatory view. It applies at a country level, product level or client/segment level and depends on the availability of sufficiently granular data.

Summarising, the behavioralisation will recognise the regulatory cost directly through the FTP rate (see Example 16) rather than charging it to the business separately.

Stable liquidity assumption (not in stress scenario) reflects the customer behaviour or product characteristic in the medium-term time horizon. It looks at the liquidity *behavioralisation* aspect which can be linked to the bank's structural liquidity risk appetite, stable funding profile, medium-term assets composition, maturity transformation and funding resource allocation. There is an internal view and a regulatory view as well. The internal view comes from the internal balance sheet modelling such as the core model of non-maturing products, actuarial study for loans (like mortgages) or bank's assets recovery assumption. The regulatory view refers to NSFR assumptions – Available Stable Factor (ASF) for liabilities and Required Stable Factor (RSF) for assets.

The stable liquidity portion, under this approach, is profiled to medium-term tenor, which is equal or higher than 1 year.

For liabilities, the 1Y point is considered to best represent the stable balance modelling for structural liquidity risk measures (like NSFR).

An extension beyond 1 year for non-maturing liabilities is considered, in this approach, as an incentive reward for balance sheet needs.

EXAMPLE 16   *Pricing NMDs taking into account regulatory costs*

The liquidity value for NMDs is calculated as a blended rate reflecting the stability factor of the product calculated by an internal model (or by applying a stability factor based on NSFR) which, in this example, is lower than the internal factor. Where the financial institution has strong evidence regarding product stability which appears to be higher than is reflected in the NSFR factor then the internal assumption should be used.

Additionally, it is assumed that the residual portion, i.e., the difference between 70%–25% = 5% is recognised 3M tenor.

Liquidity value for NMD liabilities

LCR outflow assumption	= 25%
NSFR ASF factor	= 50%
Internal core model %	= 70%

The liability is recognised with the liquidity value equal to 2Y tenor on the FTP curve (behaviouralised tenor for the product). This value also includes regulatory cost which the product is bearing due to the liquidity buffer which needs to be held against the outflow under a stress scenario (seen as the stress portion). Given that the NSFR provides an instruction related to the stability factor over 1 year, the 3-year tenor can be considered as the additional liquidity value the ALM is going to recognise for the high-quality source of funding this product represents.

The total liquidity value of this product is equal to the **blended rate:** *25%@1M FTP rate + 5%@3M FTP rate + 70%@3Y FTP rate.*

The same illustration for the asset, for example mortgages, is shown in Example 17.

EXAMPLE 17 *Pricing residential mortgages taking into account regulatory costs*

Residential mortgages

LCR inflow assumption		= 0% (assume residual tenor >1M)
NSFR RSF factor		= 65%
Behavioural maturity (including prepayments)		= 3 Y

Mortgage portion	Stress portion 0%	Residual portion 35%	Stable portion 65%
Tenor	–	1Y	3Y (Average life)

This product is charged with the liquidity costs which corresponds to 2 years tenor of the FTP curve (*35%@1Y + 65%@3Y*). Under the assumption that it is not going to expire over the next 30 days' time horizon its behaviouralisation consists of the split between the non-liquid part with a 3-year tenor (RSF) and the residual part with a liquidity tenor equal to 1 year.

As already mentioned, the liquidity profiling is meant to reflect the liquidity cost (if assets) or liquidity value (if liability). However, the FTP rate needs also to reflect the financial characteristics of the product from the interest rate risk perspective. For example, if the product reprices in line with EURIBOR 3M then the interest rate risk profiling needs to be the same, i.e., EURIBOR 3M. For the bullet fixed rate products, the interest rate risk profiling will be based on the tenor of the risk-free curve which corresponds to the maturity of the product.

The FTP profiling becomes more complex where behavioural products are concerned, for example current accounts/savings accounts (CASA). The FTP profiling has to include both the interest rate part and an adjustment for the product's liquidity value. The CASA interest rate profiling is always composed of two parts, i.e., the volatile portion of the balance which won't stay within the bank for the long term, thus it is modelled as a portion which reprices on the O/N basis (in line with the BCBS 368 requirements), and the stable portion. The stable portion is considered to be either risk sensitive (i.e., it reprices in line with the market rate), or core part, which is non-sensitive to the interest rate movements and therefore could be seen as long-term funding with the rate at 0%. This split has to be reflected in the FTP profiling. The complexity appears when the interest rate profiling is overlaid with the liquidity profiling as the total FTP rate includes internal/regulatory stressed test view (contingent liquidity cost), term liquidity value of this product (the product's stability from the liquidity perspective) and IRR behavioural model (product's rate sensitivity and its balance stability).

The FTP behaviouralisation is a methodology which attempts to capture the full (and behavioural) interest rate risk and liquidity cost/value of the product. The correct transference of interest rate risk and liquidity risk from business units to ALM is especially important in profit allocation within the bank as it directly influences business lines activities.

Additionally, the liquidity profiling encompasses the contingent liquidity costs, i.e., those which are driven by uncertainty and the stress situation. Under stress, customers' behaviour can change radically, therefore banks need to hold a liquidity buffer which protects them against unexpected cash outflows.

However, as already mentioned, holding liquidity buffers is expensive as the cost of funding them usually exceeds generated return. This contingent liquidity cost has to be allocated back to the business.

Prior to Basel III liquidity requirements, the indirect liquidity cost was allocated on a separate basis, for example once a month through a separate process. The FTP profiling allows this cost to be included in the FTP rate and to be charged back to the business upon origination of the transaction.

INTEREST RATE RISK TRANSFER UNDER FTP FRAMEWORK

The objective of Example 18 is to provide the reader with practical aspects regarding the approaches applied to transfer the IRR component from a business unit to ALM. It shows what should be considered in the transfer of the IRR component through the FTP process.

EXAMPLE 18   *Principles of transfer of the IRR component from business units to ALM*

A) FIXED RATE PRODUCTS

Fixed rate products (for the purposes of this section) are products which have a predetermined maturity and/or repricing date and are priced at a predetermined fixed rate agreed with the customer at the outset of the account (product). Additionally, fixed rate products commonly incorporate a prepayment (early redemption clause), particularly for retail products.

Common examples of fixed rate products include fixed rate loans/mortgages and term deposits.

Interest risk transfer should be achieved by:

1. Transferring the risk on a behaviourally adjusted basis (that is, including prepayment, expected pipeline drawdown, expected delinquency and any statistically justifiable behavioural adjustment to the contractual profile of the product).
2. Ensuring the business is indifferent to interest rates after inception of the product (i.e., the margin is "locked in" to ALM, and consequently the product has been fully risk transferred from the business to ALM).
3. The behaviourally adjusted profile of the product should be *"match funded"* from ALM in such a way as the profiles of the business's assets and liabilities are matched as closely as can be practically achieved.

B) FLOATING RATE PRODUCTS (E.G., TRACKER/INDEX-BASED MORTGAGES, FLOATING RATE TERM LOANS)

Floating rate products (for the purposes of this section) are products which have a predetermined maturity and/or repricing date and are priced at a predetermined fixed spread to an externally quoted, market transactable reference rate, for example LIBOR, base rate or prime rate.

In general, there are two major types of floating rate product:

1. **Tracker rate** – where the price is relative to an "externally quoted" market transactable reference rate, for example the BoE rate.
2. **Prime rate** – Products where the price is set by a bank but there is close correlation (>80%) to an external "prime" rate.

The term externally quoted refers to the rate which is set independently of a bank and is not controlled by it, and is observable by customers/the market in general.

Interest risk transfer should be achieved by:

1. Transferring risk based on the interest rate repricing tenor of the product.
2. Considering whether a behavioural adjustment is required to recognise any material change in balance based on prepayment/pipeline (etc.) up to the repricing tenor.

The effect of a behavioural adjustment is marginal when the index rate is a short-term rate, e.g., 1 or 3 months. In such circumstances, the behavioural profile of the product may be regarded as the same as the contractual profile, and consequently the FTP rate consistent with funding the entire balance at 1- or 3-month rates.

(Continued)

(Continued)

Where the index rate is for a longer term, however (e.g., 12-month LIBOR), then these effects may be more significant – particularly for a product with a short (2–3 year) maturity.

C) MANAGED RATE PRODUCTS

A managed rate product (also known as a discretionary rate product) has cash-flows which are determined solely by reference to an index rate which is set at the discretion of a bank. They also have no defined maturity date, and the index can be changed at any time by a bank (although it usually changes generally in line with the short-term external interest rate environment).

This product category includes:

- Current accounts, either interest bearing or non-interest bearing for an indeterminate period.
- Savings accounts at a changing customer rate which may/may not follow external interest rates – and remains for an indeterminate period.
- Credit cards – at a changing customer rate which may/may not follow external interest rates – and remains for an indeterminate period.

The important key aspects of these products are that they have no predetermined maturity date, and do not track/follow any external hedgeable rate. As such, there is no mitigating FTP transaction which will bring the business unit's interest rate risk exposure to zero, i.e. fully "hedged".

The behaviour of managed rate products must be measured using portfolio analysis techniques, and funding/FTP tailored to the result of that analysis. To that end, when analysing a managed rate product there are several key factors to consider:

- The core (and non-core) element of the portfolio.
- The pricing sensitivity of the product (i.e., how much of an interest rate change is passed onto the customer).
- The investment period for the element on which a bank bears all of the interest rate risk.

THE CORE/NON-CORE PORTFOLIO SPLIT

The IRR component is broken down into the following sub-portfolios:

1. The non-core element of the balance.
2. The core balance, on which the customer effectively bears the interest rate risk.
3. The core balance, on which a bank effectively bears the interest rate risk.

The financial institution needs to empirically quantify how stable the portfolio is, and how much of the balance may be relied upon to remain over different periods of time.

PRICE SENSITIVITY

Price sensitivity seeks to quantify how much of an interest rate change is passed onto the customer. Price sensitivity is influenced by many factors, including:

- External market rate, e.g., 1M LIBOR
- Client segment, e.g., Financial Institution (FI) or non-FI
- Product type, e.g., Operational Current Account (OPAC)/non-OPAC

This assessment is carried out on a qualitative and quantitative basis incorporating the experience and knowledge of business practitioners on how they would respond in specific rate move scenarios. Banks do not apply a purely quantitative approach due to distortions seen during periods of very low interest rates where price sensitivity may be understated.

A product which has a very high pricing sensitivity, for example 95%, passes almost all of the interest rate risk onto the customer. It is effectively almost a "tracker" rate product – and therefore should be primarily funded (in fact, 95% funded) at short-term interest rates if there is to be no NII volatility in the business unit. Conversely, a non-interest-bearing current account has no pricing sensitivity, i.e., the customer rate never changes. Here, the bank retains all of the NII exposure to a potential fall in short-term interest rates.

BASIS RISK QUANTIFICATION

Basis risk is not formally transferred from the business unit into the ALM, but it is instead preserved in the business unit, and monitored/managed by ALCO. Since the correlation of prime rates to short-term interest rates is high (by definition) then the LIBOR-linked funding from ALM may be regarded appropriate interest rate risk transference to ALM, with ALM accordingly including 1-month or 3-months funding in its interest rate ladders, i.e., transfer to ALM is based on LIBOR. The residual exposure (for a correlation of less than 100%) is usually not regarded as a material source of interest rate risk over the full economic cycle. However, it is a relevant exposure at a given point in time which should be monitored and measured (in absolute mismatch terms) by ALCO.

HOW IS BASIS RISK MANAGED?

Part of the ALCO remit is to identify, monitor and report basis risk on a notional basis i.e., the volume of customer assets and liabilities which are prime linked, but LIBOR (or equivalent) funded.

(Continued)

(Continued)

> The following high-level practice is a minimum expected standard for the consideration of basis risk in portfolios of loans through the ALCO process.
>
> Basis risk should be identified, measured, monitored and controlled by the ALCO. Typical risk reports included in ALCO documentation should include:
>
> - The 2-year historical time series of prime rates versus short-term interest rates.
> - The historical correlation of prime rates with short-term interest rates.
> - The notional volume of customer assets which are prime linked.
> - The notional volume of customer liabilities which are prime linked.
> - The market rate used into ALM (e.g., 1M LIBOR, 3M LIBOR).
> - Confirmation that the exposure has been considered, and in the light of the correlations, volumes of asset and liabilities involved that the exposure is not regarded as material.
> - Confirmation of the ALCO's net risk appetite for basis risk (articulated usually in the form of the maximum notional mismatch).
> - Confirmation of the ALCO's strategy for reducing any basis risk exposure it deems inappropriate in the medium term.
>
> Prime rate linked products are funded into ALM at the associated short-term market rate (e.g., 1M LIBOR). Accordingly, 1M LIBOR rates will be applied in its FTP and incorporated as such into ALM's interest rate ladder structure.
>
> In order to demonstrate the appropriateness of applying short-term market rates as the FTP for prime rate linked products, ALCO should satisfy itself that the correlation (similar to pricing sensitivity) of their local prime rate to those short-term rates is adequately high. Where the observed correlation over the last 2 years of backtested data (with minimum monthly data of, for example, 24 observations) demonstrates a correlation over 80% then the prime rate may be regarded as adequately reflective of short-term interest rates.

Concluding this section, it has to be highlighted that it not always possible to transfer IRR from a business to a central unit and, in some cases, there is a residual exposure left at the business unit. In particular, this is the case when the product is transferred on a "proxy" benchmark basis (product priced off on prime rate and short-term market rate used as proxy).

The pricing of products from the IRR perspective should differ from products at a floating rate and products at a fixed rate (short-term benchmark versus swap rate) and the behavioural/automatic options should be incorporated in the FTP rate.

An incorrect FTP methodology and framework leads to margin compression and losses at the bank level, therefore the FTP process should be an integrated part of the IRRBB framework. The losses are driven not only by the residual exposure which is not managed by ALM but also by the fact that an improper FTP process shapes the balance sheet in the wrong direction and erodes its value.

COMPREHENSIVE AND FEASIBLE IRRBB STRATEGY

Some people understand IRRBB as a regulatory buzzword, but it isn't just the term that regulators are focused on in the BCBS Standards. IRRBB has an impact on a bank's capital base as it is a potential threat to capital, and interest movements create sensitivity to the NII. A proper framework creates an opportunity for the income generation both under a near- and a long-term horizon. Mismanagement can be very expensive and have implications across different areas of a bank. In the first place, both incorrect assumptions and risk underestimation can affect the P&L of the treasury, which is responsible for ALM profitability. Secondly, it affects P&L results of the business units through FTP rates and FTP margins. Thus, the correct IRRBB assumptions impact the product profitability assessment through the interest income split.

IRRBB is one of the risk categories which falls under the ALM remit. As already mentioned, many times throughout this book, proactive management of IRRBB can be beneficial for a bank.

The first challenge consists in defining an IRRBB strategy and steering approach which is consistent with the bank's business model. In order to develop a comprehensive and feasible IRRBB strategy and steering approach ALCO has to define the extent to which the business model will rely on generating earnings through rate transformation, i.e., funding long-term repricing assets with short-term repricing liabilities and determining the level of maturity transformation which stabilises a bank's NII. Finally, there is always certain risk capacity allowed to run maturity transformation. Alongside this there is another set of questions the bank needs to answer regarding the steering approach to achieve the strategy defined. A common practice consists of providing a treasurer with a certain amount of discretion in diverging from the benchmark cash-flow profile. The steering approach is shown in Figure 5.18.

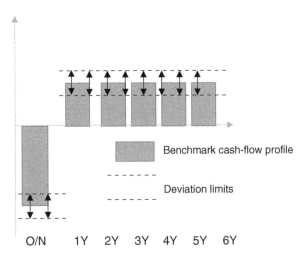

FIGURE 5.18   Steering approach in driving the IRRBB strategy.
Source: own elaboration

In other words, the steering approach is a trade-off between the Net Interest Income (NII) and Economic Value of Equity (EVE) metrics.

MANAGEMENT OF THE INTRAGROUP INTEREST RATE RISK

A common practice to deal with the interest rate risk within the group, where the subsidiary does not have its own tools to manage the interest rate risk exposure and funding risk, is to apply the principle of the match funding process. The match funding process relates mainly to items at a fixed rate (which raises the structural interest rate risk exposure) and consists in providing funding between entities within the same group, which replicates the amortisation profile of assets in order to "close" the exposure to both funding and interest rate risk. Such a structure allows the immunisation of the time bucket sensitivity and potential impact on EVE.

EXAMPLE 19   *Intragroup hedging and funding*

Bank Y funds itself through money market products and customer deposits. One of its subsidiaries is launching a new product, i.e., fixed rate assets with the average maturity of 4 years. The newly originated product will have a monthly capital repayment, i.e., it will be amortising over its life. The parent company of the subsidiary, i.e., Bank Y, will be providing funding to the subsidiary for the newly originated business. This situation is presented in Figure 5.19.

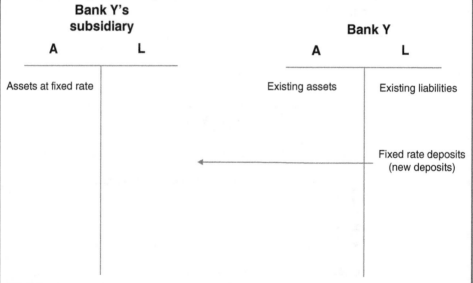

FIGURE 5.19   Intragroup funding between Bank Y and its subsidiary before putting in place the funding agreement.
Source: own elaboration

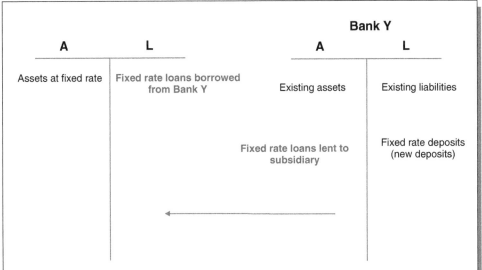

FIGURE 5.20 Intragroup funding between Bank Y and its subsidiary after the funding agreement is put in place.
Source: own elaboration

Bank Y is expected to gather new deposits in order to cover the funding needs of its subsidiary. However, this funding cannot be provided directly to the subsidiary given that these are two separate entities. In order to set up the appropriate funding structure, the intragroup funding agreement between two entities needs to be put in place. Figure 5.20 presents the intragroup funding between Bank Y and its subsidiary under an intragroup funding agreement. Under the agreement Bank Y will provide funding at a fixed rate to the subsidiary at an agreed price.

As a result, Bank Y will provide a funding facility to the subsidiary and will charge it for the arm's length cost of funds plus a servicing fee. Given the nature of the new business (assets at fixed rate) the provided funding will aim to replicate the amortisation profile of fixed rate assets in order to fully immunise the subsidiary exposure to funding and interest rate risk. This is known as the **match funding** process. Figure 5.21 shows the transfer of funding risk and interest rate risk between two entities.

(Continued)

(Continued)

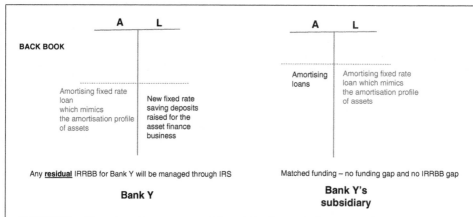

FIGURE 5.21 Transfer of interest rate risk and funding risk from subsidiary to Bank Y.
Source: own elaboration

On the consolidated basis the Group (Bank Y plus its subsidiary) will take on mismatching in terms of IRRBB and funding risk, i.e. the Group is exposed to IRRBB and funding risk as the intragroup loan will disappear as shown in Figure 5.22. However, the subsidiary does not have any open risk position because the risk is "closed" through matched funding.

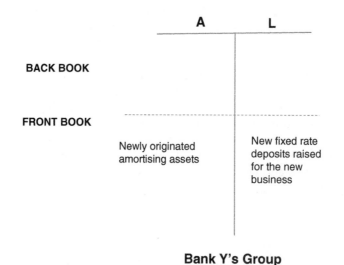

FIGURE 5.22 The Group's (Bank Y and its subsidiary) exposure to IRRBB and funding risk.
Source: own elaboration

CHAPTER 6

IRRBB stress test, reverse stress test and ICAAP

IRRBB STRESS TESTING

Stress testing plays a crucial role in a bank's IRRBB framework. The common market practice is to perform a number of stress tests for IRRBB to inform management decisions as well as to size its financial safeguards. Stress testing provides the supplementary, important tool for understanding the IRRBB positioning, it feeds into the assessment of the capital adequacy for IRRBB. The stress test is performed with an annual frequency and is aligned with the regulatory requirements for stress testing (in Europe EBA/GL/2018/04). In particular, it attempts to address the interrelation between liquidity risk and interest rate risk under an integrated approach that aims to assess the impact resulting from changes in liquidity profile and interest rates on a bank's risk profile.

This chapter describes one of the market practices for stress testing. It combines two approaches. The backbone of the stress testing is the event driven approach where the scenario is formulated based on the historical events and the way those events might affect the relevant risk factors and current IRRBB position of a bank, as of the end of the financial year (historical interest rate shocks). However, the historical scenario is usually complemented by the adoption of additional stresses, for example either the regulatory stress testing applied by the regulator or the bank's own hypothetical scenarios, which it considers plausible, and which aims to stress its IRRBB position.

IRRBB stress testing methodology

One of the potential methodologies used for stress testing, based on BCBS Standards, is to assess an interest rate exposure from two different perspectives under each constructed scenario, i.e.:

- The *earnings perspective* which focuses on the impact interest rate changes have on a bank's near-term earnings. Changes in the yield curve, due to the stress scenario, have a direct impact on a future net interest income. Hence, interest rate risk analysis from an earnings perspective will focus on assessing the earnings effects that may arise from changes in market interest rates.

■ The economic value perspective, which focuses on the impact interest rate changes may have on the economic value of the future cash flows, and thus on the economic value of both interest rate book and capital. The present economic value is affected by changes in interest rates in two ways: by the change in future interest cash flows included in the calculation, and by the change in the discount rates of all future cash flows used for this calculation.

The first step in the design of the IRRBB stress test is to analyse the IRRBB sub-categories which are material for a bank. For example, many banks have material exposure to the option risk which arises because customers have the right, but not obligation, to influence the timing and the magnitude of the cash flows of deposits. Sight deposits and savings deposits, whose maturities are uncertain for a financial institution, entail a risk for the banking book in the form of the right of withdrawal (in relation to the assumed maturity). In the environment of negative or low interest rates banks often have automatic options embedded in the banking book, for example implicit zero floor on the deposits side or embedded floor in corporate loans.

In such a case, the stress test is designed to cover the impact of both automatic and behavioural options under different scenarios.

Banks have NII sensitivity resulting from a maturity mismatch between on balance sheet assets and liabilities instruments. It is one of the principal forms of interest rate risk faced by an institution and is analysed through gap analysis and the calculation of the ΔNII under a stress scenario.

Equally important is to assume changes related to the CASA elasticity and volatility under stress scenarios.

The second step in the design of the IRRBB stress test is to calculate the IRRBB metrics according to a bank's IRRBB policy and adopted in the IRRBB measurement framework under each stress scenario (Figure 6.1).

The outcome of the stress test provides a valuable picture of the potential vulnerabilities of the financial institution and plays an important role in the definition of mitigation actions.

IRRBB stress test description

The section below provides the reader with a practical example of the stress test scenarios for IRRBB.

IRRBB metric	Threshold
ΔNII/expected NII	$\geq -10\%$
ΔEVE/OF under six scenarios	$\geq -10\%$
PV01/OF	$\geq 0.5\%$

FIGURE 6.1 Illustrative example of IRRBB metrics in a bank.
Source: own elaboration

EXAMPLE 20 *Stress testing framework – Bank Z*

SCENARIO 1: REGULATORY STRESS TEST SCENARIOS – 2017 IRRBB STRESS TEST

The ECB stress testing exercise involved six hypothetical interest rate shocks applied at the beginning of the observation period. Multiple interest rate shocks allow the exploration of potential weaknesses in the IRRBB positioning of a bank. Various IR shocks complement the standard +/–200 bps shocks. Apart from the parallel shocks, the steepener and flattener shocks were introduced in the analysis. The steepener scenario represents the increased trend in the long end of the curve in conjunction with a compression in short-term rates. Meanwhile the flattener reflects a shock similar to the 2008 Lehman episode, i.e., inversion of the curve. The aforementioned scenarios were calibrated according to the BCBS Standards methodology (BCBS, 2016).

In addition to BCBS, there is another interest rate shock purely based on the trend in the term structure of interest rates calibrated as per the end of the year 2010. The 2010 year is considered to represent the environment just before the acute phase of the Euro Area crisis. Risk dimensions for IRRBB are tested using two complementary approaches: instantaneous shock for EVE changes and 3-year time horizon for ΔNII changes. This scenario is purely based on the shifts of interest rates and does not include any changes in the behaviour of customers.

The starting point for this scenario is determined both as of December 2018 for the static scenario and taking into consideration the simulated structure of the banking book after origination of fixed rate mortgages over a period of 3 years.

THE REASON FOR THE PROPOSAL OF THE STRESS SCENARIO

The objective of this stress test, carried out by the ECB in 2017, aimed to assess the bank's exposure to interest rate risk after years of low interest rates and the potential impact of the automatic options in a negative rates scenario. The ECB has identified IRRBB as one of the key risks for banks in a low interest rates environment.

POTENTIAL IMPACT OF STRESS TEST ON BANK Z'S (IRRBB) POSITION

The risk dimensions are tested according to two complementary approaches: EVE changes under instantaneous interest rate shocks and changes in NII under a 3-year time horizon. The time horizon, for change in NII, is the main difference between the timing applied to shocks which Bank Z applies on a monthly basis for the IRRBB measurement purposes (instantaneous shock for the ΔEVE and

(Continued)

under 1-year time period for ΔNII) and the stress test described analysed (instantaneous for the ΔEVE and 3-year time period for ΔNII).

The *"Parallel up"*, *"Flattener"* and *"End of 2010"* scenarios envisage the increase in the interest rates across the whole term structure by different magnitudes. Meanwhile, the *"Parallel down"* and *"Steepener"* scenarios envisage a decrease in rates (the *"Steepener"* scenario envisages a decrease in the short rates). Bank Z, as of 31 December 2018, has EUR 2.4bn of RSA of which EUR 1.8bn has the interest rate option (floors) embedded into the contract (considered a short automatic option position). The floor is set at the level of 0% or, in some cases, 1%. Bank Z funds itself through EUR 1.96bn of deposits by retail and customer clients. For commercial reasons, for all deposits, Bank Z has decided not to cut the interest rate below the zero level.

Given that assets, for the purpose of the IRRBB measurement and stress testing, have longer behavioural maturity than liabilities, the negative implicit option value on the liabilities side, driven by negative interest rate environment, is fully compensated by the positive option implicit value on the asset side.

This situation significantly limits the exposure of Bank Z to the downward movement of the term structure of interest rates. Under the regulatory stress test scenario, the baseline curve is negative for the Euro currency up to the 4Y tenor, therefore it is expected that the application of this scenario results in the floors being *in the money* up to 4Y maturity. This significantly reduces the impact of the downward movement shock scenario. Bank Z is positioned, as of December 2018, both in terms of EVE metric and NII metric, to benefit from the upward movement of the curve.

The main impact is expected to be seen on the NII position as it includes the new business generation over the time horizon of 3 years. This is driven by important changes in the structural position of the banking book and its risk profile which Bank Z is going to undertake over the period of analysis, i.e., 3 years.

Therefore, under the 2017 stress scenario, the position of Bank Z is going to be affected because of two important factors:

1. The negative interest rate environment and the existence of floors embedded in the banking book both on the asset side (contractual floors) and on the liability side (implicit zero floor on deposits). In the scenario where the interest rates go down the value of floors is going to increase for assets. However, the existence of the short option position on the liabilities side will partially offset the increased economic value of options on the assets side.

2. The structural changes in the banking book position over the next 3-year time period, i.e. the change in the business model of Bank Z.

SCENARIO 2: HISTORICAL STRESS TEST SCENARIO "94 BOND CRISIS – THE GREAT BOND MASSACRE" – BANK Z

In January 1994, the 34th month of economic expansion, bond yields were historically low, and inflation seemed negligible. But within seven short months of that promising start, something fairly unusual happened: 1994 became the year of the worst bond market loss in history. A sharp, unexpected rise in interest rates wrecked the value of bond portfolios and turned profitable trades into money losers. Yields on 30-year treasuries jumped 200 bps in the first 9 months of the year hammering investors and financial firms. This stress began with a modest 25-basis point base rate hike in February which pushed short-term interest rates up by 2.25% by the end of the year. The total losses suffered by bond investors totalled over US$1 trillion. The acute phase of the crisis lasted 9 months.

THE REASON FOR THE PROPOSAL OF THE STRESS SCENARIO

The aim of this scenario is to assess the impact of the rise in interest rates on the treasury book portfolio, and the potential consequences on the counterbalancing capacity of Bank Z. Bank Z intends to apply this scenario on an instantaneous basis for the calculation of the ΔEVE, and 3 years for the ΔNII. It considers this scenario important given that, over the time horizon of 3 years, the treasury book is expected to grow further.

POTENTIAL IMPACT OF STRESS TEST ON BANK Z'S (IRRBB) POSITION

Where interest rates increase, the embedded automatic options become *out of the money* and their implicit value equals to zero. However, Bank Z is structurally positioned to benefit from the rates increase, therefore under this scenario it is expected to see a positive change in terms of the EVE (Bank Z has a net liability position on the medium-to-long part of the curve). Instead, it is likely to see a negative impact in terms of the ΔNII impact driven by the expected change in the banking book structure (it is going to invest in long-term assets at a fixed rate funded by short-term repricing liabilities) and, consequently, negative impact on the risk profile of Bank Z over the time of analysis (3 years). Additionally, there is an expectation of an increase in the cost of funds under this scenario, driven by the necessity of adjusting the administered rate on deposits which is partially compensated by the increase in income generated by the corporate loans side. The strong negative impact is expected to be seen on the treasury portfolio where market value is going to decrease significantly. Changes in the value of a fixed-rate asset held under available-for-sale accounting are immediately reflected in the statement of financial position through equity but it will only affect the income statement once the asset is sold. Given that forward starting interest rate swaps were used (rather than spot starting swaps), the 94-crisis scenario mostly impacts the short-term bonds as they are not hedged through the forward starting swaps.

(Continued)

SCENARIO 3: ADVERSE STRESS SCENARIO – BANK Z

Bank Z has decided to adopt the assumptions applied by ECB in its adverse macro-economic scenario designed for the purpose of a stress testing exercise run in 2018. It requires Bank Z to use the outcome of the adverse macro-financial scenario for variables such as interest rates. In addition, further assumptions such as impact on Bank Z asset growth, deposit base and liquid asset price, are taken into account under this scenario in line with the definition of this stress test.

This is a severe stress scenario which aims to assess the impact on the IRRBB and Bank Z's capacity to survive without, as an unintended consequence, rendering the underlying business model unsustainable. Given that the scope of this stress test scenario is the interest rate in the banking book, the scenario focuses on the risk coming from changes in interest rates. However, there is a strong argument for incorporating changes to assumptions over the depositor volumes as well as changes to prices.

The time horizon of the scenario is 3 years, and includes changes in the banking book structure that Bank Z is going to adopt over the 3-year time period.

The adverse scenario is based on the adverse market-financial scenario stress performed by the ECB in 2018. In the market-wide scenario banks were required to apply the assumptions related to the changes in GDP, exchange rates, interest rates and credit spreads for their banking book items in order to estimate what the potential impact might be on profits or capital. The base of the adverse scenario is deep recession, which results in a large fall in asset prices in global financial markets and an upward shift and steepening of the yield curve across all jurisdictions. The economic slowdown would result in an increase in unemployment across the European Union. An increase in unemployment and an increase in long-term bond yields would also negatively affect clients' creditworthiness and their ability to service their mortgage. Moreover, a prolonged period of low economic activity combined with a rise in corporate bond yield would increase credit risk for non-financial corporates. This would lead to a higher cost of financing and an increased level of Non-Performing Loans (NPL). There is also an increased withdrawal of the funds by non-financial bodies which causes an EU-wide uniform shock to interbank money market rates.

This scenario represents a severe global market shock, with a sharp increase in long interest rates in Europe. Overall, long-term interest rates in Europe would be higher by 85 bps in 2019. Money market rates (3-month interbank offered rate) in all EU countries would rise by 55 bps, reflecting higher credit premium for banks. Under this scenario there is no change in the monetary policy adopted by the central bank.

THE REASON FOR THE PROPOSAL OF THE STRESS SCENARIO

This scenario envisages positive rates for the duration of the stress. Consequently, it is important for Bank Z to test how its business model in the environment of the positive and rising rates is going to impact its IRRBB position (Bank Z is operating in a negative rates environment). The introduction of this scenario aims to analyse the impact on the key IRRBB metrics and to build an awareness among senior management on the impact which a rising and positive interest rates environment may cause. This is especially important in light of the current position of Bank Z in terms of the exposure to the following sub-risk categories:

(a) Gap risk.
(b) Option risk – behavioural and automatic options.
(c) Basis risk – understood herein as the difference in the velocity of refixing between market rates on assets (EURIBOR and GBP LIBOR) and administered rate liabilities.

THE POTENTIAL IMPACT OF THE STRESS TEST ON BANK Z'S (IRRBB) POSITION

Tighter financing conditions would contribute to a reduction in the availability of funding and would contribute directly to a contraction in economic activity. It is assumed that Bank Z would respond by tightening lending standards on loans to the corporate sector. The global shock is going to affect the customer's confidence and it is expected that some depositors will decide to transfer their savings to other banks. In order to make up for the lost funds Bank Z will have to sell off the portion of its liquidity buffer. For the purpose of the adverse scenario this cannibalisation of current accounts is estimated at 10%. The remainder of CASA have seen an increase of the client rate by 30 bps. Additionally, Bank Z has observed an increased level of NPL which amounts to 5% of the total pool of corporate assets and the loss in the value of the treasury book of 20%.

   In a positive and rising interest rates environment the interest rate options (floors) embedded in corporate loans are not exercised (*out of the money*) as the contractual floor is set at 0%. Therefore, it is expected to see, under this scenario, the increased sensitivity of the ΔEVE and ΔNII.

(Continued)

STRESS TESTING TABLES

1. 2017 IRRBB stress test

TABLE 6.1   Interest rates movement under 2017 IRRBB stress test for EUR currency.

	Interest rate shock size (%) for EUR				
Maturity	Parallel up	Parallel down	Steepener	Flattener	End-2010
ON	2.00%	−2.00%	−1.62%	2.00%	0.72%
1W	2.00%	−2.00%	−1.61%	1.99%	0.76%
2W	2.00%	−2.00%	−1.60%	1.97%	0.76%
1M	2.00%	−2.00%	−1.57%	1.95%	0.85%
3M	2.00%	−2.00%	−1.47%	1.84%	0.94%
6M	2.00%	−2.00%	−1.33%	1.69%	1.01%
12M	2.00%	−2.00%	−1.07%	1.42%	1.11%
15M	2.00%	−2.00%	−0.95%	1.30%	1.17%
21M	2.00%	−2.00%	−0.73%	1.08%	1.31%
2Y	2.00%	−2.00%	−0.63%	0.98%	1.38%
3Y	2.00%	−2.00%	−0.29%	0.63%	1.69%
4Y	2.00%	−2.00%	−0.03%	0.36%	1.95%
5Y	2.00%	−2.00%	0.18%	0.14%	2.14%
7Y	2.00%	−2.00%	0.46%	−0.15%	2.34%
8Y	2.00%	−2.00%	0.56%	−0.25%	2.39%
9Y	2.00%	−2.00%	0.63%	−0.33%	2.40%
10Y	2.00%	−2.00%	0.69%	−0.39%	2.42%
11Y	2.00%	−2.00%	0.74%	−0.43%	2.43%
12Y	2.00%	−2.00%	0.77%	−0.47%	2.44%
13Y	2.00%	−2.00%	0.80%	−0.50%	2.47%
14Y	2.00%	−2.00%	0.82%	−0.52%	2.43%
15Y	2.00%	−2.00%	0.84%	−0.54%	2.43%
16Y	2.00%	−2.00%	0.85%	−0.55%	2.42%
17Y	2.00%	−2.00%	0.86%	−0.56%	2.40%
18Y	2.00%	−2.00%	0.87%	−0.57%	2.38%
19Y	2.00%	−2.00%	0.88%	−0.58%	2.37%
20Y	2.00%	−2.00%	0.88%	−0.58%	2.35%
21Y	2.00%	−2.00%	0.89%	−0.59%	2.33%
22Y	2.00%	−2.00%	0.89%	−0.59%	2.30%
23Y	2.00%	−2.00%	0.89%	−0.59%	2.28%
24Y	2.00%	−2.00%	0.89%	−0.59%	2.25%
25Y<T	2.00%	−2.00%	0.90%	−0.59%	2.23%

Source: EBA IRRBB stress test 2017

TABLE 6.2 Interest rates movement under 2017 IRRBB stress test for GBP currency.

Maturity	Interest rate shock size (%) for GBP				
	Parallel up	Parallel down	Steepener	Flattener	End-2010
1M	2.50%	-2.50%	-1.88%	2.33%	0.31%
3M	2.50%	-2.50%	-1.75%	2.20%	0.31%
6M	2.50%	-2.50%	-1.56%	2.01%	0.33%
12M	2.50%	-2.50%	-1.22%	1.67%	0.38%
15M	2.50%	-2.50%	-1.06%	1.51%	0.45%
21M	2.50%	-2.50%	-0.78%	1.23%	0.60%
2Y	2.50%	-2.50%	-0.65%	1.10%	0.69%
3Y	2.50%	-2.50%	-0.21%	0.66%	1.07%
4Y	2.50%	-2.50%	0.14%	0.31%	1.39%
5Y	2.50%	-2.50%	0.40%	0.05%	1.62%
7Y	2.50%	-2.50%	0.78%	-0.33%	1.95%
8Y	2.50%	-2.50%	0.90%	-0.45%	2.05%
9Y	2.50%	-2.50%	1.00%	-0.55%	2.14%
10Y	2.50%	-2.50%	1.08%	-0.63%	2.20%
11Y	2.50%	-2.50%	1.14%	-0.69%	2.24%
12Y	2.50%	-2.50%	1.19%	-0.74%	2.29%
13Y	2.50%	-2.50%	1.22%	-0.77%	2.31%
14Y	2.50%	-2.50%	1.25%	-0.80%	2.34%
15Y	2.50%	-2.50%	1.27%	-0.82%	2.36%
16Y	2.50%	-2.50%	1.29%	-0.84%	2.37%
17Y	2.50%	-2.50%	1.30%	-0.85%	2.38%
18Y	2.50%	-2.50%	1.31%	-0.86%	2.39%
19Y	2.50%	-2.50%	1.32%	-0.87%	2.40%
20Y	2.50%	-2.50%	1.33%	-0.88%	2.40%
21Y	2.50%	-2.50%	1.33%	-0.88%	2.41%
22Y	2.50%	-2.50%	1.34%	-0.89%	2.41%
23Y	2.50%	-2.50%	1.34%	-0.89%	2.41%
24Y	2.50%	-2.50%	1.34%	-0.89%	2.41%
25Y<T	2.50%	-2.50%	1.34%	-0.89%	2.42%

Source: EBA IRRBB stress test 2017

(Continued)

2. Historical stress test scenario "94 bond crisis – the great bond massacre"

TABLE 6.3 Interest rates movement under 94 bond crisis scenario for EUR, GBP and USD currencies.

	EUR	USD	GBP
O/N	0.38%	2.75%	0.56%
O/N–1mth	0.38%	2.75%	0.56%
1–3mth	0.48%	3.13%	1.24%
3–6mth	0.73%	3.44%	1.90%
6–9mths	1.18%	3.66%	2.33%
9–12mths	1.63%	3.88%	2.75%
1–1.5yr	1.76%	3.90%	3.36%
1.5–2yr	1.97%	3.61%	3.28%
2–3yr	2.17%	3.31%	3.19%
3–4yr	2.27%	3.20%	3.18%
4–5yr	2.37%	3.02%	3.10%
5–6yr	2.32%	2.88%	3.04%
6–7yr	2.26%	2.73%	2.97%
7–8yr	2.21%	2.68%	2.92%
8–9yr	2.15%	2.62%	2.86%
9–10yr	2.10%	2.30%	2.77%

Source: own elaboration

3. Adverse stress scenario

TABLE 6.4 Interest rates movement under adverse scenario for EUR currency.

SWAP rates EUR	Adverse rates
1M	0.22
3M	0.34
1Y	0.50
2Y	0.66
3Y	0.82
5Y	1.14
7Y	1.45
10Y	1.92
20Y	2.39
30Y	3.00

Source: EBA market adverse stress scenario, 2018

ICAAP – ASSESSMENT OF THE INTERNAL CAPITAL TO COVER IRRBB

Before the BCBS Standards had been published banks had quite a lot of flexibility to come up with the amount of internal capital to cover IRRBB risks. Many banks based their approach to ICAAP based on the *Value at Risk* metric at a certain point in time. The maximum loss meant the need for potential capital coverage against risks.

The revised final guidelines on the management of interest rate risk, arising from non-trading book activities published on 19 July 2018, revised the methodological approach to ICAAP and set up the new rules to be followed. In particular, it proclaimed that institutions should base the contribution of IRRBB to the overall internal capital assessment taking into account both the impact on the ΔEVE and ΔNII. The ΔEVE must be assessed under a number of interest rate scenarios at a certain point of time. The overall level of capital should be commensurate with both the institution's actual level of risk and its risk appetite, i.e., it represents the highest negative impact which the institution can face in terms of the ΔEVE. There is the need for a buffer, in terms of ΔNII impact, to cover an immediate loss where there is an adverse movement in interest rates. This, and additional requirements, are clearly formulated by the regulator.

Institutions must consider:

- internal capital held for risks to economic value that could arise from adverse movements in interest rates and internal capital needs arising from the impact of rate changes on future earnings capacity and the resultant implications for the internal capital buffer levels;
- the size and tenor of internal limits on IRRBB exposure, and whether these limits are reached at the point of capital calculations;
- the effectiveness and effective cost of hedging open positions that are intended to take advantage of internal expectations of the future level of interest rates;
- the sensitivity of the internal measures of IRRBB to key or imperfect modelling assumptions;
- the impact of shocks and stress scenarios on positions priced with different interest rate indices (basis risk); and
- the drivers of the underlying risks.

Furthermore, the Final Report states, to calibrate the amount of the internal capital requirement for IRRBB, institutions should use a measurement system and a range of interest rate shocks and stress scenarios that are adapted to the risk profile of the institution in order to quantify the potential scale of any effects under adverse conditions. In considering whether an allocation of internal capital should be made in respect of IRRBB, an institution should take into account the following:

- The potential for actual losses to be incurred under stressed conditions, or because of secular changes in the market environment, e.g. where it might become necessary to liquidate positions that are intended as a long-term investment to stabilise earnings.

- The fluctuation of net interest income, the strength and stability of the earnings stream, and the level of income needed to generate and maintain normal business operations. Institutions with a high level of IRRBB that could, within a plausible range of market scenarios, result in losses, in the revision of the dividend policy, or a decrease in business operations, should ensure that they have sufficient capital to withstand the adverse impact of these scenarios.
- Institutions should consider internal capital buffer adjustments where the results of their stress testing highlight the potential for reduced earnings (and therefore reduced capital generation capacity) under stress scenarios.
- The actual levels of net interest income achievable under different scenarios (i.e. the extent to which margins are wide enough to absorb volatility arising from interest rate positions, changes in the cost of liabilities).

This revised approach is an attempt towards an overall standardisation of the methodological approach to IRRBB. This is also a big opportunity as outcomes achieved by different banks are easily comparable and introduce the standardised methodological approach toward risk management in general.

EXAMPLE 21 *ICAAP – allocation of internal capital for IRRBB – Bank BL*

INTRODUCTION

The objective of this part of the document is to assess the amount of the internal economic capital that needs to be considered sufficient to cover all IRRBB related risks (repricing risk, option risk and yield risk) to which Bank BL is currently exposed.

The approach adopted by Bank BL, for the calculation of the capital add-on for IRRBB, follows the following steps:

Step 1. Calculation of the impact on EVE as of 31 December 2019 (cut-off date) under the six regulatory interest rate shocks for each material currency applying both contractual and behavioural views.

Step 2. Calculation of the NIIS as of the cut-off date under parallel scenarios of +/−200 bps for each material currency and applying both contractual and behavioural view.

The worst result (the highest potential loss), in terms of the impact on the EVE for each material currency is considered as a driver in the capital assessment process for IRRBB. Additionally, Bank BL takes into account the earnings sensitivity under a parallel shock scenario and allocates a capital buffer to cover potential earnings losses for each material currency.

The calculation methodology is based on the Bank BL IRRBB measurement process as per its IRRBB policy.

IRRBB METHODOLOGICAL OVERVIEW

The methodology used for the assessment of Bank BL exposure to IRRBB is based on the change in the Economic Value of Equity (ΔEVE) measure augmented by the impact of the automatic interest rate options embedded into the banking book products.

The ΔEVE is calculated under six regulatory interest rate shock scenarios and split by material currencies (EUR and GBP):

– parallel shock up

– parallel shock down

– steepener shock (short rates down and long rates up)

– flattener shock (short rates up and long rates down)

– short rates shock up

– short rates shock down

The worst result, in terms of ΔEVE, provides an indication of the potential negative impact on the EVE under adverse changes in the term structure of interest rates. The ΔEVE is calculated under both a contractual and behavioural view. However, for ICAAP purposes, only the behavioural view is analysed (under the behavioural view Bank BL shows the worst result in terms of the impact on the IRRBB metrics).

Using this methodology, EVE results across currencies are aggregated under a given interest rate shock scenario. The methodological approach adopted focuses on the IRRBB sub-risk categories such as option risk and gap risk, which are considered material for Bank BL.

Bank BL is exposed to the option risk as a result of the existence of the automatic and behavioural options in its banking book structure. The impact of the automatic options is measured under a number of interest rate shocks and the change in the options value is added to the final ΔEVE number (as per the methodological approach presented in the BCBS Standards 2016). In addition, it monitors the overall impact of the behavioural options on the IRRBB position through the comparison of IRRBB metrics under behavioural and contractual analysis, i.e., under the assumption that Non-Maturing Deposits (NMDs) are modelled versus the assumption that they simply follow contractual maturity.

The gap risk (often known as the repricing risk) arises because the rate of interest paid on liabilities increases before the rate of interest received on assets or reduces on assets before liabilities. The extent of gap risk depends on whether

(Continued)

changes to the term structure of interest rates occur consistently across the whole yield curve (parallel risk) or differently by period (non-parallel risk). Bank BL measures and controls gap risk through the repricing gap technique and the analysis of the net mismatch for every time band and split by material currency. As per the regulatory guidelines, this is the simplest technique for measuring a bank's interest rate risk exposure to the short end interest rate risk. Additionally, it performs the net interest income sensitivity analysis (herein NIIS). The gap risk is measured through the application of the parallel shift to the interest rate curve and the calculation of the change to the Net Interest Income (ΔNII).

INTERNAL CAPITAL ASSESSMENT METHODOLOGY

In the Pillar 2 approach Bank BL examines the impact on the key IRRBB metrics (ΔEVE and NIIS) caused by the potential movement in the term structure of interest rates. This analysis is split by the material currencies (EUR and GBP) in which Bank BL operates.

The starting point for the assessment of the capital adequacy methodology is the trend in position in terms of both economic value of equity and the net interest income sensitivity under a number of predefined interest rate shocks analysed as of December 2019.

EVE SHOCKS

The change in EVE is calculated for six regulatory shocks and for all material currencies. Additionally, it is calculated both under contractual view (no behaviouralisation of the banking book) and behavioural view (items are behaviouralised).

EARNINGS IMPACT

In the second stage, Bank BL has additionally analysed both the impact on earnings under a parallel down scenario (Bank BL is exposed to the downward movements on the short end of the curve) and the impact on economic value of equity, under the more severe shock Bank BL is exposed to, over a 4-month time period (from November 2019 to February 2020). The purpose of this detailed analysis is to show the trend in the movements of key IRRBB metrics over time to ensure the conservative and appropriate capitalisation for IRRBB risks.

Based on the analysis, Bank BL decided to allocate internal capital to cover the worst outcome between ΔEVE and ΔNII within a 4-month time period. Given the same direction of the exposure in terms of both metrics (Bank BL is exposed to downward movements of the curve) there is no need to sum the result for ΔNII with the ΔEVE result.

REVERSE STRESS TESTING

The objective of the reverse stress test is to undermine the IRRBB position of a bank in terms of the breach of one or more of its key IRRBB metrics (for example, ΔNII and ΔEVE).

Thus, the starting point of the analysis is to find such a shift (positive or negative), and its magnitude, so that a bank faces the significant impact on its equity position or net income (which will be translated into the impact on its equity) which undermines its position. The likelihood of such scenario is the factor assessed by the end of the analysis.

Additionally, the analysis aims to test the potential action plan which senior management might need to undertake in order to overcome the negative impact driven by the reverse stress scenario.

CHAPTER 7

IRRBB governance and framework

According to BCBS Standards banks should have a clearly defined risk appetite statement (RAS) for IRRBB, that should be articulated in terms of the risk to both **economic value** and **earnings**. The RAS should be approved by the governing body. Banks must implement policy limits set by the governing body that target maintaining IRRBB exposure consistent with their risk appetite. Aggregate risk limits should be applied on a consolidated basis and as appropriate, at the level of individual affiliates.

RISK APPETITE STATEMENT (RAS)

Risk appetite is the level of risk that an organisation is prepared to accept in pursuit of its objectives, before action is deemed necessary to reduce the risk. It is a crucial part of the Risk Appetite Framework (RAF).

All banks are exposed to the risk of an adverse change in financial situation, resulting directly or indirectly from fluctuations in the level or volatility of market prices of assets and liabilities, and from adverse movements in interest rates, credit spreads and FX rates. This can affect their profitability, Net Interest Income (NII) and capital measures.

The key element of RAS is the assessment of the main market risks that financial institutions are exposed to:

(a) Foreign Exchange Risk
(b) Interest Rate Risk in the Banking Book
(c) Credit Spread Risk in the Banking Book

Figure 7.1 shows the market risk metrics to which a bank is willing to commit, limiting its appetite to risk and its risk capacity, and the buffer above risk appetite at which an escalation process kicks off, as described within the governance section of the RAF.

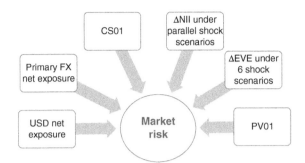

FIGURE 7.1 Market risk metrics governed by RAS and RAF.
Source: own elaboration

EXAMPLE 22 *Risk Appetite Statement (RAS) of Bank X*

Bank X holds a portfolio of treasury securities (held mainly as HQLA) which give rise to the Credit Spread Risk in the Banking Book (CSRBB). Exposure to movements in securities prices can be broken down into the exposure to interest rates and to spreads which fluctuate on a daily basis as a result of the changes in the market demand and liquidity for certain securities.

Bank X's funding strategy is primarily from customer deposits and it deploys them into the corporate assets at floating rates. As part of an asset diversification program, Bank X is planning to invest in a fixed rate mortgage product which will change its IRRBB profile. Additionally, Bank X has successfully launched a new deposit product in late 2020 (30-day savings accounts) profiled at the short term.

Bank X originates a moderate volume of loans and funding in foreign currencies (currencies other than the Euro) which are not always offset, creating an exposure to the FX risk.

FOREIGN EXCHANGE RISK

Overall Risk Appetite: **Low**

Bank X does not seek to gain competitive advantage by actively taking foreign exchange risk and seeks to hedge any foreign currency positions that arise through the normal course of business unless these are insignificant. Additionally, it has no appetite for operating FX trading positions, either internally or for customers.

Therefore, Bank X has a low risk appetite for foreign exchange risk. Internal limits are also in place to help monitor and manage this risk.

(Continued)

(Continued)

Bank X currency of domicile for all operating entities of the regulated Group is EUR. It only classifies USD as a material currency it has FX exposure to. The definition of material currencies for FX risk follows the specifications provided in the BCBS Standards, April 2016, as those FX currencies that account for more than 5% of total risk sensitive assets or liabilities. Therefore, GBP is not deemed to be material by Bank X. All other FX exposures also fall well below the 5% threshold.

INTEREST RATE RISK IN THE BANKING BOOK RISK APPETITE

Overall Risk Appetite: **Medium**

Exposure to the interest rate risk in the banking book is differentiated by various sub-categories such as:

- Gap risk (repricing risk)
- Option risk
- Basis risk
- Yield risk (exposure to the parallel and non-parallel interest rate curve shifts)

Bank X therefore assigns the following risk appetite to each of the various aspects of interest rate risk:

i. Option risk

Risk Appetite: **Low**

Bank X is exposed to option risk as a result of the existence of both automatic and behavioural options in its banking book.

It measures the impact of the automatic options under a number of interest rate shocks. There is limited risk in terms of automatic options given that these are long option positions, and they are executed only at the favour of Bank X. There are interest rate floors explicitly embedded in a portion of the Bank X asset base – typically either at 0% or at 1% – so in a low interest rate environment the optionality of the portfolio should naturally be positive. In the current interest rate environment, the implicit floor at zero on Bank X liabilities (deposits) cannot be ignored, but Bank X has of course no intention of selling interest rate options outright.

The behavioural option risk is strategically mitigated by the Group through the inclusion of the new savings account with the notice period of 3 months, which is meant to protect Bank X from the potential withdrawal of savings deposits before their contractual notice period expires. However, the residual portion of funding represents the behavioural liabilities without predetermined maturity. Consequently, appropriate modelling of the behavioural characteristics of this product class will be crucial in light of the future investment and commercial strategy of Bank X.

Bank X will apply prudential behavioural assumptions to this product category. Thereafter, once it gathers sufficient time series to perform statistical analysis of the product, it will apply the result of the behavioural modelling assumptions observed.

In addition, Bank X monitors on a monthly basis the overall impact of the behavioural options on its IRRBB position (behavioural versus contractual analysis).

ii. Gap risk

Risk Appetite: **Medium**

The gap risk arises when the rate of interest paid on liabilities increases before the rate of interest received on assets, or reduces on assets before liabilities. The extent of gap risk depends on whether changes to the term structure of interest rates occur consistently across the whole yield curve (parallel risk) or differently by period (non-parallel risk).

Bank X measures and controls the gap risk through the repricing gap and the analysis of the net mismatch for every time band and by material currency. Bank X is aware of the impact, in terms of gap risk, driven by the introduction of new products as part of the diversification strategy.

iii. Basis risk

Risk Appetite: **Low to Medium**

Exposure to basis risk is inherent in Bank X's business and can arise either directly or indirectly. In some cases, it may be possible to reduce this exposure by executing hedging, but it is not always possible to eliminate the risk entirely.

Bank X measures the extension of the basis risk by monitoring different benchmarks of assets and liabilities by every time bucket. By default, the strategy in terms of the minimisation of the exposure to the basis risk consists of strategic approaches to match the risk factors on the asset and liability side as much as possible.

Given the diversification strategy, Bank X is aware of the potential exposure to basis risk driven by potential hedges that may be needed to be put in place. In order to mitigate the exposure to basis risk the bank is going to enhance its monitoring and perform the rate sensitivity analysis of its administered rate liabilities in order to match risk factor as much as possible.

(Continued)

(Continued)

iv. Yield risk

Risk appetite: **Medium**

As Bank X is maturing, it is reasonable to assume more stickiness characteristics in its deposit products. Adoption of the diversification strategy, encouraged by the Regulator and adopted by Bank X, will imply the potential exposure to the yield risk which is understood here as the potential negative impact on its equity due to the parallel and non-parallel movement of the interest rate curve.

Bank X monitors the change in the Economic Value of Equity (ΔEVE) of the banking book on a monthly basis, applying a number of shocks, different in size and direction, to the interest rate curve.

In particular it monitors:

- Steepener
- Flattener
- Short up
- Short down
- Parallel up
- Parallel down
- An internal scenario (reviewed and approved by the Board Risk Committee)

In addition, it applies the dual view (behavioural and contractual) to understand the impact of the extension of the repricing terms of structural liabilities on the exposure to the yield risk. The yield risk will also be driven by the fixed rate bonds which Bank X is already acquiring as part of its treasury yield enhancement strategy.

In order to mitigate this risk category, Bank X is proposing to lower the ΔEVE and PV01 limits and introduce a dynamic metric in terms of VaR to be able to monitor the bond portfolio. The yield risk will also be mitigated through derivatives.

IRRBB risk appetite limits

The table below describes the interest rate risk appetite limits for IRRBB. Limits which are set up in terms of negative numbers reflect the potential loss Bank X may face rather than the variability of the metric itself.

Interest rate risk in the banking book	Risk appetite level	Notification threshold	Risk appetite limit
ΔNII under parallel shock of 100 bps/expected Total net income as per budget forecast	Low to medium	≥ −15.0%	≥ −20.0%
ΔEVE under 7 shock scenarios to Tier 1 capital (better of contractual and behavioural)	Low to medium	−5.5%	−10.0%
PV01 to Tier 1 capital	Low to medium	≥ −0.10%	≥ −0.2%

v. Net Interest Income (NII) risk

NII under parallel shock scenarios related to the expected NII under 1-year time horizon

This metric focuses on the impact interest rate changes might have on Bank X's near-term earnings. Thus, the risk analysis from an earnings perspective will focus on assessing the earnings effects that may arise from changes in market interest rates using a 1-year time measure.

The magnitude of the limit has been based on the analysis of the historical exposure of Bank X to the repricing risk. In particular, it is based on the fact that Bank X has always been strongly asset sensitive, i.e., exposed to the downward movement of the short part of the curve.

Although this exposure is limited by the existence of the automatic interest rate options which protect against the margin compression risk, and the potential loss in the NII, the limit of −20.0% against the expected total net income as budget allows for seeking out of new product opportunities and diversification of the funding base. This limit also defines Bank X's appetite for accepting variability of the profit driven by fluctuations in interest rates.

vi. Economic Value of Equity (EVE) risk

EVE under seven shock scenarios related to Tier 1 capital

This metric focuses on the impact interest rate changes might have on the economic value of future cash flows and thus on the economic value of both the interest rate book and capital. The limit is based on the better of both the behavioural and contractual basis.

(Continued)

(Continued)

The behavioural view is driven by the regulatory landscape which requires the bank to include the ALM assumptions in the analysis of the IRRBB position of the bank. One of the main assumptions is related to NMDs. Both BCBS Standards and EBA recommend that banks allocate the items without deterministic maturity according to their expected life, rate sensitivity and balance volatility. This is additionally supported by the fact that regulatory reporting is set up on that basis.

vii. PV01 related to Tier 1 capital

Bank X assesses total time bucket sensitivity through the 1 bp upward shift in the interest rate curve based on the baseline interest rate scenario.

Where $\Delta PV > 0$, it means the present value of the banking book increases after a parallel up 1 bp shift in the interest rate curve. On the other hand, $\Delta PV < 0$ means the PV is going to decrease as a result of the parallel shock up by 1 bp.

Credit spread risk in the banking book

Risk Appetite: **Low to Medium**

Bank X defines credit spread risk as the potential loss in value of a security which is caused by changes in credit spreads while the counterparty's rating remains the same. The credit spread of the issuer, for the corresponding term, is quantified through the difference between the security's market yield at the valuation date and the risk-free rate.

The credit spread is an important market risk category for Bank X given the existence of a significant amount of treasury securities, mainly held for HQLA purposes.

Appendix 1: Example of IRRBB policy aligned with the requirements of BCBS Standards

The first part of the IRRBB policy introduces the importance of IRRBB for a bank, the main IRRBB concept and IRRBB subcategories a bank is exposed to. For example, the introduction part could look like the following:

Interest Rate Risk in the Banking Book (IRRBB) refers to the current or prospective risk to Bank A's net economic value (EV), capital and earnings arising from adverse movements in interest rates that affect the banking book positions. Bank A measures the following sub-types of IRRBB:

(a) *Gap risk which arises from the term structure of banking book instruments, and describes the risk arising from the timing of instruments' rate changes. The risk to Bank A arises when the rate of interest paid on liabilities increases before the rate of interest received on assets or reduces on assets before liabilities. The extent of gap risk depends on whether changes to the term structure of interest rates occur consistently across the whole yield curve (parallel risk) or differently by period (non-parallel risk). Bank A measures and controls the gap risk through the repricing gap and the analysis of the net mismatch for every time band, and by material currency, i.e., currency which accounts for more than 5% of total risk sensitive assets or liabilities.*

(b) *Basis risk describes the impact of relative changes in interest rates for financial instruments that have similar tenors but are priced using different interest rate indices (bases). It arises from the imperfect correlation in the adjustment of the rates earned and paid on different instruments with otherwise similar rate change characteristics. Bank A measures basis risk by monitoring different benchmarks of assets and liabilities by every time bucket. By default, Bank A's strategy, in terms of the minimisation of the exposure to the basis risk, consists of an attempt to match the risk factors on the asset and liability side as much as possible.*

(c) *Option risk arises from option derivative positions explicitly embedded within the contractual term of assets which aim to protect Bank A from a decrease in the interest rates and from the optional elements embedded in customer deposits providing them with a contractual right to withdraw their balance. Bank A has decided not to charge negative rates to depositors; therefore, it is considered as an implicit short option position on the liability side. Bank A measures and monitors the impact which interest rate options might have on the changes in the economic value of equity of the banking book through their full evaluation under base and shocked scenarios.*

(d) *Yield risk – the risk arising from unanticipated non-parallel shifts of the yield curve such as steepening, flattening, inverted curve and parallel shifts on the medium-to-long part of the curve – herein this is understood as the exposure to the structural interest rate risk in the banking book.*

     In addition to the aforementioned risks that can arise from changes to the level and structure of interest rates Bank A measures material currency mismatches.

Both the Basel Standards (BCBS, 2016) and the EBA Final Report (2018) define clearly the requirement of measuring Credit Spread Risk in the Banking Book (CSRBB). This is mainly due to the fact that banks hold a significant portfolio of liquid assets under HQLA to meet regulatory requirements for liquidity.

Consequently, the IRRBB policy also needs to cover this new risk category. For example, it could introduce the CSRBB as follows:

Credit Spread Risk in the Banking Book (CSRBB) is a related risk that banks need to monitor and assess in their interest rate risk management framework. CSRBB refers to any kind of asset/liability spread risk of credit-risky instruments that is not explained by IRRBB and by the expected credit/jump to default risk, and in particular to the risk to EV represented by a change in the market spreads associated with the bank's assets.

     Bank A defines credit spread risk as a potential loss in the value of a security which is caused by changes in credit spreads while the counterparty's rating remains the same. The credit spread of the issuer, for the corresponding term, is quantified through the difference between the security's market yield at the valuation date and the risk-free rate. The credit spread is an important market risk category for Bank A given the existence of ttreasury securities, mainly held for liquidity purposes.

The IRRBB policy defines the purpose and scope of the policy. For example, it could read as follows:

The purpose of this Interest Rate Risk Policy (the Policy) is to establish principles, standards, and controls that govern the ongoing management of the Interest Rate Risk in the Banking Book (IRRBB) and Credit Spread Risk in the Banking Book (CSRBB). In particular the document aims to set up the framework around:

(a) *Identification of IRRBB and CSRBB*
(b) *Measurement of IRRBB and CSRBB*
(c) *Control and monitoring of IRRBB and CSRBB limits*
(d) *Reporting of IRRBB and CSRBB*

(e) *Stress testing of IRRBB and CSRBB*
(f) *Capital assessment for internal calculations of Pillar 2 requirements*

The policy is designed to ensure compliance with all national and international standards and guidelines that are applicable to these activities, in particular BCBS 368 Standards and EBA Guidelines and their subsequent updates.

The CSRBB methodological approach and framework is covered by this IRRBB policy and practice guide.

The section below discusses in more detail the responsibilities for the IRRBB measuring, monitoring, behavioural assumptions and controls around the IRRBB framework.

Board ownership

The IRRBB and CSRBB strategy is governed by the Board of Directors which delegates the management of Bank A's overall strategy with reference to the IRRBB and CSRBB to the Asset and Liability Management Committee (ALCO).

The Board of Directors, in line with Bank A's Risk Appetite Statement (RAS), has a medium appetite for exposure to the IRRBB and low to medium for CSRBB. ALCO has a mandate to maintain the bank's IRRBB exposure at levels that are in line with the Board of Directors' risk appetite towards IRRBB and CSRBB and expressed through high-level limits included in the RAS. Therefore, the residual exposure should be limited as specified in the Interest Rate Risk limits section of this policy.

ALCO management of IRRBB

The more detailed IRRBB and CSRBB limits are reviewed and approved by ALCO at least on an annual basis or more frequently where such an update appears appropriate. The detailed specifications of the IRRBB and CSRBB reports are agreed by ALCO.

The IRRBB and CSRBB reports are required to be presented to ALCO on a monthly basis. ALCO determines, even if all risk measures are within limit, whether it is comfortable with the bank's exposure to interest rate movements and taking into account the bank's senior management view of the market outlook. ALCO has the remit to impose other "what if" scenarios and to request changes in parameters and assumptions to see the effect on model outputs.

Risk management of IRRBB

The Bank A Risk Function owns the IRRBB policy and IRRBB/CSRBB methodologies. The Risk Function is responsible for the model update, calibration and back testing. In addition, it must assure ALCO that the appropriate IRRBB and CSRBB models have been reviewed and validated by an independent unit on at least an annual basis.

It is the responsibility of the Bank's Risk Function to ensure that any updates in the IRRBB/CSRBB framework are promptly reflected in the IRRBB policy, metrics and regular reporting as they are approved by ALCO.

The Internal Audit function is responsible for periodic and thematic reviews of this Policy in order to assess, review effectiveness and adherence to this Policy.

Treasury management of IRRBB

The treasurer is responsible for the management of IRRBB/CSRBB according to the prevailing interest rate risk strategy as set by ALCO and subject to the IRRBB/CSRBB limits.

In order to manage its interest rate risk, Bank A may establish swap lines with counterparties that enable it to execute derivatives transactions approved for this purpose.

While the accounting treatment of hedge instruments is clearly defined and leaves no scope for discretion, in many cases it is possible under hedge accounting rules to select from a range of options for accounting treatment of the assets and liabilities being hedged. Any such decision should be made by ALCO or within constraints (such as a maximum unhedged amount) to be defined by it.

The next section of the IRRBB policy goes into the methodological details of the IRRBB framework. For example, it could start with the description of interest rate shocks applied by a financial institution for IRRBB measurement purposes. The example below is a description of interest rate shocks according to the BCBS Standards.

In order to produce a quantitative estimate of IRRBB, it is necessary to assume a shock to current interest rate levels which would allow the change in EV or earnings, and ultimately the effect on equity, to be computed. The size and shape of the shock determine the measured outcome and is the key consideration in the IRRBB framework of Bank A.

Bank A applies seven interest rate shock scenarios to capture parallel and non-parallel gap risks for Economic Value of Equity (EVE) and two prescribed interest rate shock scenarios for Net Interest Income Sensitivity (NIIS). These scenarios are applied to measure the IRRBB exposures in each currency for which the bank has material positions.

In addition, Bank A quantifies and monitors the time bucket sensitivity through its PV01 profile described in the following sections.

Bank A has adopted an approach recommended under BCBS Standards (BCBS Standards, April 2016) and EBA Final Guidelines (EBA Final Report on management of interest rates risk, July 2018) for the interest rate shocks methodological approach.

Interest rate shocks

Under this approach, IRRBB is measured by means of the following six interest rate shocks:

- parallel shock up
- parallel shock down
- steepener shock (short rates down and long rates up)
- flattener shock (short rates up and long rates down)
- short rates shock up
- short rates shock down

As part of these market scenarios Bank A has set up an additional historical interest rate shock.

One of the most important parts, in the author's view, is the section related to the behavioural assumptions which a bank applies to its banking book. There has to be a clear description related to the following items:

– Non-Maturing Deposits (NMDs)

– Early prepayment of fixed rate assets

– Early termination of fixed rate deposits

– Treatment of pipeline

– Treatment of Non-Performing Loans

The example below is a description of the IRRBB section related to NMDs.

Allocation of Non-Maturing Deposits (NMDs)

From a risk perspective, the allocation of Non-Maturing Deposits (NMDs) to maturity buckets according to a gap profile is particularly important, especially because these positions are used to hedge an institution's economic exposure.

The following steps have been applied in order to allocate the NMDs to the corresponding time buckets:

1) Segmentation of the NMDs *NMDs are segmented into retail and wholesale categories. Retail deposits are defined as deposits placed with a bank by an individual person. Deposits made by small business customers and managed as retail exposures are considered as having similar interest rate risks to retail accounts and thus can be treated as retail deposits (provided the total aggregated liabilities raised from one small business customer are less than Euro 1.0 million).*

Retail deposits should be considered as held in a transactional account when regular transactions are carried out in that account (for example when salaries are regularly credited) or when the deposit is non-interest bearing. Other retail deposits should be considered as held in a non-transactional account.

2) Split between the stable and non-stable part of NMDs *Bank A distinguishes between stable and non-stable NMDs. The non-stable part consists of customers' balances which cannot be relied upon to remain with the bank for an extended period of time. This portion of NMD is allocated to the O/N time bucket or the time bucket which corresponds to the length of contractual maturity of notice accounts.*

The stable NMD portion is the portion that is found to remain undrawn with a high degree of likelihood. Core deposits are the proportion of stable NMDs which are unlikely to reprice even under significant changes in the interest rate environment. The remainder constitutes non-core NMDs. By definition, this sub-portfolio is 100% correlated to short-term interest rates. For IRRBB purposes Bank A allocates the stable non-core part to the O/N time bucket. In the case of notice accounts, non-stable and non-core parts are assigned to time buckets corresponding to their notice period.

The core balances, defined as those that are not rate-sensitive, can best be represented as providing fixed-rate funding to which a term maturity can be applied. In order to reflect the bank's risk profile characteristics in the best way possible it should attempt to perform its own statistical approach based on the behavioural analysis of the past behaviour of the customer base. Where the behavioural modelling analysis provides adequate analysis of NMDs the bank can propose, via ALCO, to adopt the result of the internal analysis.

The figure below summarises the split between the stable and non-stable part of NMDs applied by Bank A.

Split of NMDs

3) Determination of the average life of the product In order to estimate the economic life of NMD products, Bank A performs its own analysis of the decay profile of the portfolio over a certain time horizon (for the sake of statistical significance a minimum 7 years of data is typically expected).

Average life modelling assigns the life of the product by tracking the closing behaviour of the customers' accounts. This is done through tracking the decaying of the number of accounts. This represents a variation to the approach prescribed in the BCBS Standards document and is driven by the bank's willingness to pursue a more conservative approach in terms of the assumption of the average life of NMDs.

The analysis of the decay profile is done through the following approach:

Collection of the account level data and formation of the "triangle": The "triangle" is a form of representing the account level data such that the continued presence of the number of accounts opened in one month can be tracked through different age buckets. It gives the remaining number of accounts for a given age bucket for a given opening month.

Calculation of the mortality ratio for each age bucket: The mortality ratio is defined as the number of accounts closed at that age to the number of accounts that were alive at the beginning of that. All the mortality rates for each age bucket together tell how fast (or slow) the accounts closed.

Computation of the average life of accounts: Once the mortality rates are determined, it is possible to track the percentage of accounts remaining at each age.

Bank A has allocated the average maturity of 4.5 and 4 years for the retail nontransactional and wholesale NMDs respectively.

Under different scenarios, a distinction is typically made between interest rate sensitivity to falling and rising interest rates (different interest rate scenarios cause different outcomes for the deposit volatility and sensitivity). This is known as the dynamic approach in the IRRBB methodological framework as opposed to the static one. In order to show the impact of a change in market interest rates on the volume of positions with uncertain maturities, depending on the interest rate scenario, the effects on interest rate income are typically simulated. Consequently, under the dynamic approach the interaction between rate changes and behaviour is analysed.

Finally, the core section of the IRRBB policy describes the methodology which is used by a financial institution in measuring and managing IRRBB. The section below shows an example of the methodological section of the IRRBB policy.

IRRBB KEY METRICS AND MEASUREMENT PROCESSES

IRRBB measurement

Bank A looks at the IRRBB exposure from three different perspectives:

- *The earnings perspective which focuses on the impact interest rate changes might have on a bank's near-term earnings. After all, changes in the yield curve have a direct impact on future net interest income. Hence, interest rate risk analysis from an earnings perspective will focus on assessing the earnings effects that may arise from changes in market interest rates.*
- *The economic value perspective which focuses on the impact interest rate changes might have on the economic value of the future cash flows and thus on the economic value of both interest rate book and capital. The discounting factors must be representative of a risk-free zero-coupon rate or, alternatively, the rate to which market spreads have been added. An example of an acceptable yield curve is a secured interest rate swap curve or overnight index swap.*
- *Changes in Mark to Market (MtM) of the treasury book.*

IRRBB calculations

The main objectives of the IRRBB measurement process consists of the following:

- *Calculation of the NII is performed under parallel interest rate scenarios and a predefined holding period (known as a Gapping Period) – 12 months and 24 months.*
- *Calculation of the EVE sensitivity under six regulatory and one internal interest rate scenarios.*

- *Calculation of the time bucket sensitivity through a shift in the interest rates curve upward by 1 bp.*
- *Assessment of the gaps in repricing and the direction of the overall exposure of Bank A to the movement of interest rates.*
- *Assessment of the bank's exposure to the basis risk through refixing gap analysis.*

Additional metrics implemented with reference both to the IRRBB and CSRBB involves:

- *Calculation of the maximum potential loss on the treasury portfolio through the calculation of the parametric Value at Risk metric.*
- *Calculation of the CSRBB on the asset portfolios through the estimation of the impact the widening credit spread would have on the asset price.*

The next section provides methodological details related to the calculation of main IRRBB metrics applied to the banking book and described in the IRRBB policy. However, though it may seem to be a repetition of concepts already discussed in Chapter 2, the intention is to show the practical application of these concepts in the daily management of IRRBB in a small bank.

Gap analysis

Bank A uses the maturity gap as the technique for measuring a bank's interest rate risk exposure and the base for the calculation of the IRRBB metrics. It distributes interest-sensitive assets (RSA), interest-sensitive liabilities (RSL) and Off-Balance Sheet (OBS) positions into the 19 time bands according to their maturity (if fixed rate) or time remaining to their next repricing (if floating rate).

To evaluate earnings exposure, RSL in each time band are subtracted from the corresponding interest RSA to produce a repricing gap for that time band.

Using the maturity gap method, Bank A oversees its overall position to the interest rate risk through the monitoring of the total gap amount under the horizon period of 1 year. From a practical standpoint it monitors the direction of the total gap (known as directional gap) and its magnitude.

Changes in expected earnings (earnings-based) measure

The building blocks for constructing an earnings-based (NII) measure are the aggregated notional repricing cash flows of assets and liabilities for the 19 time buckets. This section describes the methodology for the NII volatility calculation using a simplified approach.

A cash flow in a certain time bucket could consist of several positions with different fixed terms that reprice in that time bucket. Therefore, it is in principle impossible to determine precisely the interest rate after repricing, since it will depend on the tenor of the single instrument. However, for parallel interest rate shocks, the precise repricing term does not matter since for parallel shocks the yield curve is shocked equally at all tenors. In addition, the shock to the forward rates will be equal to the shock to the yield curve. Therefore, it does not matter at which rate a position will reprice when calculating the change in NII. This is because the change in NII is calculated by taking the difference between a baseline and a shocked interest rate scenario, and the only variable that changes between the two scenarios is the shock magnitude that is added to the risk-free component.

In order to calculate the change in the NII due to the parallel interest rate shock, Bank A allocates the Risk Sensitive Assets (RSA) in each time band and subtracts the Risk Sensitive Liabilities (RSL) to produce a repricing gap for that time band. This gap can be multiplied by an assumed change in interest rates to yield an approximation of the change in net interest income that would result from such interest rate movement.

The bank calculates the NII in two parallel interest rates scenarios:

1. For EUR currency by +/–200 bps
2. For USD currency by +/–250 bps

It is important to highlight that this approach is designed to generate interest rate sensitivities (in other words the difference between earnings projections in stressed versus base cases) rather than the base case valuations or earnings projections themselves.

The model assumes that all instruments are accounted for on an accrual basis and that their book value is par. As such it also ignores second-order effects such as the pull-to-par behaviour of assets whose book prices are materially different from their par amount.

Changes in the Economic Value of Equity (EVE) (economic based) measure

EVE measures the theoretical change in the net present value of the balance sheet excluding equity. The measure therefore depicts the change in equity value resulting from an interest rate shock. With this method, the value of equity in alternative stress scenarios is compared with the value in a base scenario. This base interest rate scenario is the present value of the assets less liabilities in the current interest rate environment. All cash flows from on-balance sheet and off-balance sheet interest rate-sensitive items in the banking book may be included in the computation.

The market value of equity is computed as the present value of asset cash flows, less the present value of liability cash flows, without including assumptions on the interest rate sensitivity of equity. The balance sheet is then revalued under the alternative interest rate scenarios and the difference between the value of equity in the base scenario and the alternative scenario is calculated.

The accuracy of the valuation of the balance sheet positions is extremely dependent upon the cash flows calculated and the discount rate used. Theoretically the discount rates used should match the duration and risk of the cash flows. In the model there is the assumption that the cash flows in certain time buckets are discounted with the rates at the mid-point of the time bucket.

There is also an assumption related to the fact that the timing of the cash flows and their size do not differ in the various scenarios as a result of customer behaviour.

In reality, there is a specific relationship between the interest rate scenario and the extent of prepayment and growth of deposits. The cash flows are discounted by the risk-free curve (without including the commercial spreads).
The benefits of the EVE model are:

- *interest rate risk is measured in terms of economic value;*
- *it enables basis and yield curve risk as well as convexity to be measured properly.*

The disadvantages of the EVE model are:

- *it is a static method in the sense it shows a snapshot in time of the risk based upon the current portfolio or balance sheet composition;*
- *it cannot make allowance for the market valuation of future (forecast) growth in existing or new business activities.*

Calculation of the EVE measure   *The gain or loss in economic value of equity $\Delta EVE_{i,c}$ in scenario i and currency c is calculated as follows:*

Under each scenario i, all notional repricing cash flows are slotted to the respective time bucket $k \in \{1, 2, \dots, K\}$. Within a given time bucket k, all positive and negative notional repricing cash flows are netted to form a single long or short position, with the cancelled parts removed from the calculation. Following this process across all time buckets leads to a set of notional repricing cash flows $CF_{i,(k)}$, $k \in \{1, 2, \dots, K\}$.

Net notional repricing cash flows in each time bucket k are weighted by a continuously compounded discount factor: $DF_{i,c(tk)} = exp(-R_{i,c(tk)} \cdot t_k)$ that reflects the interest rate shock scenario i in currency c and where tk is the midpoint of time bucket k. This results in a weighted net position, which may be positive or negative for each time bucket. The discount factors represent the risk-free rate (OIS curve).
These risk-weighted net positions are summed to determine the EVE in currency c under scenario i (excluding automatic interest rate option positions which the Group might have).

$$EVE_{i,c} = \sum_{k=1}^{K} CF_{i,c}(k) * DF_{i,c}(t_k) / DF_{0,c}(t_k)$$

The EVE in currency c under base scenario is calculated as:

$$EVE_{0,c} = \sum_{k=1}^{K} CF_{0,c}(k) * DF_{0,c}(t_k) / DF_{0,c}(t_k)$$

EVE in currency c associated with the base scenario is equal to the principal. This is driven by the model assumption to map instruments as zero coupons, consequently it is a better approximation to assume they have a par value rather than to assume they behave as a real zero-coupon instrument.

Finally, the full change in EVE in currency c associated with scenario i is obtained by subtracting $EVE_{0,c}$ from the EVE under shocked interest rate term structure $EVE_{i,c}$ and by adding the total measure for automatic interest rate option risk $KAO_{i,c}$ as follows:

$$\Delta EVE_{i,c} = \sum_{k=1}^{K} CF_{i,c}(k) * DF_{i,c}(t_k) / DF_{0,c}(t_k) - \sum_{k=1}^{K} CF_{0,c}(k) * DF_{0,c}(t_k) / DF_{0,c}(t_k) + KAO_{i,c}$$

In this regard, if $\Delta EVE_{i,c} > 0$ then the economic value of the banking book is going to increase. Meanwhile, where it is $\Delta EVE_{i,c} < 0$ Bank A faces a reduction in its economic value.

$KAO_{i,c}$ is an add-on for the calculation of the change in value of the automatic interest rate options, whether explicit or embedded.

Time Bucket Sensitivity Analysis (PV01)

Sensitivity analysis is a method for calculating the change in the present value of items due to a shift in the interest rates curve. The sensitivity (ΔPV or PV01) of the transaction is calculated as the difference between its Present Value (PV) determined with the current market rates and its present value under a 1 bp shock in interest rates scenario (PV_{shock}).

The traditional approach consists of positioning cash flows, fair value and sensitivity at the date at which the flow is expected to occur (according to its contractual or modelled maturity).

Bank A assesses the time bucket sensitivity through the 1 bp upward shift in individual rates that makes up the interest rate curve based on the baseline interest rate scenario. In normal circumstances the overall PV01 of Bank A's portfolio will be closely approximated by the sum of the individual time bucket sensitivities.

Where $\Delta PV > 0$ it means the PV of the banking book increases after a parallel up 1 bp shift in the interest rate curve. On the other hand, $\Delta PV < 0$ means Bank A's banking book PV is going to decrease as a result of the parallel shock up by 1 bp.

Automatic options measurement

Bank A has a significant number of automatic Interest Rate Options (IROs) which are explicitly embedded in corporate loans on the asset side. Therefore, it is a holder of those options (a long option position). It also has a short option position as the result of the (implicit but still automatic) zero floor on the interest rates paid on retail deposits.

The IROs aim to limit the exposure to the decrease in interest rates through the application of floors. According to the BCBS Standards, in order to calculate the change in economic value of the banking book under interest rate shocks, those options have to be stripped out from the host contract and evaluated separately through full evaluation under the base and shocked scenarios described hereafter.

The subsequent change in the value of options is added to the change in the economic value of the banking book for every interest rate shock and material currency. The option value change is given by:

■ *An estimate of the option value to the option holder, given:*

– Yield curve in currency c under shocked interest rate scenario i;
minus:

■ *The value to the option holder given the yield curve in currency c at the valuation date.*

In a positive interest rate environment, the Black 76 model is typically used to price the vanilla interest rate options such as floors, caps and swaptions. However, given that the majority of the Group's floors are embedded in the loan contracts which are denominated in Euro currency, and at the moment short-term interest rates are negative, it is impossible to apply the Black formula to derive the full options value (time plus implicit value) through the standard model. Consequently, under the negative interest rates environment Bank A intends to apply the Bachelier model (known also as the model under normal distribution assumption). The normal model allows valuation of options with negative strikes and negative forward rates.
The following formula needs to be applied to calculate the value of each floorlet.

$$P = e^{-rT} \left[(K - F) \times N(d_1) + \sigma \times \sqrt{T} \times n(d_1) \right]$$

and

$$d_1 = \frac{(F - K)}{\sigma \times \sqrt{T}}$$

where:

■ *F is the forward rate, K is the strike level, σ is the annualised absolute volatility of the underlying rate and T is the time to expiration in years.*

In addition, $N(d_1)$ represents the cumulative normal distribution function and $n(d_1)$ the standards normal density function. The sum of all floorlets for every option contract provides the value of the floor.

Bank A needs to include in the calculation of its IRRBB metrics:

■ *Intrinsic value of the long and short automatic option position for NIIS calculation purposes.*
■ *At least intrinsic value of the long and short automatic option position for ΔEVE calculation purposes.*

IRRBB RISK APPETITE LIMITS

Bank A's risk appetite for IRRBB is set on the basis of the amount of Tier 1 affected by adverse interest rate movements and interest earnings volatility Bank A is willing to assign to such risk. The core part of the banking book items such as NMDs will be allocated at a term to the extent that can be statistically supported and confirmed by internal modelling and expert judgment.

The exact parameters for risk appetite are reviewed at least annually. Bank A must adhere to the approved limits in place to limit its risk, and risk positions must be managed to remain within these limits.

IRRBB limit allocations must be presented to ALCO and must be consistent with the following requirements:

- *There must be exposure monitoring established for ΔEVE, ΔNII, PV01, CR01 on a behavioural basis.*
- *The IRRBB limits, for ΔEVE, ΔNII are set in terms of negative numbers, indicating in this way the potential loss it is facing.*

IRRBB ESCALATION AND REPORTING PROCESS

The following metrics must be monitored and reported to ALCO on a monthly basis and should not exceed the allocated limits:

- *NII sensitivity (ΔNII/total budget net income)*
- *EVE sensitivity (ΔEVE/Tier 1)*
- *PV01*
- *CS01*

In addition to the above metrics the Group monitors:

- *Repricing gap for the banking book items*
- *Refixing gap for the items indexed to different risk factors and material currencies*
- *Total amount of the CSRBB*

If any IRRBB moves to be in excess of the limit, the escalation procedures must be followed.

Appendix 2: Example of IRRBB model manual

BCBS Standards highlight the importance of the documentation and validation of all models related to the IRRBB framework in a bank. In particular, there is a requirement to have in place documentation with the objective of allowing a smooth model validation process. The section below provides an example of documentation of a simple IRRBB model (set up in Excel) based on BCBS Standards.

A) THE PURPOSE OF THE MODEL

The main objectives of the IRRBB model are as follows:

- Calculation of the Net Interest Income sensitivity (NIIS) performed under predetermined interest rate risk scenarios, certain assumptions and a predefined holding period (herein gapping period).
- Calculation of the change in the Economic Value of Equity (ΔEVE) performed under a number of predetermined interest rate risk scenarios and assumptions.
- Time bucket sensitivity analysis through the calculation of the change in the present value of items due to the shift in the interest rates by 1 bp (PV01).
- Allocation of the stable and non-stable parts of the Non-Maturing Deposits (NMDs) according to the assumptions related to the balance volatility, rate sensitivity and average life of the product.
- Calculation of the change in the value of automatic options embedded in the structure of the bank's banking book.

B) COVERAGE

With relation to the bank's interest rate risk exposure, the model looks at it from two different perspectives:

- The earnings perspective, which focuses on the impact interest rate changes have on the bank's near-term earnings. After all, changes in the yield curve have a direct impact on future net interest income. Hence, interest rate risk analysis from an earnings perspective will focus on assessing the earnings effects that may arise from changes in market interest rates.
- The economic value perspective, which focuses on the impact interest rate changes may have on the economic value of future cash flows and thus on the economic value of both interest rate book and capital. The present economic value is affected in two ways by changes in interest rates: by the change in future interest cash

flows included in the calculation, and by the change in the discount rates of all future cash flows used for this calculation.

The output of the model allows an assessment of its exposure to the following interest rate risk subcategories:

- **Gap risk** – results from the maturity mismatch between on-balance sheet assets and liabilities and off-balance sheet instruments. It is one of the principal forms of interest rate risk faced by the institution and it is analysed through maturity gap and scenario analysis in the model.
- **Yield curve risk** – results from non-parallel shifts in the yield curve and changes in the form of the yield curve. It relates to the changing relationship between interest rates of various maturities for the same index or market. The model captures yield curve risk through the application of seven interest rate risk shocks in two scenarios (contractual versus behavioural).
- **Option risk** – arises when a customer of an institution has the right but not obligation to influence the timing and the magnitude of the cash flows of an asset, liability or off-balance sheet instrument. Sight deposits and savings deposits whose maturities are uncertain for the institution entail a risk for the banking book in the form of the right of withdrawal (in relation to the assumed maturity). This kind of option risk is known as a behavioural option risk.
- **Basis risk** – results from a change in the relationship between the yields/yield curves of the long and short positions with the same maturities which means that the long and short positions no longer fully hedge each other. This change will affect the net interest margin as a result of changes in the spreads received or paid on instruments that are repriced at that time. The aim of the model is to assess the bank's exposure to the basis risk through the refixing gap integrated in the model.

C) SCOPE

The model focuses on quantitative aspects of the interest rate risk in the banking book (IRRBB), in particular the measurement and simulation (if required) of the sensitivity to the movement of the interest rate curves of all positions included in the banking book for the model purposes. The model calculates the IRRBB metrics for every material currency, i.e. those currencies accounting for more than 5% of total risk sensitive assets or liabilities.

As a result, the IRRBB position is calculated by material currency and at the consolidated level, where all immaterial foreign currency positions are converted into EUR currency by the FX rate at the valuation date. The scope of the model can be extended in the event that any additional currencies trigger the materiality threshold.

The model includes, for the purpose of the IRRBB analysis, the undrawn committed credit lines.

The model has the following applications:

- As a measurement tool for internal analysis of the exposure of the bank, and monitoring whether risk appetite is satisfied, i.e., if the IRRBB limits are not breached.

- Assessment of the internal capital allocation for the interest rate risk under Pillar 2. Each bank is responsible for holding sufficient capital in relation to interest rate risk.
- Simulation of the potential impact on the IRR position of the bank driven by the new business strategies undertaken.
- Calculation of the IRRBB metrics for the purpose of IRRBB stress testing.

D) DESCRIPTION OF THE MEASUREMENT TECHNIQUES

The following section describes the measurement techniques used by the model. The model evaluates the IRRBB exposure with reference to the following time horizons:

- **Short-term horizon** – 12M and 24M for the short-term exposure to the interest rate risk for the purpose of the NIIS calculations.
- **Whole banking book time structure** – from O/N to >25 years for the assessment of the change in the EVE (structural interest rate risk exposure).

E) THE CALCULATION OF NET INTEREST INCOME SENSITIVITY (NIIS)

To evaluate earnings exposure, RSL in each time band are subtracted from the corresponding RSA to produce a residual gap for that time band. The model estimates the NIIS rather than the NII itself and the sensitivity is assessed under the parallel interest rate curve shifts. In order to calculate the NIIS, the gap in each time band is multiplied by an assumed change in interest rates. It yields an approximation of the change in NII that would result from such an interest rate movement. The size of the interest rate movement used in the analysis is based on the shift by currency prescribed in the BCBS Standards. The bank recognises, however, some limitations presented by this method:

- it considers only the transactions existing in the banking book at the date of the analysis (no new business assumption),
- it disregards different maturities of the transaction within the same time buckets (all transactions falling into the same time bucket have the same risk profile),
- it allows an estimation only of uniform movements of the interest rates,
- it assumes that assets and liabilities in maturity will be reinvested/refinanced within the gapping period (without altering the balance sheet structure) – there is no new business strategy applied here.

The impact on interest income resulting from the movement of interest rates is calculated as a product between the changes in the interest rates and the difference between interest rate risk sensitive asset and liabilities:

$$\Delta NII = \Delta j \times GAP = \Delta j \times (sensitive\ assets - sensitive\ liabilities)$$

Thus, the delta of interest margin is the function of two elements:

- interest rates movements, Δj,
- difference between assets and liabilities, GAP.

The total GAP is obtained by summation of the subsequent $GAPs$ weighted for the time factor. This time factor represents the time between the central value of the bucket (mid-point) and the end of the gapping period:

$$\Delta NII = \sum_{i=0}^{n} GAP * (T - t) \times \Delta j$$

where:

> T represents the length of the gapping period, t maturity related to the i-th time bucket, Δj shock in the interest rates curve.

The model applies the repricing flow approach where the sensitivity is caused by the flows in repricing as opposed to the stock analysis where the sensitivity is caused by unmatched position in terms of the ourstanding gap position.

TRADITIONAL APPROACH – REPRICING FLOWS
NII sensitivity calculated with the traditional repricing gap methodology

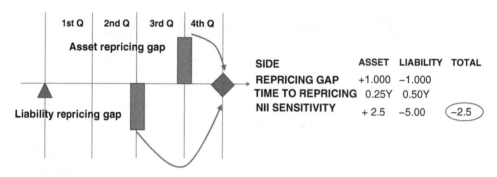

Maturity (repricing) gap analysis according to the repricing flows approach.

ADVANCED APPROACH – REPRICING STOCKS
NII sensitivity calculated as differential change in funding costs for unmatched position

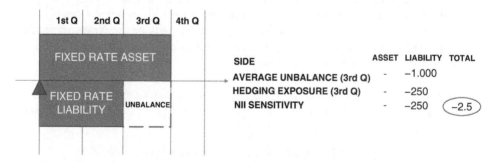

Maturity (repricing) gap analysis according to the repricing stocks approach.

The method presented above, applied in the model, is static. That is, in the evolution of the balance sheet from the perspective of the new business production, NMDs customer behaviour and the future evolution of the interest rates are not taken into consideration in the model. The bank recognises though that, under different scenarios, a distinction is typically made between interest rate sensitivity to falling and rising interest rates (different interest rate scenarios cause different outcome for the deposit volatility and sensitivity). The bank applies the static IRRBB model assumptions, i.e., constant balance sheet from the impact on earnings perspective (replacement of items *like for like*) and run off from the economic perspective, therefore the interaction between rate changes and behaviour is not analysed. Consequently, the assumed NMDs run off may not apply in some stress scenarios. This creates the potential for model enhancement in terms of the distinction between different interest rate scenarios and resulting deposits run off through the application of simulation techniques.

The bank calculates the NIIS under two parallel interest rates scenarios:

- For EUR currency by +/–200 bps
- For GBP currency by +/–250 bps

Again, it is important to highlight that this approach can be used to generate interest rate sensitivities rather than base case valuations or earnings projections.

The model assumes that all instruments are accounted for on an accrual basis and that their book value is par.

The changes in NII (ΔNII) driven by the parallel shifts in the interest rate curves are related to the expected NII over the predefined time horizon (respectively 12 months and 24 months) through the equation:

$$NIIS\ ratio = \Delta NII\ /\ NII$$

The model allows for the analysis of the maturity gap of the bank through the allocation of the RSA, RSL and derivatives to the respective time bands according to their re-set date (if floating) and/or expiration date (if fixed).

Using the maturity gap technique, the bank monitors its IRRBB position through observing the *directional gap* mismatching according to the expectation of the future movements of the interest rate curve and analytical understanding of the maturity profile of the balance sheet. In particular, where the total $GAP > 0$ the bank is exposed to re-investment risk, meaning that when interest rates increase the bank's NII is going to be impacted positively. On the other hand, where interest rates decrease it is going to show losses. Where the total $GAP < 0$ the bank is exposed to refinancing risk, meaning that when interest rates increase it is going to incur losses. On the other hand, it realises profits if interest rates decrease. In this sense, the directional gap strategy consists in the adjustment of the sign of the GAP (increasing it when there is an upward movement expectation for interest rates and reducing it when there is downward pressure from the market).

One of the most important limits of maturity gap analysis consists in the impossibility of the identification of the parameters (risk factors) to which the transaction is linked and NII sensitivity that is driven by non-perfect indexation is not captured. Imperfect indexation arises in the following situations:

- Rate fixing period different to the interest payment period.
- The presence of financial spreads.
- Weight of indexation parameter not equal to 1.
- Average indexation.

The bank, at least partially, overcomes these limitations through the introduction of the refixing gap analysis in its suite of IRRBB metrics, and through the assumption that all instruments are accounted for on an accrual basis and that their book value is par. As such it also ignores second-order effects such as the pull-to-par behaviour of assets whose book prices are materially different from their par amount.

An example of the bank's maturity gap is presented in the graph below.

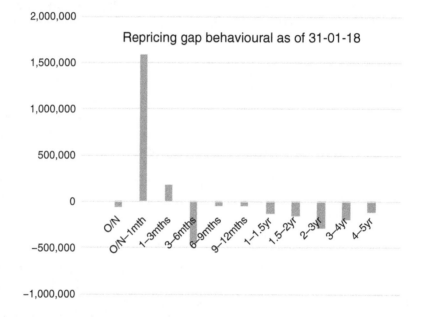

The refixing gap analysis enriches details provided by the maturity gap. It provides information about existing mismatching between assets and liabilities at the floating rate indexed to the different risk factors (EURIBOR 3M, LIBOR 1M, etc.) grouped in monthly time buckets within a predetermined time horizon of 12 months. Unlike the maturity gap, the refixing analysis takes into consideration all the refixing dates of accounts related to assets and liabilities under the gapping period. It is important information for the bank since it allows containment of the risk of mismatching and high sensitivity driven by interest rate fluctuations. It is also an important tool for setting the hedging strategy and for containing a negative impact on the interest income of the bank.

The refixing method is static. That is, the evolution of the balance sheet from the perspective of new business production and the future evolution of interest rates are not taken into consideration.

An example of the bank's refixing gap is presented in the graph below.

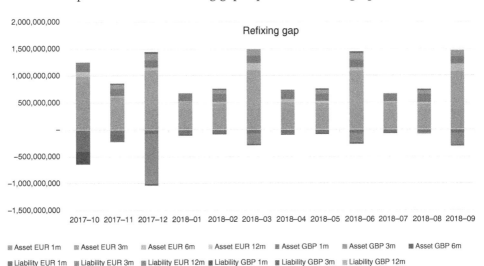

F) THE CALCULATION OF THE ECONOMIC VALUE OF EQUITY VOLATILITY (ΔEVE)

Maturity gap analysis also facilitates the analysis of the effects of the interest rate changes on the economic value of capital. In principle this analysis is based, firstly, on the determination of the cash flows of the transactions and the subsequent mapping of them on the corresponding time bands. In order to obtain the overall measure of the structural risk exposure, the change in the present value of gaps is related to the Own Funds (OF) of the bank, indicating in this way the percentage of its own funds that will be affected by any interest rate movement.

The ΔEVE measures the change in the market value of equity resulting from the upward and/or downward interest rate shocks. With this method the value of equity in alternative interest rate scenarios is compared with the value in a base scenario. This base interest rate scenario is the present value of the assets less liabilities within the current interest rate environment. The balance sheet is then revalued using the alternative interest rate scenarios and the difference between the value of equity in an alternative scenario and in a base scenario is calculated. The accuracy of the valuation of the balance sheet positions is extremely dependent upon the cash flows calculated and the discount rate used. Theoretically, the discount rates used should match the duration and risk of the cash flows. In the model there is an assumption that the cash flows in particular time buckets are discounted with the rates at the mid-point of the time bucket. There is also an assumption related to the fact that the timing of the cash flows and their size do not differ under the various scenarios as a result of customer behaviour. In reality, there is always a specific relationship between the interest rate scenario and the extent of prepayment and growth of deposits.

The benefits of the EVE model are:

- Interest rate risk is measured in terms of economic value.
- The method enables basis and yield curve risk as well as convexity to be measured properly.

The disadvantages of the EVE model are:

- It is a static method in the sense it shows a snapshot in time of the risk based upon the current portfolio or balance sheet composition.
- It cannot make allowance for the market valuation of future (forecast) growth in existing or new business activities.

The loss in economic value of equity $\Delta EVE_{i,c}$ under scenario i and currency c is calculated as follows:

- Under each scenario i, all notional repricing cash flows are slotted to the respective time bucket $k \in \{1, 2, \ldots, K\}$. Within a given time bucket k, all positive and negative notional repricing cash flows are netted to form a single long or short position, with the cancelled parts removed from the calculation. Following this process across all time buckets leads to a set of notional repricing cash flows $CF(k)$, $k \in \{1, 2, \ldots, K\}$.
- Net notional repricing cash flows in each time bucket k are weighted by a continuously compounded discount factor: $DF_{i,c}(t_k) = \exp(-R_{i,c}(t_k) \cdot t_k)$ that reflects the interest rate shock scenario i in currency c and where tk is the midpoint of time bucket k. This results in a weighted net position, which may be positive or negative for each time bucket. The discount factors represent the risk-free rate (OIS curve).

These risk-weighted net positions are summed to determine the EVE in currency c under scenario i (excluding automatic interest rate option positions which the bank might have).

$$EVE_{i,c} = \sum_{k=1}^{K} CF_{i,c}(k) * DF_{i,c}(t_k) / DF_{0,c}(t_k)$$

The EVE in currency c under base scenario is calculated as:

$$EVE_{0,c} = \sum_{k=1}^{K} CF_{0,c}(k) * DF_{0,c}(t_k) / DF_{0,c}(t_k)$$

EVE in currency c associated with the base scenario is equal to the principal. This is driven by the model assumption to map instruments as zero coupons. Consequently, it is a better approximation to assume they have a par value rather than to assume they behave as a real zero-coupon instrument.

Finally, the full change in EVE in currency c associated with scenario i is obtained by subtracting $EVE_{0,c}$ from the EVE under shocked interest rate term structure $EVE_{i,c}$ and by adding the total measure for automatic interest rate option risk $KAO_{i,c}$ as follows:

$$\Delta EVE_{i,c} = \sum_{k=1}^{K} CF_{i,c}(k) * DF_{i,c}(t_k) / DF_{0,c}(t_k) - \sum_{k=1}^{K} CF_{0,c}(k) * DF_{0,c}(t_k) / DF_{0,c}(t_k) + KAO_{i,c}$$

In this regard, if $\Delta EVE_{i,c} > 0$ then the economic value of the banking book is going to increase. Meanwhile, where it is $\Delta EVE_{i,c} < 0$ the bank faces a reduction in its economic value.

$KAO_{i,c}$ is an add-on for the calculation of the change in value of the automatic interest rate options, whether explicit or embedded.

G) TIME BUCKET SENSITIVITY ANALYSIS (PV01)

Sensitivity analysis is a method for calculating the change in the present values of items due to a shift in the interest rates curve. The sensitivity (ΔPV) of the transaction is calculated as the difference between its Present Value (PV) determined with the current market rates and its present value under the shocked interest rates scenario (PV*):

$$\Delta PV = PV * - PV$$

The traditional approach consists in positioning cash flows, fair value and sensitivity at the date at which the flow is expected to occur (according to its contractual or modelled maturity).

In the model, time bucket sensitivity is assessed through the upward parallel shift by 1 bp in the interest rate curve based on the baseline interest rate scenario (PV01). Net notional repricing cash flows in each time bucket k are weighted by a continuously compounded discount factor: $DF_{i,c}(t_k) = \exp(-R_{i,c}(t_k) \cdot t_k)$ that reflects the interest rate move by 1 bp in currency c and where tk is the midpoint of time bucket k.

H) TREATMENT OF THE AUTOMATIC OPTIONS

The bank has automatic interest rate options (IROs) which are explicitly embedded in the corporate loans on the asset side. Therefore, the bank is a holder of those options (a long option position). In addition, the bank has a short option position with 0% strike on liabilities (deposits) as there is no willingness to cut depositor rates below 0% where rates are negative.

The IROs aim to limit the exposure of the bank to a decrease in interest rates through the application of floors. The level of these floors is set at 0%. According to the BCBS Standards, in order to calculate the change in economic value of the banking book under interest rate shocks, those options have to be stripped out from the host contract, and they should be revaluated separately through full revaluation under base and shocked scenarios described herein.

The subsequent change in the value of options is added, at the final stage of the calculations, to the change in the economic value of the banking book for every interest rate shock and by material currency.

An estimate of the change in the option value to the option holder is given as:

- the option value determined in currency c and under shocked interest rate scenario i;

 minus

- the option value determined in currency c at the valuation date under base scenario.

In a positive interest rate environment, the Black 76 model is used as a best practice to price the vanilla interest rate options such as floors, caps and swaptions. However, given that most of the bank's floors are embedded in the loan contracts which are denominated in Euro currency and, at the same time, short-term interest rates in Euro currency are negative, it is impossible to apply the Black formula to derive options value through the standard model. Consequently, in a negative interest rates environment, and with the aim of calculating the impact of the options on the overall position of the bank, the model allows the application of the Bachelier model which is known also as the model under normal distribution assumption. The normal model allows valuation of options with negative strikes and negative forward rates.

The following formula is applied to calculate the value of each floorlet.

$$P = e^{-rT}\left[K - F) \times N(d_1) + \sigma \times \sqrt{T} \times n(d_1)\right]$$

and

$$d_1 = \frac{(F - K)}{\sigma \times \sqrt{T}}$$

where:

F is the forward rate, K is the strike level, σ is the annualised absolute volatility of the underlying rate and T is the time to expiration in years.

In addition, $N(d_1)$ represents the cumulative normal distribution function and $n(d_1)$ the standard normal density function. The sum of all floorlets for every option contract provides the value of the floor.

The Bachelier model calculates the total option value, i.e., the intrinsic option value and time value. On the liability side, the bank is not willing to apply negative rates to depositors (and charge them for holding funds within the bank). Consequently, there is an implicit short option position (floor) hold by the bank. The impact of these options is calculated through full revaluation under base and shocked scenarios.

I) CASH FLOW BUCKETING

The model projects all future notional repricing cash flows arising from RSA and RSL and OBS items onto 19 predefined time buckets into which they fall according to their repricing dates, or onto the time bucket midpoints retaining the notional repricing cash flows' maturity.

The bank applies the time buckets schedule as shown below.

O/N	O/N–1mth	1–3mths	3–6mths	6–9mths	9–12mths	1–1.5yr	1.5–2yr	2–3yr	3–4yr
0.00280	0.04170	0.16670	0.37500	0.62500	0.875	1.25	1.75	2.5	3.5

4–5yr	5–6yr	6–7yr	7–8yr	8–9yr	9–10yr	<15yr	<20yr	>20yr
4.5	5.5	6.5	7.5	8.5	9.5	12.5	17.5	25

Time bucket mid-point in years

Interest rate curve and valuations

J) INTEREST RATE CURVE AND VALUATIONS

For the purpose of valuation, the known cash flows are discounted off the risk-free curve without consideration of the product margins. This is driven by the fact that inclusion of the margin components and discounting them at risk-free rates could create potential issues with the overestimation of the economic value of the instrument. The model does not project the future cash flows based on the forward rate. Instead, the NIIS and ΔEVE are calculated to provide a static risk picture at the cut-off date. In addition, the model does not evaluate the positions at the single instrument level. All positions which reprice or expire at a certain time bucket are grouped together and assessed at the residual gap level.

The model uses the OIS curve which is considered to be representative as a risk-free curve, for EUR and GBP currencies. The mid points of time buckets are interpolated linearly:

$$y = y1 + (x - x1) * (y2 - y1) / (x2 - x1)$$

where:

$x, x1$ and $x2$ is the length of time bucket and $y, y1$ and $y2$ are interest rates for the respective time buckets.

K) ITEMS WITHOUT DETERMINISTIC MATURITY – CURRENT ACCOUNTS AND SAVINGS ACCOUNTS (CASA)

The interest rate risk arising from sight deposits with uncertain maturities and where there is no close correlation between changes in interest income and market interest rates requires particular attention. Various techniques are used by banks to determine the effective maturity of these positions. These techniques can vary from basic to sophisticated. Given the underlying assumptions, relating to interest sensitivity and volume characteristics, these techniques are subject to model risk. For these reasons, deposit characterisation models need to be checked by periodic valuation, sensitivity analysis and stress testing. The technique applied by the bank is described in the following sections.

In the gap report constructed in the model, a distinction is made between positions with uncertain maturities that are interest-sensitive and those that are not interest-sensitive. Interest-sensitive positions, where the interest income is sensitive to the movements in market interest rates, are allocated to the short-term maturity bands of the gap report. With regard to the positions that are not interest-sensitive, there are a number of possible allocation techniques depending on assumptions regarding customer behaviour. From a risk perspective, the allocation of positions with uncertain maturities to maturity segments according to a gap profile is particularly important if these positions are used to hedge an institution's economic exposure.

The following steps have been applied by the bank to model and allocate the NMDs to the corresponding time buckets.

1) Segmentation of the NMDs

NMDs are segmented into retail and wholesale categories. Retail deposits are defined as deposits placed with a bank by an individual person. Deposits made by small business customers and managed as retail exposures are considered as having similar interest rate risk characteristics to retail accounts and thus can be treated as retail deposits (provided the total aggregated liabilities raised from one small business customer are less than EUR 1.0m).

Retail deposits should be considered as held in a transactional account when regular transactions are carried out in that account (for example when salaries are regularly credited) or when the deposit is non-interest bearing. Other retail deposits should be considered as held in a non-transactional account.

Moreover, the bank distinguishes them by location, currency (EUR, USD) and product category (current accounts or savings accounts).

2) Split between the stable and non-stable part of NMDs

The bank distinguishes between stable and non-stable NMDs. The non-stable part consists of customers' balances which cannot be relied upon to remain with the bank for an extended period of time. This portion of the NMD is allocated to the O/N time bucket or to the time bucket which corresponds to the length of their contractual maturity for notice accounts.

The stable NMD portion is the portion that is found to remain undrawn with a high degree of likelihood. Core deposits are the proportion of stable NMDs which are unlikely to reprice even with significant changes in the interest rate environment. The remainder constitutes non-core NMDs. By definition, this sub-portfolio is 100% correlated to the short-term interest rates. For IRRBB purposes the bank allocates the stable non-core part to the O/N time bucket. With notice accounts, non-stable and non-core parts are assigned to time buckets corresponding to their notice period.

The core balances, defined as those that are not rate-sensitive, can best be represented as providing fixed-rate funding, to which a term maturity can be applied. In order to reflect the IRRBB profile in the best way possible the bank should attempt to perform its own statistical approach based on the behavioural analysis of the past behaviour of the customer base. Where the behavioural modelling analysis does provide adequate analysis of NMDs the bank can propose via ALCO, subject to the approval of the Risk Committee, to adopt the result of the internal analysis.

In this particular example, the bank classifies as core 50% of the maximum proportion permitted in the BCBS Standards (BCBS, 2016) as per the table below.

	Cap on proportion of core deposits (%)	Total maturity of core deposits (years)
Retail/non-transactional	35%	4.5
Wholesale	25%	4

The figure below summarises the split between the stable and non-stable part of NMDs applied by the bank.

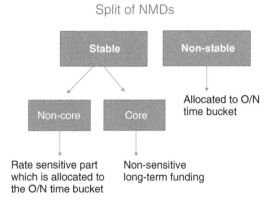

Split of NMDs

3) Determination of the average life of the product

In order to estimate the economic life of NMD products the bank performs its own analysis of the decay profile of the portfolio over a specific time horizon (for the sake of statistical significance a minimum 7 years of data is typically expected).

The average life modelling assigns a life to the product by tracking the closing behaviour of the customers' accounts. This is done through tracking the decaying of the number of accounts. This represents a variation in the approach prescribed in the BCBS Standards document and is driven by the bank's willingness to pursue the more conservative approach in terms of the assumption of the average life of the NMDs.

The analysis of the decay profile is done through the following approach:

i. Collection of the account level data and formation of the "triangle": The "triangle" is a form of representing the account level data such that the continued presence of the number of accounts opened in one month can be tracked through different age buckets. It gives the remaining number of accounts for a given age bucket for a given opening month.

ii. Calculation of the mortality ratio for each age bucket: The mortality ratio is defined as the number of accounts closed at that age to the number of accounts that were alive at the beginning of that bucket. All the mortality rates for each age bucket together tell how fast (or slow) the accounts close.

iii. Computation of the average life of accounts: Once the mortality rates are determined, it is possible to track the percentage of accounts remaining at each age.

The bank has allocated the overall maturity of 4.5 and 4 years for the retail non-transactional and wholesale NMDs respectively.

Under the different scenarios, a distinction is typically made between interest rate sensitivity to falling and rising interest rates (different interest rate scenarios cause a different outcome for the deposit volatility and sensitivity). However, the bank's IRRBB model is static, therefore the interaction between rate changes and behaviour is not analysed. Consequently, the assumed run off may not be applied in some stress scenarios. This creates the potential for model enhancement in terms of the distinction between different interest rate scenarios and resulting deposit balance volatility and rate sensitivity through the application of the simulation techniques.

Modelling techniques of items without deterministic maturity – Current Accounts and Savings Accounts (CASA)

In order to reflect its risk profile characteristics in the best way possible the bank should attempt to perform its own statistical approach based on the behavioural analysis of the past behaviour of the customer base. Where the behavioural modelling analysis provides adequate analysis of NMDs the bank can propose via the ALCO, subject to the approval of the Risk Committee, to adopt the result of the internal analysis. This section describes in detail the methodological approach for internal modelling of NMDs.

The bank is mainly funded by non-maturing deposits, both savings and current accounts. The way these products are modelled has significant implications in terms of the exposure to the interest rate risk and liquidity risk. The whole picture of risks a bank is running can change, driven by changes in the customers' behaviour. For this reason, understanding the main underlying factors is of crucial importance for the bank.

Usually, the balance fluctuations are a function of multiple factors, including the macroeconomic environment as well as the product pricing structure. Presumably, by increasing the rate paid to the consumer, inflows of deposits will in turn increase. It is recognised that the customer–financial institution relationship indicates positive correlation which may exhibit a linear or even exponential relationship over a particular interest rate interval. Consequently, it is the main objective of the bank to understand the rate-balance elasticity equation of the deposits base.

Regardless of the methodology used, the first step in current account modelling is to apply a correct segmentation scheme. The main goal of product segmentation is to preserve the underlying balance and rate characteristics of products/product subdivisions for the full deposit modelling, while also ensuring a minimum threshold of materiality and simplicity. As already mentioned, for the sake of the deposit behavioural modelling, the bank has adopted the segmentation applied in the BCBS Standards.

Once segmented, NMDs are slotted into the appropriate time bucket midpoint. Non-stable deposits are considered as overnight deposits for accounts without a notice period. In the case of notice accounts, they are allocated to the time bucket corresponding to the length of the contractual notice period.

The bank distinguishes between the stable and the non-stable parts of each NMD category using observed volume changes over the previous 2 years. The stable NMD portion is the portion that is found to remain undrawn with a high degree of likelihood. Core deposits are the proportion of stable NMDs which are unlikely to reprice even with significant changes in the interest rate environment. The remainder constitutes non-core NMDs. In order to establish the split between the stable and non-stable part of CASA, the bank applies a simplistic way of estimating balance volatility, i.e., by modelling it singularly as a function of time.

In this approach, the model fits the product balances to find the exponential trend line and the variation of actual balances around the trend line. It then sets the trend line at a certain confidence level. The following part describes the exponential model applied by the bank. Under this model the product balances are modelled to fit balances to an exponential curve of the form:

$$Balance = B_0 e^{rt}$$

where:

B_0 represents the initial balance and r denotes the fixed growth rate.

Obviously, this simplified approach neglects the fact that, in practice, the growth rate of balances is not constant over time but depends on different factors, both internal and external (for example interest rate and product pricing). It allows for future model enhancements.

The exponential model can be converted to a linear relation through the log function:

$$\ln(Balance) = \ln(B_0) + rt$$

A regression model is utilised to compute the growth rate of the natural logarithm of the balances, and the standard error of the estimate, σ_{Fit}.

To ensure that the probability of core balances dropping below the actual balances is minimal, the fitted equation is lowered with some multiple of standard deviation; 99.9% approximately corresponds to 3.1 standard deviation shift in balances for a normal distribution. The growth rate is decreased by n*σ, or 3.1 times the standard deviation, to decrease the chance of the total balance level falling below the core level to 0.1% of the time, or approximately one month in every 83 years. The resulting core balance equation is:

$$Balance_{Core} = B_0 e^{rt - n\sigma_{Fit}}$$

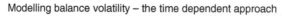

Modelling balance volatility – the time dependent approach

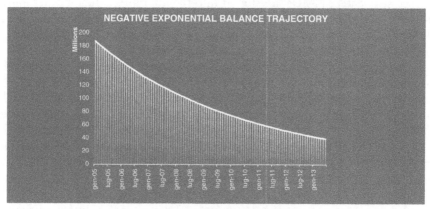

Exponential functional form $B(t) = B_0 \exp(-\beta^* t)$ can be used to model this movement and issue forecasts going forward.

The significance of the regression parameters is analysed for R Square and P-value.

SUMMARY OUTPUT

Regression statistics	
Multiple R	0,837421572
R Square	0,701274889
Adjusted R Square	0,698287638
Standard Error	0,298780376
Observations	102

ANOVA

	df	SS	MS	F	Significance F
Regression	1	20,95659388	20,95659388	234,75592235	,49163E-28
Residual	100	8,92697133	0,089269713		
Total	101	29,88356521			

	Coefficients	Standard Error	t Stat	P-value	Lower 95%	Upper 95%	Lower 95,0%	Upper 95,0%
Intercept	19,06561717	0,059605073	319,8656784	2,4159E-152	18,9473624	19,18387194	18,9473624	19,18387194
X Variable 1	-0,015394713	0,001004762	-15,32174671	5,49163E-28	-0,017388132	-0,013401293	-0,017388132	-0,013401293

For the purpose of the IRRBB analysis the bank applies two scenarios, i.e., a behavioural view where the NMDs are modelled according to the methodology described above, and the contractual based on the contractual characteristics.

INTEREST RATE SHOCKS

In order to produce a quantitative estimate of IRRBB, it is necessary to assume a shock to current interest rate levels which would allow the change in EV or earnings, and ultimately the effect on equity, to be computed. The size and shape of the shock determines the measured outcome produced by the model.

In the model, seven interest rate shock scenarios are set up to capture parallel and non-parallel gap risks for EVE and two prescribed interest rate shock scenarios for the NIIS. These scenarios are applied to measure the IRRBB exposures in each material currency analysed in the model.

In the model, IRRBB is measured by means of the six scenarios as prescribed in the BCBS Standards:

- parallel shock up
- parallel shock down
- steepener shock (short rates down and long rates up)
- flattener shock (short rates up and long rates down)
- short rates shock up
- short rates shock down

As part of the market scenarios the model applies an additional historical interest rate shock chosen because of the significant increase in interest rates:

- 1994 crisis (aggressive global interest rates increase)

INTEREST RATE SCENARIOS

The model applies two interest rate risk scenarios for which each of the interest rate shocks is applied, i.e. behavioural and contractual.

Interest rate shocks – underlying assumptions	
Behavioural view	**Contractual view**
Non-Maturing Deposits (NMDs) follow the behavioural view through the application of modelling assumptions.	NMDs follow the contractual view.

Interest rate shocks – underlying assumptions

Behavioural view	Contractual view
No prepayment rate applied to fixed rate assets (as there is no statistically backed analysis at this stage).	No prepayment rate applied to fixed rate assets.
Time deposits follow their contractual maturity (there is no facility for early redemption except in extreme cases – such as the death of a depositor – which are ignored on the basis that they are of negligible frequency).	Time deposits follows their contractual maturity.
For the purposes of NII, time deposits falling under maturity are replaced by products with the same financial characteristics and amount (constant balance sheet assumption).	For the purposes of NII, time deposits falling under maturity are replaced by products with the same financial characteristics and amount (constant balance sheet assumption).
For the purposes of EVE there is an assumption that time deposits are in run off.	For the purposes of EVE there is an assumption that time deposits are in run off.

IRRBB MODEL COMPOSITION

The section below describes the components of the IRRBB model provided by the author.

Position capture

The sheet "Position capture", in the model, shows the maturity gap of the banking book of the bank. It reflects the picture of the exposure to the interest rate risk within a short time period (12 months), and in the medium to long term (beyond 1 year). It captures the positions (both at the fixed rate) which mature and need to be reinvested (if assets), or refinanced (if liabilities), and the floating rate which will reset its rate, generating in this way the interest rate risk exposure. The gapping period is split into 19 time buckets, thereby giving information about time when risk is present. The more precise the information about timing related to the presence of risk, the more accurate is the measure of exposure to the interest rate risk. It is worth highlighting at this point, that even if it delivers the fast view from the interest rate risk perspective, it does not consider the structure and the positions of the subsequent repricing gaps related to the given position. Instead, it "sees" only the first risk date of the position in fixation.

For example, if the bank has an amount of liabilities which reprice in January 2021, April 2021, July 2021 and October 2021 (the liability is indexed to LIBOR 3M), under the maturity gap approach, the model will see only the repricing in January 2021 if analysed in December 2020 (the cut-off date of the analysis).

The fixed rate items (for example, corporate time deposits) are allocated to the respective time buckets according to their contractual maturity.

Consequently, the "Position capture" sheet provides the model user with an important analysis of the distribution of risk sensitive items over time and its interest rate risk exposure.

The model also manages the off-balance sheet positions according to the following rules:

- Long positions are treated as assets and allocated to the respective time bucket according to their expected expiration or repricing date.
- Short positions are treated as liabilities and allocated to the respective time buckets according to their expiration or repricing date.

The following off-balance sheet positions can be treated in the model:

- Interest rate swaps
- Forward rate agreements (FRA)
- Cross currency swaps

Examples and underlying assumptions:

(a) Allocation of the floating rate loan with residual maturity of 5 years indexed to EURIBOR 1M.

The cut-off date is 31 December 2020.

Based on the characteristics above the loan is allocated to the O/N–1M time bucket.

(b) Allocation of the fixed rate loan bullet with the expiration date as of December 2025

The cut-off date is 31 December 2020.

Based on the characteristics above the loan is allocated to the 4–5yrs time bucket.

(c) Allocation of the EUR 400m amortised loan at fixed rate with the following amortisation schedule:

2022: EUR 100m

2023: EUR 100m

2024: EUR 200m

The cut-off date is 31 December 2020.

Based on the characteristics above the loan is allocated to the following time buckets:

1.5–2yrs: 100m

2–3yrs: 100m

4–5yrs: 200m

(d) Allocation of the Euro 400m amortised loan at floating rate indexed to EURIBOR 1M with the following amortisation schedule:

2022: EUR 100m

2023: EUR 100m

2024: EUR 200m

The cut-off date is 31 December 2020.

Based on the characteristics above the loan is allocated to the O/N–1M time bucket.

(e) Allocation of the undrawn revolving loans

Not included in the calculations for IRRBB.

(f) Allocation of equity

Not included in the calculations for IRRBB.

(g) Allocation of Non-Performing Loans (NPLs)

Allocated according to the expected schedule of loan recovery.

(h) Allocation of fixed assets

Not included in the calculations for IRRBB.

(i) Treatment of the fixed rate bonds in the treasury model

The model maps fixed rate securities as zero coupons, consequently it approximates they have a par value rather than assuming that they behave as real zero-coupon instruments.

Consolidated in EUR (in 000)–Baseline scenario–behavioural

ASSETS

Balance Sheet - ASSETS	Non Int	O/N	O/N–1mth	1–3mths	3–6mths	6–9mths	9–12mths	1–1.5yr	1.5–2yr	2–3yr	3–4yr	4–5yr	5–6yr
Cash & Central Bank balances	95,410	95,410	0	0	0	0	0	0	0	0	0	0	0
Treasury securities held as AFS	50,856	0	30,000	20,856	0	0	0	0	0	0	0	0	0
Placed Interbank	0	0	0	0	0	0	0	0	0	0	0	0	0
Retail loans	0	0	0	0	0	0	0	0	0	0	0	0	0
Corporate loans	1,193,458	0	1,109,508	17,073	66,878	0	0	0	0	0	0	0	0
Revolving loans	0	0	0	0	0	0	0	0	0	0	0	0	0
Syndication loans	0	0	0	0	0	0	0	0	0	0	0	0	0
Other corporate loans	0	0	0	0	0	0	0	0	0	0	0	0	0
All other assets	1	1	0	0	0	0	0	0	0	0	0	0	0
Total Assets	**1,339,725**	**95,411**	**1,139,508**	**37,929**	**66,878**	**0**	**0**	**0**	**0**	**0**	**0**	**0**	**0**

LIABILITIES

Balance Sheet - LIABILITIES	Non Int	O/N	O/N–1mth	1–3mths	3–6mths	6–9mths	9–12mths	1–1.5yr	1.5–2yr	2–3yr	3–4yr	4–5yr	5–6yr
Retail Current Accounts non-transactional in Malta - seg 1	0	0	0	0	0	0	0	0	0	0	0	0	0
Retail Current Accounts non-transactional in Belgium - seg 1	0	0	0	0	0	0	0	0	0	0	0	0	0
Retail Savings Accounts - Malta - seg 2	0	0	0	0	0	0	0	0	0	0	0	0	0

Consolidated in EUR (in 000)–Baseline scenario–behavioural

Retail Savings Accounts - Belgium - seg 2	-122,788	-79,813	0	-1,622	-2,433	-2,433	-2,433	-4,865	-4,865	-9,730	-9,730	-4,865	0
Me3 retail	-780,203	0	0	0	-518,055	-16,384	-16,384	-32,769	-32,769	-65,537	-65,537	-32,769	0
Me3 wholesale	-2,692	0	0	0	-2,050	-46	-46	-92	-92	-184	-184	0	0
Me12 retail	-70,844	0	0	0	0	0	0	-49,072	-3,629	-7,257	-7,257	-3,629	0
Me12 wholesale	0	0	0	0	0	0	0	0	0	0	0	0	0
Wholesale in Malta - seg 1	0	0	0	0	0	0	0	0	0	0	0	0	0
Wholesale in Belgium - seg 1	0	0	0	0	0	0	0	0	0	0	0	0	0
Wholesale in Malta - seg 2	0	0	0	0	0	0	0	0	0	0	0	0	0
Wholesale in Belgium - seg 2	-761	-571	0	-8	-12	-12	-12	-24	-24	-49	-49	0	0
All other currencies NMD	-2,173	-2,173	0	0	0	0	0	0	0	0	0	0	0
Term Time Deposits	-129,867	0	-1,658	-4,336	-3,036	-5,461	-12,634	-16,809	-15,657	-49,295	-17,744	-3,237	0
Total Deposits	**-1,109,329**	**-82,556**	**-1,658**	**-5,966**	**-525,585**	**-24,335**	**-31,509**	**-103,631**	**-57,035**	**-132,052**	**-100,501**	**-44,499**	**0**
Borrowed Interbank	0					0							
Other liabilities	0												
Senior securities issued (incl covered bonds)	0					0							
Sub debts	0												
Tier 1 Securities	0												
Tier 1 Equity & Reserves	0												

0

Consolidated in EUR (in 000)–Baseline scenario–behavioural

		Balance	Non Int	O/N	O/N–1mth	1–3mths	3–6mths	6–9mths	9–12mths	1–1.5yr	1.5–2yr	2–3yr	3–4yr	4–5yr	5–6yr
BS	Total Liabilities	−1,109,329	0	−82,556	−1,658	−5,966	−525,585	−24,335	−31,509	−103,631	−57,035	−132,052	−100,501	−44,499	0
	Net Mismatch	230,396	0	12,854	1,137,850	31,963	−458,707	−24,335	−31,509	−103,631	−57,035	−132,052	−100,501	−44,499	0
	BS Cumulative Net Mismatch	230,396	0	12,854	1,150,704	1,182,667	723,959	699,624	668,115	564,484	507,449	375,397	274,896	230,396	230,396
Off-Balance Sheet	Off-Balance Sheet	Balance	Non Int	O/N	O/N–1mth	1–3mths	3–6mths	6–9mths	9–12mths	1–1.5yr	1.5–2yr	2–3yr	3–4yr	4–5yr	5–6yr
	IRS	0	0	0	0	0	0	0	0	0	0	0	0	0	0
	FRA	0	0	0	0	0	0	0	0	0	0	0	0	0	0
	Fx Forwards/Swaps	−4,656		0	−2,801	−1,855	0	0	0	0	0	0	0	0	0
	Undrawn Revolving Loans	0		0	0	0	0	0	0	0	0	0	0	0	0
	OBS Asset Repricing	0	0	0	0	0	0	0	0	0	0	0	0	0	0
	OBS Liability Repricing	−4,656		0	−2,801	−1,855	0	0	0	0	0	0	0	0	0
	OBS Net Mismatch	−4,656		0	−2,801	−1,855	0	0	0	0	0	0	0	0	0
	OBS Cumulative Net Mismatch	0	0	0	−2,801	−4,656	−4,656	−4,656	−4,656	−4,656	−4,656	−4,656	−4,656	−4,656	−4,656
Total	Total Net Mismatch	225,741	0	12,854	1,135,049	30,108	−458,707	−24,335	−31,509	−103,631	−57,035	−132,052	−100,501	−44,499	0
	Total Cumulative Net Mismatch	225,741	0	12,854	1,147,903	1,178,011	719,304	694,968	663,459	559,828	502,793	370,741	270,240	225,741	225,741

Market capture

The model calculates ΔEVE and PV01 based on the prevailing yield curve at the cut-off date.

The section contains the following tables for interest rates:

- Scenario moves – used in the determination of the shocked interest rate curves and indicating the magnitude of the shock by each shock scenario.
- Shocked interest rate curves – used in the calculation of ΔEVE.
- Actual moves applied – used in the calculation of ΔNII
- The prevailing yield curve at the date of the analysis needs to be updated manually.

The model allows for negative rates, and the curves under the section labelled "New Curve" incorporate the full size of the downward shock (there is no zero floor for the downward movement of the interest rate curve).

The size and shape of the shocked interest rate curve is based on the scenarios prescribed by the Basel Committee on Banking Supervision (BCBS) Standards (BCBS, 2016). These scenarios are calculated in the sheet "Basel shocks scenario" which feeds the sheet "Market capture". There is one additional historical scenario named "94 crisis" which represents the global economic crisis and significant increase in interest rates.

Scenario Moves

94 crash	O/N	O/N–1mth	1–3mths	3–6mths	6–9mths	9–12mths	1–1.5yr	1.5–2yr	2–3yr	3–4yr	4–5yr
EUR	0.38%	0.38%	0.48%	0.73%	1.180%	1.63%	1.76%	1.965%	2.17%	2.27%	2.37%
USD	2.75%	2.75%	3.13%	3.44%	3.660%	3.88%	3.90%	3.605%	3.31%	3.20%	3.02%
GBP	0.56%	0.56%	1.24%	1.90%	2.325%	2.75%	3.36%	3.275%	3.19%	3.18%	3.10%
CHF	0.38%	0.38%	0.48%	0.73%	1.180%	1.63%	1.76%	1.965%	2.17%	2.27%	2.37%
JPY	0.38%	0.38%	0.48%	0.73%	1.180%	1.63%	1.76%	1.965%	2.17%	2.27%	2.37%
NOK	0.38%	0.38%	0.48%	0.73%	1.180%	1.63%	1.76%	1.965%	2.17%	2.27%	2.37%

Parallel up	O/N	O/N–1mth	1–3mths	3–6mths	6–9mths	9–12mths	1–1.5yr	1.5–2yr	2–3yr	3–4yr	4–5yr
EUR	2.00%	2.00%	2.00%	2.00%	2.00%	2.00%	2.00%	2.00%	2.00%	2.00%	2.00%
USD	2.00%	2.00%	2.00%	2.00%	2.00%	2.00%	2.00%	2.00%	2.00%	2.00%	2.00%
GBP	2.50%	2.50%	2.50%	2.50%	2.50%	2.50%	2.50%	2.50%	2.50%	2.50%	2.50%

Parallel down	O/N	O/N–1mth	1–3mths	3–6mths	6–9mths	9–12mths	1–1.5yr	1.5–2yr	2–3yr	3–4yr	4–5yr
EUR	−2.00%	−2.00%	−2.00%	−2.00%	−2.00%	−2.00%	−2.00%	−2.00%	−2.00%	−2.00%	−2.00%
USD	−2.00%	−2.00%	−2.00%	−2.00%	−2.00%	−2.00%	−2.00%	−2.00%	−2.00%	−2.00%	−2.00%
GBP	−2.50%	−2.50%	−2.50%	−2.50%	−2.50%	−2.50%	−2.50%	−2.50%	−2.50%	−2.50%	−2.50%

Short up	O/N	O/N–1mth	1–3mths	3–6mths	6–9mths	9–12mths	1–1.5yr	1.5–2yr	2–3yr	3–4yr	4–5yr
EUR	2.50%	2.47%	2.40%	2.28%	2.14%	2.01%	1.83%	1.61%	1.34%	1.04%	0.81%
USD	3.00%	2.97%	2.88%	2.73%	2.57%	2.41%	2.19%	1.94%	1.61%	1.25%	0.97%
GBP	3.00%	2.97%	2.88%	2.73%	2.57%	2.41%	2.19%	1.94%	1.61%	1.25%	0.97%

Short down	O/N	O/N–1mth	1–3mths	3–6mths	6–9mths	9–12mths	1–1.5yr	1.5–2yr	2–3yr	3–4yr	4–5yr
EUR	−2.50%	−2.47%	−2.40%	−2.28%	−2.14%	−2.01%	−1.83%	−1.61%	−1.34%	−1.04%	−0.81%
USD	−3.00%	−2.97%	−2.88%	−2.73%	−2.57%	−2.41%	−2.19%	−1.94%	−1.61%	−1.25%	−0.97%
GBP	−3.00%	−2.97%	−2.88%	−2.73%	−2.57%	−2.41%	−2.19%	−1.94%	−1.61%	−1.25%	−0.97%

Flat-tener	O/N	O/N–1mth	1–3mths	3–6mths	6–9mths	9–12mths	1–1.5yr	1.5–2yr	2–3yr	3–4yr	4–5yr
EUR	2.00%	1.97%	1.89%	1.77%	1.62%	1.49%	1.30%	1.08%	0.79%	0.48%	0.24%
USD	2.40%	2.37%	2.27%	2.10%	1.92%	1.75%	1.51%	1.23%	0.87%	0.48%	0.17%
GBP	2.40%	2.37%	2.27%	2.10%	1.92%	1.75%	1.51%	1.23%	0.87%	0.48%	0.17%

Steep-ener	O/N	O/N–1mth	1–3mths	3–6mths	6–9mths	9–12mths	1–1.5yr	1.5–2yr	2–3yr	3–4yr	4–5yr
EUR	−1.62%	−1.60%	−1.52%	−1.40%	−1.26%	−1.13%	−0.95%	−0.73%	−0.45%	−0.15%	0.08%
USD	−1.95%	−1.92%	−1.82%	−1.65%	−1.47%	−1.30%	−1.06%	−0.78%	−0.42%	−0.03%	0.28%
GBP	−1.95%	−1.92%	−1.82%	−1.65%	−1.47%	−1.30%	−1.06%	−0.78%	−0.42%	−0.03%	0.28%

NII details

The sheet "NII details" calculates the NIIS at the portfolio level. The bank believes that the split at portfolio level, instead of the analysis at the residual *GAP* level, is particularly important given the materiality of the automatic options embedded in the corporate loans portfolio and customer deposits. The model calculates the impact, in terms of NIIS, driven by the shock scenario applied both at the behavioural and contractual level. In addition, the analysis is performed both by material currency and at the consolidated level.

Deposit characterisation

The sheet "deposit characterisation" allocates a deposit with uncertain maturity to its respective time bucket according to:

(a) Deposit balance volatility
(b) Deposit rate sensitivity
(c) Average life of the product

The balance volatility model determines what level of balances will remain with the bank in the long term given a level of confidence. As an output, the balance volatility model divides the balances into two portions: stable balances, which remain with the bank under almost all market conditions; and non-stable balances, which fluctuate over time due to market and idiosyncratic reasons and typically characterised as short term.

Characterisation of administered rates for deposit products ascertains the significance of market rate changes on the rates paid by the bank. By modelling the behaviour of interest rates paid, relative to market rates, a better understanding of repricing behaviour and the sensitivity of interest expenses to market rates can be gained, i.e., how do rates paid to customers vary with market conditions?

This determines the effective duration and value of deposits.

Additionally, the rate sensitivity modelling is a key aspect of allocating FTP and in determining which assets the bank can match with minimal risk.

The interest rate paid to depositors of indeterminate maturity products is generally a combination of one or more market rates, and an idiosyncratic "fixed" component. The repricing frequency for the market driven component is simply the maturity associated with that rate. The fixed component is assumed to have a repricing frequency equal to the average life of the product.

Average life modelling assigns a life to each product by tracking the closing behaviour of the customers' accounts. This can be done through tracking the decaying of the number of accounts or through decaying of the balances.

The parameters related to the deposit volatility, rate sensitivity and average life of the product have to be introduced into the IRRBB model, as they are calculated by the application of regression techniques.

There are two model assumptions related to the treatment of NMDs:

(a) NMD modelled where the assumptions related to the product stickiness, rate sensitivity and average life are made.
(b) NMD contractual where there are no assumptions made on the product.

Model

The sheet "Model" sheet is the calculation engine which produces the following interest rate metrics:

1. **Total interest rate mismatch** – this shows the net mismatching for each time bucket. This information is particularly important in the daily management of hedging strategies and balance sheet composition.
2. **PV01** – time bucket sensitivity measure – it calculates the change in value of the banking book after shocking the yield curve by 1 bp.
3. **Historical scenario – 94 crash EVE** – it calculates the change in value of the banking book where the yield curve is shocked according to the bond crisis in 1994.
4. **EVE changes** – under "parallel up, parallel down, short up, short down, steepener and flattener" scenarios.
5. **Earnings sensitivity – ΔNII** – impact on earnings resulting from +/– parallel shift in yield curve in 12-month and 24-month gapping periods.

The change in the economic value of the automatic options embedded in assets and liabilities is calculated in the sheet "Option summary" through the application of the regulatory shocks.

The change in the option value and, consequently, its impact under a given scenario is calculated as per the following equation:

$$KAO_{i,c} = \text{intrinsic option value of option in currency } c \text{ under base scenario} -$$
$$\text{intrinsic option value of option in currency } c \text{ under shocked scenario}$$

All above metrics are calculated both under behavioural (NMD modelled) and contractual (NMD as per contractual terms) view.

Dashboard

The IRRBB dashboard shows the following results metrics:

1. ΔNII/expected net interest income under the gapping period of 12 months.
2. ΔEVE/Tier 1 capital calculated by interest rate shock and by material currency.
3. Total PV01 and PV01 by time bucket (time bucket sensitivity).

The above metrics are calculated for every material currency, both under behavioural and contractual views.

Economic value analysis - behavioural–ratio				
	EVE sensitivity	EAR 3m	EAR 12m	EAR 24m
94 crash	15%			
Parallel up	15%		61%	
Parallel down	44%		–8%	
Short up	10%			
Short down	4.01%			
Flattener	6%			
Steepener	1.29%			
Worse	1.29%		–8%	
Threshold	–15%		–15%	

References

Adam, A. (2007) *Handbook of Asset and Liability Management*. Chichester: Wiley.

Alessandri, P. and Drehmann, M. (2010) An economic capital model integrating credit and interest rate risk in the banking book. *Journal of Banking and Finance* 34: 730–742.

Baldan, C., Zen, F. and Rebonato, T. (2012) Liquidity risk and interest rate risk on banks: Are they related? *IUP Journal of Financial Risk Management IX* (4): 27–51.

Basel Committee on Banking Supervision (2004) Principles for the management of interest rate risk, July.

Basel Committee on Banking Supervision (2010) Basel III: International framework for liquidity risk management, standards and monitoring, December.

Basel Committee on Banking Supervision (2011) Basel III: A global regulatory framework for more resilient banks and banking systems – revised version, June.

Basel Committee on Banking Supervision (2013) Basel III: The Liquidity Coverage Ratio and liquidity risk monitoring tools, January.

Basel Committee on Banking Supervision (2014) Basel III: The Net Stable Funding Ratio, January.

Basel Committee on Banking Supervision (2016) Standards, Interest rate risk in the banking book, April.

Cadamagnani, F., Harimohan, R. and Tangri, K. (2015) A bank within a bank: How a commercial bank's treasury function affects the interest rates set for loans and deposits. *The Prudential Regulatory Authority, Bank of England Quarterly Bulletin Q2 2015*, Vol. 55, No. 2, pp. 153–164.

Choudhry, M. (2017) Strategic ALM and Integrated Balance Sheet Management: The Future of Bank Risk Management, *European Finance Review*, August.

Choudhry, M. (2018) *The Moorad Choudhry Anthology: Past, Present and Future Principles of Banking and Finance*. London: Wiley.

Enthofer, H. and Haas, P. (2016) *Asset Liability Management Handbook*. Vienna, Austria: Linde.

European Banking Federation (2019) "European Banking Industry Common Understanding of Credit Spread Risk in the Banking Book (CSRBB) defined by the European Banking Authority (EBA) Guidelines on the Management of Interest Rate Risk Arising from non-Trading Book Activities". EBF_036633. Brussels 8 May 2019.

European Central Bank (2017) *Sensitivity Analysis of IRRBB – Stress test 2017*. Frankfurt: ECB.

Forsgren A, Gill F.E., Wright M.H., (2002) Interior methods for nonlinear optimization. *SIAM Rev* 44(4):525–597.

Guidelines on institutions' stress testing", 19 July 2018.

Kaufman, G.G. (1984) Measuring and managing interest rate risk: A primer. *Federal Reserve Bank of Chicago Economic Perspectives*, Vol. 8, No. 1, pp. 16–29. Chicago, IL: Federal Reserve Bank of Chicago.

Lubinska, B. (2014) Review of the static methods used in the measurement of the exposure to the interest rate risk. *Financial Sciences* 4 (21): 25–41.

Lubinska, B. (2020) *Asset Liability Management Optimisation*. Chichester: Wiley.

Lusignani, G. (1996) La gestione dei rischi finanziari nella banca. Bologna, Italy: Il Mulino.

Newson, P. (2017) *Interest Rate Risk in the Banking Book*, London: Risk Books.

Nocedal, J. and Wright, S.J. (2006) *Numerical Optimization, Springer Series in Operations Research and Financial Engineering*. New York: Springer.

Office of the Comptroller of the Currency (OCC) (2011) *Supervisory Guidance on Model Risk Management*. New York: OCC.

Parramore K., Watsham T., (2015) Numercial Methods, [in:] *The PRM Handbook, Mathematical Foundations of Risk Management* vol. II, Prmia.

PRMIA (2015a) *Professional Risk Managers' Handbook: Financial Instruments*, Vol. I, Book 2, pp. 209–221. Wilmington, DE: PRMIA Publications.

PRMIA (2015b) *Professional Risk Managers' Handbook: Numerical Methods*, Vol. II, pp. 203–218. Wilmington, DE: PRMIA Publications.

Resti, A and Sironi, A. (2007) *Risk Management and Shareholders' Value in Banking: From Risk Measurement Models to Capital Allocation Policies*, John Wiley & Sons Ltd.

Widowitz, M., Vogt, P. and Neu, P. (2014) Funds transfer pricing in the new normal. In Bohm A., Elkenbracht-Huizing M. (eds), *The Handbook of ALM in Banking: Interest Rates, Liquidity and the Balance Sheet*. London: Risk Books.

Index